Litton Forbes

Two Years in Fiji

Litton Forbes

Two Years in Fiji

ISBN/EAN: 9783337471934

Printed in Europe, USA, Canada, Australia, Japan

Cover: Foto ©Andreas Hilbeck / pixelio.de

More available books at **www.hansebooks.com**

BY

LITTON FORBES, M.D., L.R.C.P., F.R.G.S.

LATE MEDICAL OFFICER TO THE GERMAN CONSULATE,
APIA, NAVIGATOR ISLANDS

LONDON
LONGMANS, GREEN, AND CO.
1875

PREFACE.

THE greater portion of this little work was written during a voyage from London to New Zealand. The Author's object has been to give the reader an idea—faint and imperfect, perhaps, but as far as it goes truthful—of the kind of life an Englishman may expect to lead who makes Fiji his home. The work professes to be written mainly from the point of view of a planter, and lays no claim either to original research or scientific accuracy.

As regards the orthography of Fijian names the spelling used is that which was introduced by the missionaries and subsequently adopted, without modification, by the Government of Cacobau, and also by Commodore Goodenough and Mr. Layard in their report, presented to both Houses of Parliament. Though awkward at first to English readers, this spelling will probably establish itself in all official circles, as it offers the advantage of being uniform and of reproducing fairly enough the native pronunciation of proper names. Attention to the following simple rules will enable the English reader to pronounce correctly, 'Vaka viti,' every Fijian word he is likely to meet with :—

1. All vowels are pronounced as in French or Italian.

2. The letter B is never sounded without an *m* before it, e.g. Bua is pronounced *M*bua; Bau = *M*bau; Cacobau = Thako*m*bau; bokola = *m*bokola.

3. C is always pronounced as *th* in *thin*: thus, *C*acobau = *Th*akombau; *C*akadrovi = *Th*akandrovi; *C*olo = *Th*olo.

4. D, G, Q are always pronounced as if *n* preceded them, e.g. Cakadrovi = Thaka*n*drovi; Bega = Be*n*ga; oqa = o*n*go.

The account of the formation and ultimate collapse of the Government established by Cacobau and a few whites in 1871, is written chiefly from personal recollections, supplemented by private letters from residents in Fiji, and by the 'Fiji Gazette' and 'Fiji Times,' two newspapers published at Levuka. The former of these was the private property of the Government, and consequently its organ; the latter represented the views of the oppositionists, and therefore of the great body of planters. The 'Fiji Times' used frequently to publish letters from individuals which were interesting as throwing light on the condition of society in the outlying portions of the group, and on the real motives which induced many to favour an autonomy in Fiji.

It is impossible to write about the South Sea Islands and make no reference to missionary enterprise. The missionaries themselves, in their published writings, claim to have effected so much, and have returned such profuse thanks for the success which they consider has been vouchsafed to them, that a plain man is apt to be surprised and disappointed when he learns from actual observation the real state of the case. Christianity was first introduced, and subsequently propagated, in Fiji by Tongan influence. It has always been, and is even now, more or less of a political matter with Fijian chieftains; for until quite lately to *lotu*, or turn Christian, meant nothing more than to acknowledge the supremacy of Bau. As a body the missionaries at present in Fiji are a deserving set of men; but a very short acquaintance with native character will be sufficient to show that much of the good they claim to have effected is, to say the least, somewhat hypothetical.

The Author acknowledges his obligations to Mr. Calvert's 'Fiji and Fijians,' a work which, for intimate knowledge of the country and people of which it treats may be placed side by side with Lane's 'Modern Egyptians;' also to Doctor Peachey's 'Cotton-growing in Fiji;' and to an article in 'Fraser's Magazine,' on the 'Labour Traffic,' by the Earl of Pembroke.

It may be thought that this sketch of Fijian life and politics ends somewhat abruptly. As a matter of fact, however, the political events recorded in the last chapter close a distinct period in the history of Fiji, beyond which it seemed unnecessary to go. With the arrival of the Imperial Commissioners, and subsequent annexation of the group to the British Crown, a new era commences, not for the Fiji Islands alone, but probably for all the island groups of the South Pacific, too long unknown and neglected.

LITTON FORBES.

AUCKLAND: *January* 1875.

CONTENTS.

CHAPTER I.
PAGE

Causes of the 'rush' to Fiji—I take Shipping to the Islands—Ratu Joey—Fijian Women—Canoes—First View of Ovalau—Passage through a Coral Reef—Arrival at Levuka . . . 1

CHAPTER II.

Manton's Hotel—Nicknames—'Old Hands'—Reindeer—Town of Levuka—Totoga—Bathing in Levuka River—Dinner at Manton's—An uncomfortable Night 15

CHAPTER III.

Levuka in the Daytime—Visit to King Cacobau—Queen Lydia—Leave Levuka—Voyage to Tavinni—Imported Labourers—Soloman Islanders—A Pioneer of Civilisation—Hotel at Vuna—A Tropical Forest 30

CHAPTER IV.

Cotton-growing in Fiji—A Plantation Breakfast—The Cotton-house—Labourers' Quarters—Sickness—Difficulties attending the Instruction of certain Islanders—Labourers at Work—Overseers—Tanna Men—Soloman Islanders—Erromango Men—Tokalaus—Ra Men—Fijian Labourers Returning to their Homes . 55

CHAPTER V.

Another Plantation—Salt Beef—Bachelor Planters—Starting a Cotton Plantation—Purchasing Land—Sources of Trouble with the Natives—Advantages of Possessing an entire Island—How to Procure Labourers—House-building—Native Servants—Sowing Cotton-seed—Feeding Labourers on a Plantation—Cotton-picking—Cotton-ginning—Uses of Sea Island Cotton—Cotton-growing as a Commercial Speculation—Elements of Uncertainty in it—Living on Credit—Commercial Morality—Death of a Planter—Omens—A Fijian Mekè—Night Air . . . 86

CHAPTER VI.

A Fiji Canoe Voyage—Scenery along the Coast—Shipwreck—Old Hands—A Deserted Plantation—Dangers of Canoe Travelling—Arrive at Wairiki—A Native Teacher 125

CHAPTER VII.

Wairiki—Tiu Cakou's House—Monotony of Savage Life—*Tappa*-making—Tiu Koominooa—Ethics of Trading with Savages—British and American Subjects—Hotel at Wairiki—Two Residents 141

CHAPTER VIII.

Tropical Rain—The Fijian Language—Professional Poisoners—Medical Science in Fiji—Fijian Idiosyncrasies—The Mat Fever—French Missionaries 163

CHAPTER IX.

Voyage to Ngalena—Fijian Girls—House-building for a Chief——A Fijian Dinner—Kava Making and Drinking—How a Chief transacts Business—An American Planter—Fijian Half-castes—The Land Question—Position of Englishmen in Fiji . . 180

CHAPTER X.

A Hurricane—Its Effects at Wairiki—On the Group generally—Increased Demand for Native Labourers—A Labour-vessel—Ocean Islands—Tanna Boatmen—A Perilous Voyage—Straits of Somo-Somo—Leave Fiji for Rotumah 204

CHAPTER XI.

Voyage to Rotumah—Natives—Rotumah Mats—An Extinct Volcano—Ancient Inhabitants—A Feast—Cocoa-nuts—I Practise Medicine with Success—Missionaries—Civil War—Blown away—I return to Fiji 222

CHAPTER XII.

Method of Procuring Labourers in Rotumah—Labour-producing Islands—Trading with Savages—Pigeon English—Soloman Islanders—Banks Islanders—Tokalaus—Dangers of Labour-getting—Head-money—Tricks of the Trade—Mr. Consul March and the 'Carl'—The Labour-trade not Slavery—Exaggerated Statements current in England—Causes of these—Treatment of Labourers on Plantations in Fiji—Traffic in Natives within the Limits of Fiji—Suggestions for the Conduct of the Trade generally 246

CHAPTER XIII.

Political Changes—Social Condition of Fiji in 1871—Old and New Settlers—Business Relations between Fiji and the Australian Colonies—Anomalous Position of the British Consul—Causes which led to the Formation of a Government—A *coup d'état*—Previous Attempts to Form a Government—The Tovata League—Methods by which the Ministers consolidated their Power—The Constitution Act—The House of Delegates—Position of Native Chiefs—*Personnel* of the Ministry—Maafu and Tiu Cakou Join the Government—Attitude of England towards the New State—Orders in Council—Ministerial Doctrines—The Government loses Popularity 275

CHAPTER XIV.

The Government Consolidates its Power—The Supreme Court—The Police Court—The Case of Rees—Parliamentary Opposition Disarmed—Issue of Paper-money—More Grievances—The 'Ku Klux'—Fall of the Ministry—Accession of Mr. Thurston—Mr. Woods Premier—The Ba River District—Native Outrages—Conduct of the Ministers who Visited the District—Political Action of the Planters—A Civil War imminent—Interference of H.M.S. 'Dido'—Last Session of the Triennial Parliament—Unsettled State of the Country generally—Threatened Secession of Maafu—Attempt to Enfranchise Natives—Collapse of the Attempt at Self-government—Arrival of Commodore Goodenough and Mr. Consul Layard 311

TWO YEARS IN FIJI.

CHAPTER I.

Causes of the 'Rush' to Fiji—I take shipping to the 'Islands'—Ratu Joey—Fijian Women—Canoes—First View of Ovalau—Passage through a Coral Reef—Arrival at Levuka.

FOR some six years previous to 1870, the Australian Colonies had been in a very depressed condition. A sudden fall in the price of wool, a succession of bad seasons, and over-speculation in Sydney and Melbourne, had been perhaps chiefly to blame for this result. So bad, indeed, was the state of things towards the close of 1870, that not a few persons emigrated from the Colonies instead of to them. In many districts of Queensland and New South Wales men found it almost impossible to get remunerative employment; and but for the favourable physical conditions of Australia, coupled with the elasticity peculiar to young communities, there must have resulted great and widespread distress. Even as it was, many homes were broken up, and their inmates compelled to seek a living in distant and unsettled parts of the country.

It was about this time and under these circum-. stances that the Fijis first began seriously to attract the attention of Australian Colonists. These islands are situated some 2,000 miles to the north and east of Sydney. For nine months of the year the voyage is almost certain to be a fine-weather one. There are no south-west gales or dreary Newfoundland fogs to be encountered, but, instead, the mariner may reckon on tolerably smooth seas and a genial trade-wind, and need trouble himself only about a few stray reefs and islands that lie in his course. As soon as it became known that Fiji was likely to offer a field for adventurous spirits, a 'rush' at once commenced from Australia. Shiploads of passengers, and cargoes of odd-looking wares, fit for savage buyers, were despatched in quick succession from Melbourne, and Sydney, and Auckland. Still the demand increased, and, as new ground was being broken, became more than equal to the supply. Colonial merchants were opening up a new and lucrative trade with the long-neglected Islands. Their returns were quick and their profits large, and Fiji at length became a word in everyone's mouth. What Virginia was in the days of Queen Anne, or Melbourne some twenty years ago, to the adventurous men of that day, the South Sea Islands were now becoming to the people of New South Wales and Victoria. Men told each other that population alone was needed to develope all the capabilities and latent wealth of the new land; and though few had any real knowledge on the subject, all seemed to take for granted that the Islands must be exceptionally fertile and rich. Finally, in 1871, there was a grand stampede of all restless whites from Australia and New Zealand to Fiji.

The small island trading-vessels could with difficulty find room for the crowds of eager men that rushed on board, jostling each other, and filling to suffocation the tiny cabins. Many who could not pay their passages deemed it a favour if they were allowed to 'work' them. As always happens in circumstances of this kind, not a few infatuated persons gave up settled employment and secure situations, tempted by the alluring prospects that the 'Islands' seemed to offer. To all appearance, history was once more about to repeat itself; and much of the old South Sea Bubble infatuation was to take possession of sober-minded clerks and merchants. A company was started in Melbourne which, it was hoped, might some day rival Hudson's Bay in extent, or the East Indian Corporation in wealth and political importance. The shares of this new Company—the Polynesian—were bought up readily enough; and sufficient money was soon forthcoming to pay off the American debt which Thakombau (Cakobau), King of Bau, had been unfortunate enough to incur.

On Christmas Day, 1870, I found myself on board

the 'Young Australia,' bound for Fiji. For many months past I had been urged to 'go down to the Islands,' as the phrase was in Sydney, and had at last accepted what was thought to be a good appointment. My fellow-passengers numbered in all some twenty men. Everyone carried his revolver, and, although this was quite unnecessary, still it looked like business, and seemed the proper thing to be done by men bound to the Cannibal Islands. The vessel we were to sail in was small, and swarmed with cockroaches, rats, earwigs, and other vermin; though I learned by-and-by that, compared with Fijian craft, she might be considered almost free from such pests. During the first part of the voyage the weather was unpropitious, and we were obliged to 'heave-to' for three days, near Lord Howe's Island, one of the most stormy and ill-omened spots in the South Pacific. By-and-by the bad weather spent itself, and before long we succeeded in picking up the trade-winds, and then the rest of the voyage was made over smooth seas, and under skies brighter than those of Italy or Egypt. On the twenty-fifth day out, the high land of Kadavu, the most southerly island of the Fijian group, was sighted. The breeze continuing fair, the island itself was soon passed. All night long the ship held on her way with undiminished speed, and next morning at sunrise lay in the very centre of the Fiji group, not ten miles from Levuka, its capital. Every man expected to breakfast on shore at the very least. Boxes and portmanteaux were dragged out of dark recesses in cabins or under tables, where they had been securely wedged throughout the voyage; tail-coats and tall hats were once more the order of the day, and, in a word, there was that general attempt at dressing to go on shore which is so familiar to those who have ever made a voyage in a sailing ship.

But alas for the vanity of human wishes! The wind which had hitherto befriended the ship now fell 'dead calm.' The vessel lay like a log on the water, slowly rising and falling to the long rollers as they came up from the south. Hour after hour we were mocked by delusive appearances of a breeze, but none came; and finally the gloom of evening settled down on us, still in the same spot as at sunrise. One by one the stars came out, and those of us who were accustomed to Australian skies missed some familiar friends. On this night the constellations looked pale and sickly, and their light seemed scarcely able to struggle through the dull heavy atmosphere that hung round us. Every now and then a lurid flash of lightning would dart along the horizon, illuminating for a moment some distant and low-lying island; and then all would be darker than before. The swell was becoming heavier hour after hour, and we could hear with unpleasant distinctness its sullen roar on the coral reefs far to leeward. The barometer had been falling steadily, and now stood unusually low. It was now the middle of January—a treacherous and anxious month to all who sail the Southern Ocean:

for January is one of the three 'hurricane months,' and during its continuance sudden and violent storms may be looked for. The captain of our vessel had been wrecked only the year before near the spot where we now were, and had escaped by what seemed to himself little short of a miracle. He began now to feel somewhat uneasy; and no wonder, for if the wind should blow strongly from a certain quarter, our destruction would be inevitable, and, all things considered, it looked exactly as if it would blow.

Next morning the sun rose in a haze of cloud, and the calm continued as before. We were still pretty nearly in the centre of the group, and surrounded on all sides by islands. To the east lay Ovalau, with its sharply-defined mountains and valleys, and somewhat nearer Wakaya. This latter is one of those little gems that stud the broad bosom of the Pacific, and cause sober-minded writers to rave about the beauty of coral islands generally, as though they were all equally lovely. A few years before the time of which I write, Wakaya had been purchased from the natives for a few cases of gin and some 20*l.* of English money; to-day it is valued at 10,000*l.* sterling. Away to the west, far as the eye could reach, might be seen the hazy and uncertain outlines of 'Vauna Leon,' the 'Big-land,' while between it and our ship lay the Island of Koro, which has sometimes been called the 'Garden of Fiji,' so great is its natural fertility. Koro has ever been a favourite residence of King Thakombau, who visits it whenever he wishes to escape from the attentions of white men or the worry of Fijian politics. Hence his annoyance was great when he found that, under the self-appointed government of 1871, his dear island was to be taken out of his hands, and to become a security for money raised in Melbourne and Sydney. To the south could be seen, though far away, the blue outline of Batique, famed throughout Fiji for its beautiful and costly mats. More distant than any other land, the giant peak of Ritova loomed against the morning sky. Behind it, we knew, lay Viti Leon, or 'Big Fiji,' the home of heathens and cannibals, and the grave, in years past, of many a hardy pioneer of civilisation and progress.

As the day wore on, the heat increased, and the sky became as it were of brass. The rays of the sun reflected from the mirror-like surface of the sea smote us with tenfold force. It seemed as if the wind would never come. 'How long is this to last?' men asked each other gloomily. The captain looked melancholy, and began to tell a dismal story about having been on one occasion nine days within sight of his port, and finally after all blown out to sea; nor would he be sure that such might not be our fate on this occasion. At length, after many hours, towards sunset a light air was seen to be creeping up from the south. This soon freshened into a good sailing breeze, and before long the 'Young Australia' was careering through the water in gallant style. By-and-by the pilot boat came alongside, and the Levuka pilot, an American ex-captain, jumped on board. He was followed by a crowd of natives, all more or less nude. Most of these natives, though quite regardless of their general toilet, had apparently lavished no little care on their head-dresses. Some had plastered their hair with a coat of lime, others had saturated it with cocoa-nut oil, and then dusted it over with sandal-wood, while others, again, wore a quantity of flowers twined either singly or in small bunches among their wiry locks. This last was without doubt the most becoming way of adorning the head, as it was also the simplest. Foremost among those who climbed the ship's deck was Ratu (master) Joey, Thakombau's youngest son. At this time he was a handsome boy of some twelve years of age. His skin, though brown, was lighter in colour than that of the majority of Fijians, and was, moreover, soft and delicate as that of an infant. His hair fell in great yellow masses over his shoulders, and was adorned with a few red hybiscus flowers, which contrasted well with his swarthy features. As he stood on the deck surrounded by his followers he looked every inch a chief. His high lineage from the kings of Bau showed itself in every gesture—the more so, perhaps, because he was surrounded by a crowd of hereditary bondsmen, as the Fijian natives are almost to a man. I met Joey many times after this, but as he grew older he lost much of his early beauty. When last we met he was dressed, I grieve to say, in a tall hat and frock coat, and looked so unlike his former self that it was with difficulty I recognised my friend. The missionary love for broadcloth and respectability had destroyed all that was interesting about him, at any rate from an artistic point of view, and transformed him into something not unlike a civilised snob. Latterly Joey has frequently appeared in Sydney at missionary tea-meetings, where his presence has served to demonstrate the success of missionary enterprise in general, and of Fijian missions in particular.

But to return to the ship. There was by this time a great number of natives on deck, and a few years ago there would have been no small danger of their attempting some mischief. But times had changed in Fiji since the days of Tanoa; and the natives of Levuka at any rate were as unlikely to attack a vessel as the inhabitants of Greenwich or Gravesend. Many indeed who came on board set to work with hearty good-will, handling the sails, and going aloft to point out the openings in the reef. The majority of them stared at every object that met their gaze, with a dull unintelligent curiosity. They seemed, in fact, principally interested in trying to get something to eat. Among the number were a few women. They wore their hair closely cropped, and their ears were slit in such a manner as to enable them to carry a pipe and some tobacco where an Englishwoman would carry her ear-rings. Let me say at once that these women had nothing attractive about them, in which respect they differ vastly from their sisters in Samoa and Tahiti. They were timid and unintelligent, to say nothing of being hideously ugly, which of course they could not help. They turned a deaf ear to the many flattering compliments which some of the passengers paid them, and shrank away cowering along the bulwarks and among the water-casks. All this time canoes had been constantly arriving alongside from the town of Levuka. Their occupants kept up a ceaseless din, trying in vain to sell their freights of bananas, cocoa-nuts, pine-apples, fowls, pigs, and other wares. These canoes, though varying in size, were all made on the same principle. They consisted of trees hollowed out, sharpened at both ends, and prevented from rolling over in the water by an outrigger. In size canoes vary a good deal, some carrying only one man, while a first-rate war canoe will carry as many as two hundred. Such a canoe is built of planks sewn together with cocoa-nut fibre. It is propelled by sails, has houses for the chiefs on deck, and indeed possesses every appliance for an ocean voyage, except the all-important one of seaworthiness. These large canoes are bad 'sea-boats,' and become water-logged in anything like 'heavy' weather. They are, however, very fast, particularly in 'beating to windward,' in which respect they would be probably more than a match for our fastest yachts, especially in light winds. Canoes of the outrigger type are common throughout the South Pacific groups, with the exception of the Solomon Islands. They are driven either by sails or paddles, or sometimes by one paddle, like a Venetian gondola, though according to the size of the canoe any number may be used. Some of the canoes that came alongside were manned by tiny children, all perfectly naked, and looking the picture of health and good-humour. These little creatures plied their paddles with great skill, and seemed as much at home in their small crafts as the Arab boys at Aden do in the water. In many of the canoes I noticed an earthen pot containing embers (mbuka). These were carried in order to light pipes and cigars, for matches are too costly a luxury for the ordinary native. The Fijian cigar, or more properly cigarette, is made from native-grown tobacco, wrapped up in a piece of banana leaf. And now a chance presented itself of learning a little Fijian. My first sentence was 'Kautamai buka,' 'bring me a light,' and very useful even this instalment of the language proved subsequently.

Meantime the ship had been steadily advancing, and was now close up with the land. And here I will venture to remark that all descriptions of scenery, save by a master hand, are of necessity tame and uninteresting to the general reader. So well is this fact known to readers of light literature, that there are many who skip such passages altogether, and with such persons I have an undisguised sympathy. Consequently, I shall not inflict any elaborate description of Ovalau or its capital Levuka on my readers. Looking at the island a little distance from the shore the traveller is reminded of the first view he obtains of Ceylon from the Indian Ocean. There is the same tropical vegetation, though perhaps not quite so abundant, the same straggling cocoa-nut trees, the same dark sombre rocks, with here and there patches of red-looking earth. But on a nearer approach the view is more pleasing. The hills of Ovalau, though bleak enough near the summits, are seen to be covered with a thick growth of underwood, and divided from one another by deep valleys. Here the vegetation is of the most varied and delicate hues, while the lights and shadows, as they fall on the valleys and hill-sides, from every passing cloud, are all that a lover of the picturesque could desire. About the hills themselves, too, there was a rugged grandeur, together with a wealth of fertility and beauty, that went far to compose a noble landscape. At their base nestled the small town of Levuka, the outpost of white civilisation in the farthest East. At the period of my first visit it was but a tiny village, and consisted chiefly of a line of houses along the beach, with a few cocoa-nut trees scattered at intervals among them. The greater part of these houses was roofed with galvanised iron, and the rays of the setting sun playing upon them recalled the domes and minarets of an Eastern city. One or two large houses stood out from among the smaller ones, and caught a stranger's eye. The largest of these was the French missionary chapel, while the other was the cotton house and ginning establishment of Messrs. Smith. At the back of the single row of houses which formed the town, the hills in many places rose abruptly, forming as it were a wall of solid rock. From this at midday the rays of the sun were thrown back upon the unfortunate inhabitants with a force that at certain seasons of the year was almost insupportable. In front of the houses ran the sea beach, which was thus the main street of the town. Beyond this the eye rested on a sheet of calm clear water, which formed Levuka Harbour. Further out to sea lay the coral reef, forming a natural breakwater, upon which the Pacific rollers summer and winter spent their forces in vain.

And now the vessel was about to enter the harbour, but to do this it had first to pass through an opening in the coral reef. This was indeed a veritable Scylla and Charybdis, where rash pilotage or uncertain steering must have ended in disaster. As the critical moment arrived, some additional natives stationed themselves aloft on the fore-yard, whence they could see the rocks that lay ahead of the ship. In the neighbourhood of coral islands this look-out from aloft is always necessary. Fortunately for the navigator the water is so clear in these latitudes that rocks and shoals may be seen a long way off even though many feet below the surface, and unmarked by the curl of the smallest wave. *Tau* 'keep up,' *ule* 'keep away,' were now the commands constantly heard from the native pilot. The schooner answered her helm well; but every now and then, looking over the side, one could see the jagged masses of coral rock that she had grazed past, or sailed over with but a few inches of water to spare. The breakers formed an unbroken line of foam north and south as far as the eye could reach, and seemed to bar all further progress. But gradually approaching this formidable barrier, we could see a narrow opening, on each side of which the waves were breaking with terrific violence. The chief danger to be apprehended in passing through a coral reef is that the wind should suddenly fall light. When this happens, a vessel loses steerageway, and, drifting helplessly on one wall of the entrance, soon becomes a wreck. There is neither time nor room to cast anchor even if the great depth of water allowed any such manœuvre. Fortunately on this occasion no untoward accident happened. We passed in safety through the narrow passage, and a few moments afterwards lay securely in Levuka Harbour. The rattle of the anchor as it went over the bows proclaimed that the voyage was ended, and that for some of us a new phase of life was about to commence.

CHAPTER II.

Manton's Hotel—Nicknames—'Old Hands'—Reindeer—Town of Levuka—Totoga—Bathing in Levuka River—Dinner at Manton's—An Uncomfortable Night.

IMMEDIATELY on landing in Fiji, newcomers usually repaired to a house that was familiarly known as 'Manton's.' Like the 'Tabard' in Chaucer's day, the 'Mitre' at Oxford, or 'Shepherd's' at Cairo, so Manton's at Levuka was the hotel of the place. It possessed a character, an individuality, that placed it above all other hostelries. It was at once an hotel, a club, and a general rendezvous for all the idle, and some of the busiest, men in Levuka. If you wanted a man, the first place you would naturally look for him would be at 'Manton's bar;' and if you did not find him there, you had only to go into the billiard-room, where your search would in all probability be successful. And talking of 'Manton's bar,' let me say, as it were in parenthesis, that the amount of drinking that there went on, and indeed in Levuka generally, was something portentous. Although it had fallen to my lot to see some heavy drinking in America, in up-country villages, and in gold diggings in Australia, Fiji outdid all former experiences. Here every man seemed harassed by a perpetual thirst, and drank freely and often. Not to invite a stranger to drink with you was considered mean—to refuse to pledge him was a positive insult. This constant 'nipping,' as it used to be called, was one of the least satisfactory features of Fijian society in the early days. Much of the craving for drink so noticeable in Fiji might perhaps justly be laid to the score of climate. After a few years' residence in tropical countries, especially in those where the climate is as moist as in Fiji, some stimulant would seem to be a physiological necessity. Holland gin was the favourite drink of the citizen of Levuka ; and if a man will drink in hot countries, this perhaps is the least unwholesome of all spirits. In Fiji it was drunk by everyone, and seemed at any rate less pernicious than the brandies and sodas of India.

Entering Manton's with the other voyagers, and standing at the bar, it was not long before one of the bystanders invited me to 'have something.' This gentleman's name I found subsequently was Jones ; but there were so many other Jones's throughout the group, and as this particular one came from Sydney, what more natural than to call him 'Sydney Jones,' and by this name he was always known. It was the same with Smith. In a community so essentially Anglo-Saxon as Fiji, there would be many Smiths— so many indeed that it might be a difficult task to distinguish one member of the family from another. The community, therefore, as it were in self-defence, conferred on each individual Smith a suitable nickname which men could easily learn and remember. Most of these names were taken either from some personal peculiarity or some previous passage in the individual's life, and some of them were odd enough. There was, for example, 'Cornopean Smith,' so called from his musical attainments; 'Pegged-leg Smith,' from his wooden leg; 'Peg-leg's brother,' 'Dr. Smith,' 'Smith of Nandy,' 'J. C. Smith,' 'J. C. Smith's brother,' and, best known perhaps of all, 'Daphne Smith,' so called after the schooner 'Daphne'—a vessel whose chequered career fills many volumes in the Foreign Office, and for a long time occupied the attention of the lawyers and law courts of New South Wales. All these nicknames were conferred and accepted in good part, and their evident utility was the best apology that could be offered for them.

Leaving the reeking atmosphere of the bar-room, and stepping on to the verandah, I found it thronged with planters, storekeepers, sailors, natives, and idlers of all kinds. There was no necessity for much ceremony in Fiji in 1871. It chanced to be an idle time, too, of the year, and men, clad for the most part in shirts and trousers, lounged about the doors and passages of the hotel, glad to dissipate their *ennui* by talking to a new arrival. Many of these men thus loitering about in rough garments, and so unkempt in appearance, had seen much 'better days,' as the phrase is, and were 'gentlemen' by birth and education. There was Captain A., from a line regiment, who had exchanged his London club, maugre himself, for a reed hut in the midst of a cotton-field; there was Lieut. B., an old navy man, who, possessing only merit without interest, and thereby finding his promotion somewhat retarded, had quitted the service in disgust; there was Captain C., another navy man, who had commanded a gunboat in the Crimea, and been badly wounded, and was now on half-pay; there was the Honourable L., who had sense enough to drop this vain title and work like a man. Then came a few University men; next some wealthy traders from Australia; then a host of men who had been unfortunate in all parts of the known world, and who would be equally unfortunate in Fiji; and finally there was a somewhat mysterious man, who was pointed out as a 'Special Correspondent.' Here and there one met a few of the very old settlers, the patriarchs of the community as they might fairly have been called. These men had settled in Fiji in the days when cannibalism and lawlessness of every kind were rife. They had seen much that was savage and strange, and had lived, as a rule, hard lives. Many of these had degenerated not a little, and in habits and appearance resembled natives more than civilised men. They belonged to a genus sometimes known by the name of 'beach comber,' sometimes 'loafer,' sometimes of 'old hands,' or, in New Zealand, where representatives of the same class are found, of 'Pakehah maorie.' These men are veritable waifs and strays of humanity, and represent a class which is to be found, though in decreasing numbers, all over the South Pacific. The history of many of these men is extremely curious, and the lives of some of them, if written in a novel, would seem too strange even for fiction. Some of these 'old hands' were originally convicts who escaped years ago from the prisons of Van Diemen's Land or New South Wales. They had preferred a doubtful chance of life and liberty among the cannibals to the certain misery of years of servitude. Others of them had deserted from the ferocious discipline of the king's ships or the weary monotony of whaling voyages; while others, again, were shipwrecked mariners who had been saved alive while their comrades had been drowned or eaten. Such men it was who formed the old race of white residents in the South Sea Islands. The race to which they belonged is well-nigh extinct, but a few members of it may nevertheless still be met with, preserved like fossils in a later formation.

Leaving the bar and the verandah, I passed into an inner room, intending to write a letter for a vessel that was about to sail. It was the 'hurricane season,' and the weather was intensely hot and disagreeable. The thermometer showed about 84° F., but the mere number of degrees was no measure of the oppressiveness of the atmosphere. The horizon on all sides was dark and lowering, while great masses of cloud hung about as if only waiting a favourable opportunity to pour their contents on the town beneath. Everything was damp and sticky, the ground saturated with moisture, and the air laden with warm unwholesome vapours. No one cared to wear his coat; and, indeed, such a garment would have been as much out of place in that room as in a Turkish bath. Close to me sat an American professional gambler, keeping a 'Faro bank' against all comers. He was a middle-aged man, square-jawed, and powerfully built; he had served in Mexico, and had been with the redoubtable Walker in Nicaragua. He considered the world generally as his home; and it used to be said of him, and probably with truth, that 'what he did not know was not worth knowing.' In looking at him I was often reminded of the description of some of the grim old sergeants or *sous officiers* of the time of Napoleon I. The adventures of this man's life would probably have made an interesting romance; but he was an essentially silent being, and never cared to speak of the past. Close to him sat a young fellow of quite an opposite turn of mind. He had once been well known in London circles, but had eventually seen fit to emigrate to New Zealand, where he had been successful as a steeple-chase rider, and finally had followed the 'rush' to Fiji. He was now in Levuka, waiting for remittances. Apparently this was his chronic condition, as, during all the time I knew him, he was always waiting for 'supplies.' As I sat vainly trying to write, he kept up a desultory conversation on men and things in general. But he ceased somewhat suddenly, and his gaze became more earnest, as 'Reindeer,' a well-known Fijian woman, entered the room. She, too, had had adventures, and hair-breadth escapes. On one occasion she was pursued by her justly incensed husband, and only saved her life by a leap of some twenty feet off a cliff into the sea. Then she took refuge among the white settlers, and, being fairly honest and clever, had gained a footing in the hotel. She was now past middle age, but still retained traces of former good looks. She was accompanied by Susan, a young girl of some eighteen summers, tall and handsome, and full of fun and impudence. C. told me she was his 'weakness,' and such was apparently the case. At any rate, he pretended, for some time, to talk to Reindeer, as if to lull suspicion, but suddenly made a feint at Susan. Susan started off, without a thought as to where she was going, and came full tilt against the table at which I sat. As she weighed over twelve stone, the result was not for a moment doubtful. Over went table and writer and ink-bottle in one indiscriminate ruin, and poor Susan on the top of all. My friend did not hesitate to pursue his advantage; but when the confusion was at its height, one of the barmaids came in, and the two Fijians fled away as quickly as they could. The white ladies of Fiji do not bear their coloured sisters much good-will; nor do the Fiji women forget to requite their contempt with a cordial hatred.

A disturbance such as the above was far too common to excite much attention. No one took any notice of it, not even the gamblers, though at one time their 'bank' seemed in some danger of being demolished. But though no one cared for the noise or inconvenience caused by Susan, everyone felt that it was a suitable occasion for a general drink. The opportunity was too good to be allowed to go to waste, and soon the well-known formula 'What'll you take?' was heard in all parts of the room. Some took gin and bitters, the majority gin and water, while one unfortunate suffering from liver complaint, was fain to content himself with soda-water. I could not help noticing that no one paid, and on enquiry found that everything was to be had on credit. This was a pleasant change from the stern suspicion of London tradesmen; but even this easy-going system was found to have its drawbacks. It was, of course, useless to think of writing letters in the din of conversation that followed the general drinking-match; and as there was yet an hour to dinner, a stroll round the town seemed the best thing that one could do.

Levuka at this time was a small place, but for its size busy and prosperous. It possessed, indeed, only one street, and that contained but one row of houses. They were built close to the water's edge; not so close, however, as not to leave a narrow strip of shingly beach, which formed the main street. This street extended about a mile in length, north and south, and was of very unequal breadth—in some places so narrow that two persons could scarcely walk abreast, in others so broad that an Australian coach-and-five might easily have been turned in it. There were no vehicles, or, indeed, beasts of burden of any kind, in Fiji in 1871, except a few horses which had been imported as an experiment, and which were not found to answer. All carrying was done by the natives, who, like the Coolies in India or Egypt, preferred to carry their loads on their heads. The first vehicle ever seen in Levuka happened, curiously enough, to be a bath-chair, imported from Sydney by a planter who had been unfortunate enough to break his leg. This machine was left one day standing opposite a shop, and King Thakombau happening at the moment to be passing by, jumped in, and insisted on his courtiers wheeling him up and down 'the Beach' till he got tired of the amusement.

Nearly every house in Levuka was a store of some kind, and public-houses were the most frequent of all. Between many of these houses there were large gaps of unoccupied land, the ownership of which was very frequently in dispute. Some of the stores were built of galvanized iron, but by far the greater number were of wood, and were very roughly put together. After walking about half a mile in one direction, I found the town ended abruptly in a building larger and more pretentious than any that had as yet been met with. This turned out to be the store and cotton-house of Messrs. Hennings, the boldest and most successful merchants of Fiji, and the firm who had made cotton-growing, so far as one firm could, a recognised and profitable industry. Had it not been for the liberality of this firm to the earlier settlers, Fiji would probably not be as well known as it is to-day. Indeed, nearly all the capital on which the older plantations were worked was advanced by Mr. Hennings—advanced, too, without any legal security whatever.

Though Levuka proper might be said to end at Hennings' store, there was a kind of suburb tacked on to it, which extended perhaps a quarter of a mile further on. This was called Totonga (F. Totoga), and consisted almost entirely of native huts. In this suburb the French missionaries had established themselves. The mission was presided over by two Marist Fathers, under the spiritual guidance of the Bishop of Typasa *in partibus*. Totonga had been once a large native town, and in days gone by been surrounded by a strong war-fence. This had subsequently been allowed to go to ruin, and the warriors who had manned it had departed, if not from the world, at any rate from their old camping-ground. Some distance beyond Totonga was the American consulate, built on a lofty rock, whence a huge wooden eagle could survey at leisure the town that lay beneath. Beyond this there were no houses, and the eye could roam at will over an unbroken expanse of ocean, or rest on a small strip of rich land, covered, down to the water's edge, with cocoa-nut trees and various tropical plants.

Owing to the formation of the hills behind the town, the area available for building purposes was very limited. In some places the bare rock rose up to a considerable height, and afforded no spot on which to build even a native house. Above this rockwall the hills stretched backwards in undulating valleys, covered with verdure, and affording excellent pasturage for cattle. In one spot the ascent was not quite steep, and here, at a height of about 300 feet above the town, a few houses had been built. They were not, however, very fashionable, the difficulty of reaching them being perhaps the cause. But as the lower town grows, their prospects must improve, and eventually the whole face of the hill will probably be laid out in terraces and villas for a future generation of wealthy planters.

Retracing my steps, I once more repassed 'Manton's,' and soon found myself at the other end of the Liliputian capital. On my way I could not fail to be struck once again by the great proportion of the public-houses to all other shops of every kind. It would not be an exaggeration to say that every second house along that beach dealt in spirits, either wholesale or retail, and the difficulty was to know how they could all be supported by such a small community. The population, however, was a thirsty one, and as there were no import duties the profits must have been as large as the consumption.

The north-end of Levuka was bounded by a stream which separated it from a native village of the same name, the residence of the Chief. In the bed of this stream were several large pools of water, which formed excellent bathing-places. The sun was now low in the west, and it was the time when in the South Sea Islands groups the natives are wont to take their swim. The Levuka river was soon swarming with tiny black children far more merry and joyous than European children of the same age would be. Nor did their seniors despise the luxury they were enjoying. With not much more preparation than would be necessary in the case of a Newfoundland dog, the grown-up native could plunge into the water, and swim about to his heart's content. The natives were not indeed overburdened with clothes, but of what little they were possessed they took the greatest care. Their miserable bit of tappa (native cloth) was laid on the bank and folded up with as much care as if it had been one of Poole's masterpieces. The place of soap they supplied by the rind of a species of shaddock, or sometimes by an alkaline earth, which was indeed no bad substitute. During the day the weather had been unusually hot and oppressive even for Fiji, and the mosquitoes and flies more than ordinarily troublesome. Under such circumstances, a cold bath was not only a real luxury but an absolute necessity. Accordingly C., who had joined me, and whom I had not seen since his adventure with Susan, pointed out a good spot above where the natives were. We were both soon enjoying a good swim. But scarcely had we finished when it was as though the whole white population had turned out to a man, moved by some common impulse. Everyone had come to have his bath before dinner, as was the universal custom in Levuka society. On they came, young and old, planters, merchants, and sailors; in a word, all the white men in the place—sometimes singly, sometimes in twos or threes, carrying soap and towels, till there could not have been fewer than forty or fifty round the largest pool. The water, however, ran clear and strong, and there was no inconvenience or overcrowding. This last half-hour of daylight was perhaps the pleasantest time of the whole twenty-four hours. All was mirth and jollity. Business and cares were laid aside, and every man unbent his brow and shared in the good-fellowship around him. It would be hard to say how many new acquaintances I made that evening in the water, but the number was not small. In the Fijian society of that day there was no stiffness or pretension—no setting up of one man over another; all that came afterwards with the establishment of 'law and order,' and the assumption of the kingship by Cacobau. As it was, men felt rather drawn towards each other than antagonistic. Everyone was more or less dependent on his neighbour, and was more or less a pioneer of civilisation, intent on opening up a new country, and if possible making his own fortune, but not meanly jealous of others who might succeed better than himself. In the midst of all our fun, the sun set abruptly, and in a very few minutes afterwards the shades of night had gathered around the spot. The river was once more left in solitude or to the natives, while the whites hastened to that great *table d'hôte* which Manton daily provided for his guests.

Dinner at Manton's was a pleasant enough affair. We were waited on by boys from Rotumah or other South Sea Islands, clad in flannel liveries. These little fellows were excellent waiters, and in their cheerful service and beaming countenances it would have been difficult to recognise the marks of that 'slavery' which has given such offence to some writers. The cook was a Chinese, or 'Chinaman,' as Celestials are generally called in Australia, and, like all his nation, was very good so long as he was well watched. The dinner consisted of pork, fowls, salt beef, sardines, yam and taro; and this *ménu* seldom underwent any change. I did not at the time think it a very excellent repast; but a neighbour said to me, 'When you have been six months on a plantation you will change your mind,' a prophecy verified in even less time. After being for many months half starved on tough salt beef and unpalatable yams, I came to regard a dinner at the Levuka Hotel as an almost regal repast. Compared to plantation fare, it was indeed a banquet of Lucullus. So great was the difference between the meagre fare of a planter in the outlying districts and the generous diet of Manton's, that the sudden change from the one to the other has not unfrequently produced serious and even fatal illness. Many a poor fellow has dated the commencement of his death-sickness from a casual indulgence in the pleasures of that hospitable board, when debilitated by hard work and an insufficiency of wholesome food.

Dinner ended, everyone hastened to the verandah, where, fanned by the cool land breeze which sets in shortly after sunset, he could enjoy coffee and cigars, unmolested by natives or mosquitoes. Everything, as usual, was obtained on credit, and indeed it was well understood, though no one exactly said so, that payment was contingent on the success of the next cotton crop. About ten o'clock the quiet men retired to their beds, to be up next morning at the earliest streak of dawn. Those more merrily inclined wandered about the town, like the Caliph Haroun, in search of adventures. Others preferred the billiard-room, and others the bar; while others, again, sang catches under the verandah, making night hideous with their noisy mirth. But had the night been as still and hushed as is the Sabbath night in a Scotch village, I should have found it equally impossible to sleep. The hotel rooms were hot and close, and the air both within and without so oppressive that one could hardly breathe. The mosquitoes passed through the curtain at will, and tormented me beyond all endurance. A man in the next bed, who had been drunk for some days, or at any rate on the spree, had dropped asleep in his clothes, and now snored abominably. I tossed about fitfully on the bed, and put into practice every device I had ever heard of for wooing sleep, but in vain. As the night wore on, the noises of the hotel one by one died away, and at length I fell into a distempered sleep, broken at frequent intervals by some mosquito more venomous than his fellows. When I awoke, the sun was high, and I felt wearied and unrefreshed. The air seemed just as hot and moist and sickly as the night before. My companion also awoke about this time, and seeing daylight declared it 'was time to have a drink,' in which he was good enough to ask me to join him.

CHAPTER III.

Levuka in the Daytime—Visit to King Cacobau—Queen Lydia—Leave Levuka—Voyage to Taviuni—Imported Labourers—Soloman Islanders—A Pioneer of Civilisation—Hotel at Vuna—A Tropical Forest.

THE early morning, as everyone knows, is the pleasantest time of day in the tropics. Though 'Manton's' was close and ill-ventilated, the land breeze that came down from the mountains behind the town, and swept through the verandahs, was deliciously cool and fresh. It was, and probably always will be, the fashion in Levuka to bathe early in the morning, and, consequently, at the hour of seven A.M. the little river presented almost as busy a scene as at five P.M. of the evening before. Breakfast was nominally at eight o'clock, but so many persons were constantly dropping in, late risers, new arrivals from other islands, *et hoc genus omne*, that it was insensibly prolonged into luncheon, and could scarcely be said to be over before two o'clock in the day. The great recommendation of Fijian society at this time was the absolute freedom of action enjoyed by each individual. Everything was sacrificed to comfort. Fashion and public opinion exercised no sway in Levuka, and were quite powerless to make anyone do what he did not like. You might come to breakfast at almost any hour, with the certainty of finding something to eat; you might come to table in any guise you liked, and be sure of finding some one dressed as strangely as yourself. The morning up to twelve o'clock was the time when all business was transacted. After that hour, most men seemed to think they had worked sufficiently for the day; and, indeed, many persons had so little business to do, that they must have found these short hours more than sufficient. I found plenty of time to stroll about the town, to peer into native huts, to visit the various hotels, and to be introduced to so many pleasant fellows, that it became at last quite impossible to recollect their names or their faces. I had brought some letters of introduction from the Colonies; but, as is generally the case in new countries, they went for nothing. If friends at home could only know of how little use the letters are, which they have been at the trouble of procuring for some son, or brother, or cousin, who goes out to make his fortune at the other side of the world, they might save themselves much unnecessary trouble. As a rule, letters of introduction are said to be worth only a dinner, but in Fiji they were not worth even a luncheon. In two days you might easily become acquainted with everyone who was worth knowing in Levuka; and, as to the other islands or plantations, you had only to present yourself at a planter's house to ensure a hospitable welcome. On this, my second day in Fiji, I had no lack of acquaintances. I explored the town in company with a number of idle agreeable men, who had left their plantations for a few weeks, and were anxious to make the most of their holiday. This they did in the only way open to them, viz., by visiting one house of refreshment after another, paying for each other's 'drinks,' and discussing all the scandal and business of the group. As wool is the staple of conversation in Australia, so is cotton in Fiji, although, indeed, sugar has lately become a somewhat formidable rival. The men whom I have mentioned formed a class quite distinct from the ordinary citizens of Levuka. Their occupation was cotton-growing, and they worked on their lands and among their labourers for some ten or eleven months every year, the rest of the time being spent in Levuka, for purposes either of business or of pleasure. Their company was ever on the move, changing and renewing itself. The boat-loads of passengers that went away one afternoon were replaced by fresh arrivals next morning. This would continue for several weeks during the 'dull' season, the arrivals exceeding in number the departures, until at length the town would be said to be full of 'strangers.' Sometimes a larger craft than usual would bring down almost all the settlers from a certain district. Then 'Manton's' would be filled to overflowing. Beds would be extemporised on billiard-tables, on verandahs, on chairs, on the bar—anywhere, in fact, where a very tired man might be supposed to be able to sleep. Men were sometimes obliged to sleep in their boats in the harbour for lack of room on shore, but the season of year generally rendered this a very disagreeable matter. Meanwhile, all this overcrowding and discomfort used to be borne with the greatest good-humour. Everyone seemed to be on friendly terms with his neighbour, and anxious to make the best of untoward circumstances. The reason of this was in no small degree owing to the fact that, at this time, everyone in Fiji felt more or less drawn towards his fellow-men by a common bond of similar interests, hopes, and dangers. I remained long enough in Fiji to see this kindly feeling among the settlers sadly changed; to see it give place to mutual contempt and distrust, which threatened even to end in anarchy and bloodshed. But at the time of which I write, no political troubles had as yet come upon the country. In 1871 Levuka was a pleasant enough place to live in, at any rate, for a short time. One heard the latest news, received home letters that may have been lying at the post-office for weeks or months—my first batch of letters were seven months old—met friends whom perhaps you had not heard of for years, and all this amid the popping of champagne and soda-water, the rattling of billiard-balls, and cheery songs carolled forth by men whose hearts were even lighter than their purses. It was a kind of Homeric banquet, that lasted not nine days, but as many weeks; and, if truth be told, soon became somewhat wearisome. There were no amusements of any sort to be had, except drinking, and gossiping, and billiards; and to men who were not devoted to such pursuits, life in Levuka became, after a while, extremely dull and monotonous.

As I had been now some time in King Cacobau's dominions, I should have failed in proper respect had I postponed any longer visiting his majesty. I had heard so much about him from the works of missionaries and others, so many stories were current about his anthropophagous propensities, his great stature, his numerous wives, his conversion to Christianity, and other interesting traits of character, that I looked forward to making his acquaintance with a good deal of eagerness. Accordingly, taking a friend with me who spoke Fiji well, I presented myself before the King. The entrance to his palace was somewhat small and low—so low, indeed, that the visitor had to go down on hands and knees before he could pass through the doorway. The palace itself was built in native fashion, and might be considered a good specimen of Fijian architecture. The interior consisted of one large room, subdivided at the further end into two smaller compartments by a screen of handsomely dyed native cloth. Cacobau was seated on a heap of mats, and close by him was the queen, a woman of very large proportions. The king was dressed in strictly native costume. The upper part of his body was uncovered, while his legs were swathed in ample folds of coloured tappa. This 'tappa,' or Fijian linen, was as stiff as repeated applications of white of egg could make it, and must have been far from comfortable wearing. It is manufactured by the women from the inner bark of the paper mulberry (*Broussonetia*; Fiji, *malo*), and when thoroughly dry is painted over with grotesque designs, somewhat resembling those of an Egyptian mummy-cloth. I and my companion seated ourselves on a mat before his majesty, such being the approved posture of respect among Fijian courtiers, and commenced an animated conversation. After the usual salutation, 'siadra na Turang' ('good morning, chief') we were mutually introduced to each other, the King by the title of 'vuni-valu,' or 'root of war.' A pleased smile stole over the old man's face at the delicate compliment contained in this appellation; for, though now a converted man, and consequently a changed being, he had been, in his fighting days, a warrior of no mean order. Then I was presented to his notice somewhat as follows :—' This chief is from Sydney; he is a man-of-death (*matai ni mati* = doctor); he is come to stay with you in Fiji.' Cacobau seemed to take an interest in me at once. He requested me to feel a strange lump, or, to speak accurately, 'callous,' about the size of a walnut behind his right ear, the result of having lain for seventy years on a wooden pillow. This wooden pillow is a universal institution throughout the Fijian group, and in its simplest form is shaped exactly thus ⊓ ⊓. It is made of bamboo, or sometimes of hardwood, and is of course extremely uncomfortable to persons not accustomed to it. I learned to use it after a time, but could never get rid of a fearful stiffness in the neck which it always brought on. This pillow is perhaps one of the strangest freaks of fashion to be found in any country. Its origin is said to be due to native vanity, which could not suffer the elaborate *coiffure* of heathen times to be crushed and destroyed by a pillow of the ordinary kind.

During my visit our conversation never flagged, and Cacobau, if wearied by the audience, had too much natural politeness to show it. We described to him some of the great battles of the Franco-German war. He knew both nations well by name, having at various times been on board some of their ships that had visited Fiji. He seemed much interested in the accounts of the number of men killed and wounded on both sides, and in the rapidity with which breech-loaders could be fired. He asked especially how it was possible to find so many men, especially during the winter months. The significance of this question I understood afterwards, when I had learned something of Fijian warfare. But now it was time to say good-bye. The King had satisfied his curiosity. I had shown him the works of my watch, and had counted the beats of his pulse. While this was being done he had shown a little nervousness and anxiety regarding the result, for Cacobau, like all his countrymen, was superstitious, and lived in constant dread of an evil eye, or a charm, or a philtre. He concluded by asking me if I wanted to buy land, as every white man did, and whether I had plenty of money, to all which questions my companion gave the answers he thought most suitable for royal ears. He himself all the time had an eye to business, and told me he intended with this object to have a separate interview with Queen Lydia. This royal lady had, I believe, been at one time a great beauty, but in her case age had spared savage charms no more than it spares civilised ones. At the time of my visit she was about fifty years of age. To say she was fat would give but a faint idea of the truth. Her size was simply enormous, and her weight, if calculated in pounds, as the American custom is, must have amounted to some hundreds. She was dressed in a style very different from what European notions of a queen would suggest. She was dressed, indeed, much in the same way as the King was, the upper portion of her body being quite uncovered. But scanty as her robes were, they were, after all, infinitely more becoming than the gaudy and vulgar imitations of Sydney fashions which are now gradually becoming popular in Fiji. Queen Lydia was not perhaps quite so intelligent as Cacobau. She had, however, a ready wit, and a great deal of native dignity; and among her own women in her own house one could imagine that she could be a very stern Penelope. Her complexion was lighter than that of most Fijians. This lightness of complexion is said to be owing to the fact that ladies of rank do not work or expose themselves to the sun's rays as meaner women must do; hence, like long nails among the Chinese, or small feet in Europe, this fairness of skin has come to be regarded as a mark both of beauty and high birth.

My stay in Levuka had now extended over a fortnight, and I was beginning to grow heartily tired of the place. An intending settler soon perceives that he can learn really nothing of Fiji by a mere residence in the chief town; and if he be in earnest about his work, will lose no time in going further afield. The large and beautiful island of Tavinni, in my mind the gem of the whole group, lies some ninety miles to windward of Ovalau, and affords a good starting-point from whence to explore Vanna Leon and other islands. Its climate is good, its inhabitants peaceably disposed, its fertility undeniable, while, further, it is more thickly settled with whites than any island of its size in the Fijis. To these advantages it adds that of possessing several good harbours, with deep water, and a plentiful supply of native food; and if land is here dearer than in most other parts of the group, it is because it is at once more productive, and the title you obtain to it more secure. All these advantages decided my choice of Tavinni as a place to settle on; and learning that a vessel was bound from Levuka to Vuna, a town on the island, I lost no time in securing my passage.

Leave-taking did not occupy long; and with a hurried adieu to one friend, a wave of the hand to another, and a stirrup-cup or more properly anchor-cup with a third, I rushed up-stairs to pack for the voyage. When I reached my room I found it empty, swept, and garnished, and many things that I had left lying about that morning apparently cleared away. 'Holloa, waiter,' I cried to a smart little Rotumah boy, who filled that office at Manton's, 'Where are my clothes'? 'Ou sa nikila—don't know,' was the only reply I could elicit. All doubts were, however, soon cleared up, for in a very short time I learned that my wardrobe had been stolen, and was probably safely hidden away in some native hut. I was told somewhat later that such occurrences were by no means rare in Levuka, and that each man must guard his own property if he hoped to keep it. I betook myself after this to 'Reindeer,' hoping to discover the thief, but in vain; and indeed everyone professed such profound ignorance on the subject that I was convinced that all further enquiry was useless. Nothing remained, therefore, but to submit to the loss philosophically. Later on, when I became more acquainted with native character, I found I had only myself to blame, for having exposed such tempting articles as shirts and coats to the cupidity of Fijians, many of whom made it their regular business to prowl about the hotels, and carry off every loose article they could lay their hands upon. Honest natives no doubt exist, but they are to be found so rarely that no prudent man will count on their existence in his own immediate neighbourhood.

And now the hour for the ship to sail had come and gone, and as yet there were no signs of her being ready. By-and-by it was announced that she would not start that tide, but would wait until the next morning. By that time, however, some new cause of delay had been found, and so on for five successive days. It was the old story, the *malua*[1] of Fijian life, and a tropical climate infecting the white men who had come to settle in the country. This word is one of the first a new comer learns, and perhaps it is the one he will hear most used during his stay in the islands. It is an ill-omened word in a new country, and both in the past and present of Fijian history has blighted many an enterprise of great pith and moment. It were well for Fiji if this word could be wholly blotted out from her vocabulary, but of this there is apparently little chance. At length *malua* had brought us to the sixth day, and then we were allowed to go on board and prepare in real earnest for the long-deferred departure. The sails had been set, the windlass manned, and the word 'up anchor' was about to be given, when without warning the wind fell flat calm. With the angry surf that was roaring outside the reef, and the huge rollers that were chasing each other in through the opening, it would have been madness to attempt to sail out of the harbour without a good breeze on. All through the long hours of a hot summer's day we waited in vain for a wind, but it was not till daylight next morning that a land breeze came to our aid. This breeze proved a true one, and as it gradually freshened the

---

[1] Literally, by-and-bye; a word of very frequent use in the Fijian language.

little brig 'drew away' clear of the coral reef and great rollers, and by midday Ovalau and Levuka lay well astern.

Next morning we found ourselves near the island of Koro. Owing to light winds we had made scarcely thirty miles in twenty-four hours. But it was now the 'rainy season'—those four months of the tropical year so dear to every reader of 'Robinson Crusoe.' During that time the 'trade-winds' blow feebly, and sometimes cease altogether. Our vessel, too, was in bad 'trim,' and instead of 'beating to windward' as a respectable craft should do, drifted ignominiously sideways like a crab. Hence from Koro to Tavinni our progress was of the slowest, nor was it till the fourth day out that we dropped anchor at Vuna Point. Yet the whole distance was under ninety miles.

As this was my first trip in a labour-vessel, and my first experience of imported labourers, I may perhaps be permitted to describe the craft and her crew somewhat in detail. She was a small brig of some hundred tons, and belonged to that class of slow safe vessels that used to come out from England to the Colonies some thirty years ago. Her interior consisted mainly of a large hold without divisions or partitions of any sort. The floor of this was formed by the ship's ballast, and on this the imported labourers had spread their mats, and ate and slept. Their 'quarters' were roomy enough and well-ventilated, and were all the better for not being lumbered up with berths, as is the case in many emigrant ships. She was commanded by a captain (by courtesy) well known to all gentlemen engaged in the labour trade for his uniform success in procuring workmen. His mate was a Norfolk Islander, a direct descendant in the third generation of one of the mutineers of the 'Bounty.' He was a good seaman, brave as a lion, and liked the excitement and high pay that were to be had on board labour-vessels. Under these officers were an average crew of some six white sailors who had been shipped in Sydney, and who little cared, and possibly little knew, what people in Exeter Hall were thinking and saying about their doings. The brig had now just returned from a four months' cruise in that *terra incognita*, the Soloman Archipelago. She had procured in all forty-four labourers, and these had agreed to work in Fiji for the space of four years.

The Soloman Islanders are perhaps the most ferocious and intractable cannibals to be found throughout the whole expanse of the South Pacific. Those whom we had on board the brig were certainly an unpleasant lot of people to contemplate. They were perfectly naked, or, in some cases, wore the merest apology for a garment. Their skins were ebony black, their bodies ill-formed and dwarfish, their faces hideous with an ugliness peculiarly their own, and stamped, moreover, with an expression of truculence and cunning cruelty that allowed of no misunderstanding. Some of their number were apparently aged men; and nearly all of these suffered more or less from a chronic disease of the skin. This I recognised as a form of pityriasis, and it was commonly said by white men who had seen much of the natives to be caused by eating human flesh. Whether this was the opinion of the Islanders themselves, or whether it was a mere sailor's 'yarn,' does not much matter, as it is probably false. One thing, however, is certain, and that is, that persons thus afflicted in Fiji always go by the name of 'old maneaters,' and are regarded with more than the usual amount of aversion by the whites. The forty-four islanders on board the brig numbered amongst them a few tolerably well-formed and intelligent individuals. Two of them, who could speak a little broken English, acted as interpreters for the rest. Their food on board ship consisted wholly of yams and cocoa-nuts, supplemented by a little rice. Flesh, except of men, they were supposed not to care about. In fine weather they would congregate on deck, gesticulating and chattering in a strange jargon that no one could understand. During the voyage they had learned to pull together, and with a little teaching would probably have made average sailors. They were treated with very scant courtesy by the white crew, but, all things considered, were far from badly off. None of those horrors of the 'middle passage,' about which some fine writing has been inflicted on the public, ever came under my notice during my stay in Fiji. In rainy weather the labourers used to keep below, and amuse themselves eating yams, and making spears and arrows for imaginary campaigns, or, viewing their actions by the light of later catastrophes, shall it not be said rather that they were nursing schemes of savage vengeance against their white employers? If such was really the case, they lost, on this occasion, a rare opportunity of giving effect to their designs; for so unsuspicious were all the whites on board that, if attacked, they would have been taken unawares, and massacred to a man. Of course, as is generally the case in such catastrophes, there were plenty of arms on board—to wit, revolvers, Sniders, Enfields, muskets, cutlasses, and other weapons, but in the hurry of a general attack no one probably would have found them ready for use. In all likelihood the white passengers on board would have met the same miserable fate that befell their countrymen on board the 'Neva' a few months later.

Besides natives there were other passengers, and among the number some white women and their children. The tiny cabin of the brig was not more than about ten feet square, stifling in its closeness, and swarming, moreover, with cockroaches, earwigs, fleas, and other vermin. In spite of the heavy rain that fell so ceaselessly, most of us men preferred the deck, more especially as the unfortunate children below howled dismally all through the long night watches. And, indeed, this was not to be wondered at, for the ship was but a sorry place for any woman or delicate infant. The second night out was one of intense misery. I sat on the wet deck, sheltered indifferently by a waterproof coat, the gift of some good Alcestis before leaving England. Next to me was F——y, a man who, had his lot been cast in other times or circumstances, could hardly have failed to have left a name for himself. He was essentially a pioneer of civilisation in the widest acceptation of the term. He was a worthy member of that band of adventurous spirits of which England, since the days of Drake and Frobisher, has been so prolific. Without the savage coarseness and rough cruelty that too often disfigure the American of the far West, he had all the hardy courage, the native wit, the love of adventure, and the iron nerves that distinguish the American backwoodsman. His fertile brain soon devised a means of bettering our forlorn condition; and, by the help of a sail lashed to windward, we passed the night in comparative comfort. F——y possessed a true Tapleian humour. His spirits rose in exact proportion as difficulties increased. His whole life had been spent in wanderings to and fro in New Zealand, Australia, India, China, and the great Southern Ocean. Hitherto it had not been a success; for, though he had made other men's fortunes, he had not made his own. Alas, how many brave fellows scattered broadcast over many new countries resemble him in this particular! The battle assuredly is not always to the strong. People at home cannot realise what founding a 'new country' means. We read so glibly the narratives of adventure, of rare ability, of superhuman courage; success seems so natural and so easy a result, that we are apt to undervalue the kind of men who can do such things. Their number is small, as those who have been present on occasions when men are really tried can tell. There were some such in Fiji, and still are—broad-browed men of great physical as well as mental power, sometimes well educated, but more frequently destitute of bookish lore, and trusting rather to quick powers of perception and steady nerves. Unfortunately for themselves, men of this type generally lack one quality very needful in an age of excessive competition, viz., steady perseverance. Hence it comes to pass that other and meaner men outdistance them in the race for wealth or power. But for all that, their memories are very dear to some who have tasted the pleasure of their intimate acquaintance, and who are not careful to judge all things by the touchstone of mere success.

Then we had other passengers on board of quite a different turn of mind. There was a phlegmatic Dutchman, who drank brandy and treated his friends all round in a manner so unusual for him that he excited their astonishment quite as much as he won their approbation. After the voyage was over, indeed, a case of brandy belonging to the cargo was found out of its place, and open. No one could explain the mystery, and, as there was no law, no one, except the unfortunate owner, paid for the damage. 'Let it sweat,' was the usual coarse verdict in those days. There was another passenger on board who was sick unto death. Poor fellow! his last days on earth were sad enough. By a strange coincidence I found that his brother had 'proctorised' me just before I left Oxford, and in such an out-of-the-way place as Fiji this little circumstance served to cement our acquaintance. Before the voyage was over we became friends, and I believe I was enabled somewhat to soothe the weariness of his last moments. He had always been delicately nurtured, and was but ill-fitted for the rough life, the hard fare, and the trying climate of the tropics. He died when success seemed to be almost within his grasp, as did many another white man before that sickly summer was ended.

But at length the tedious voyage was drawing to its close. On the fourth morning from Levuka we found ourselves rounding the end of a dangerous reef that runs out to sea from Vuna Point, and scares away all cautious mariners. Seen at a safe distance this reef presented a grand sight. It differed from the reef at Levuka in that it did not encircle a placid lagoon, but, like a gigantic breakwater, stretched boldly out to sea, and defied the elements. As they encountered this adamantine barrier, the long Pacific rollers would pause for one moment in their stately march, and the next, rearing themselves sharply against the clear sky, would fall with a mighty crash, wrapping the coral rocks in foam. As the reef extended so far, an opportunity was presented of studying the waves in every stage of their formation. In one place, nothing would be visible but spray and broken water; in another, a perpendicular wall of water might be seen to rush on in eager haste, only the next moment to bury itself in its own ruins; while high over all hung the perennial canopy of mist which, when the sun shone, gave birth to innumerable rainbows. Vuna Reef needed no 'Inchcape Bell' to tell its position, for it uttered a sullen and ceaseless roar, ever loudest in calm weather or before a shift of wind. Heard in the stillness of a calm tropical night, though many miles away, this reef gave forth an ominous sound—a seeming knell, appalling enough to the seaman who felt his bark drawn within the influence of a strong current that in all weathers sets towards this spot. We, however, had nothing to fear, for the breeze was fresh and steady, and we soon anchored in a snug little harbour under the shelter of the high lands of Tavinni. Here, on the property of a planter, a rough hotel had been extemporised for the benefit of stray travellers, and here, accordingly, all took up their quarters for the time being.

This hotel unfortunately proved to be a place very different from Manton's genial house. Here were no cheerful companions, no afternoon bathe, no hospitable board, no influx of new faces. The refreshment bar at Mugby Junction was not more dismal than the bar of the Vuna Hotel. The landlord was a solemn taciturn man. He had a nervous way of constantly adding up his accounts, and repeating the result *sotto voce* to himself. He had been unfortunate in New Zealand, and would declare roundly that he believed he would be eventually more unfortunate in

Fiji. He was one of those men who are to be met with every now and then in new places, who have always apparently worked hard and yet have never succeeded in bettering themselves. This ever-present want of success may perhaps connote some mental deficiency, but in not a few of these cases there would seem to be no sufficient reason why the individuals should not succeed as well as other men around them. Sometimes one feels inclined to adopt the hypothesis that the stars have shed a baleful light on their nativity, and that the poor fellows are only the victims of untoward circumstances. In the case of our host, I learned that he left Fiji shortly after this time, and returned to New Zealand, not much the better pecuniarily for his two years in the islands. However, during my stay at Vuna, I received much civility from him, and I should be glad to hear that he has eventually succeeded in making an independence. As regards the Vuna Hotel of old days the less said the better. And yet, as it affords a fair example of the kind of accommodation that travellers still expect to find in many parts of Fiji after leaving Levuka, it may be well to give a short description of it. The whole house then consisted of four rooms, one of which formed the 'bar,' another the dining-room, while the other two were the bedrooms. These rooms were all equally hot, damp, and ill-ventilated. The beds were of the roughest kind, and very far from clean. The mosquito curtains, composed of heavy 'navy blue' calico, shut out not only the mosquitoes, but also every breath of air. The first night that I tried to sleep within their folds I was glad to throw them open, and endure for hours the torments of mosquitoes in exchange for a few mouthfuls of fresh air. It was now about seven o'clock in the morning, and after three days and nights in the little brig a good wash was an absolute necessity, and accordingly my first enquiry was, 'Landlord, when can I have a bath?'

'You can't get no bath here,' was the laconic reply.

'Well, let me have a basin and some water, at any rate.'

'Well, you can get a basin if you like, and I suppose you know where the water is—we don't do much washing here;' and with this he turned away and left me to my own devices. At length, after a great deal of delay, a basin was actually brought. It was an ancient one, seamed and scarred in all directions, with the dirt of years engrained into its substance. By a gesture the water-butt was pointed out to me, and thither I repaired full of confidence. It must be said that on Vuna Point there was no river and only one spring, which unfortunately existed on the property of a rival and hostile planter, who would by no means permit anyone to use the water. Consequently, all the water used for drinking and other purposes came from the clouds, and was kept either in barrels or iron tanks. In this case it was in an old barrel, and as I dipped the basin in I started back in horror. The sea that mocked the Ancient Mariner in that eternal calm was not more alive with loathsome forms than was that decaying water-cask. It seemed literally swarming with animalculæ. If you have ever seen a drop of impure water under the microscope of some philosopher you can form an imperfect idea of what I beheld in the water we were all about to drink. A cloud of mosquitoes hovered low over its surface, and stung me as I looked at them. I called the host's attention to the sanitary condition of his water supply, but he did not vouchsafe an answer. He was busy at his old work, adding up phantom accounts; and I could hear the words barely uttered —' six gins, three sodas, one brandy is one dollar fifty, and I hope as I may ever see it.' With such a man remonstrance was useless; so, straining out the diatomaceæ, the retiferæ, and what not, as best I could, I plunged my head into the cool water. After this I felt sufficiently revived to look about me with some feeling of interest, and as it wanted half an hour to breakfast I started on a voyage of discovery. It was now that I obtained my first view of tropical scenery. Although Ovalau is a fertile island, it cannot for a moment compare with Tavinni in either beauty or richness of vegetation. When first seen, however, from seaward, Tavinni, especially the western portion of it, is not at all striking. The coast is low and flat, and the hills that rise behind it, though covered with verdure, are not such as to give the traveller any very exalted notion of their beauty. But on landing he will probably confess that the accounts of the fertility of Fiji which have reached him, and especially of the north-eastern portions of it, have not been exaggerated.

Leaving the hotel and walking inland I found myself in the centre of a grove of tall cocoa-nut palms. These trees, at once the glory and the wealth of the South Sea Islands, were in full bearing. The luscious nuts hung in large clusters from their summits, almost lost in the crown of giant leaves that surrounded them. The grass beneath them was of a delicate green, marvellously soft and fragrant, and still wet with the morning dew. Passing further on, the cocoa-nut trees became fewer and fewer, while their places were supplied by trees of other kinds. In spots where the sun's rays had penetrated through the mass of dense foliage that overhung the ground, the soil had quickly responded to the light and warmth with a crop of flowers or fruits. Here rose the banana, weighed down with its clusters of golden fruit, while the pineapples that grew in profusion at its base tempted the traveller with their treacherous offerings. The hibiscus and cactus, clothed with red flowers, grew broadcast, and struggled for an existence with a host of other flowering annuals. The air was laden with the scent of lemon blossoms and jasmine, of limes and oranges, while high above all the breadfruit tree, one of God's choicest gifts to these islands, reared its massive stem and sombre foliage. The fruit, indeed, was not yet ripe, but even now could be seen the promise of an ample harvest. All seemed so strange and gorgeous, every beauty of tree and grace of flower was scattered with so lavish a hand, that I scarce knew what most to admire. I wandered on further, and soon found myself in the thick of the tropical forest. The air was no longer balmy, but hot, moist, and sickly. The grass here never dried, but grew long and rank, and was matted together with creeping plants that hung down in festoons from the branches above them. Here the breadfruit contended with the orange and the wild nutmeg; here grew the ivi tree, with whose flowers Fiji maidens are wont to deck their hair, and whose bitter nuts serve as food in years of scarcity; here was the banyan tree, with its giant roots stretching down like long arms from its branches; and here was the *resi*, so highly prized by native craftsmen, for it alone will resist the corroding action of seawater, and of it all war-canoes must be built. Besides all these there were trees, and ferns, and flowers whose mere names would convey but a poor idea of their noble forms and rare beauty. The denseness of their foliage shut out the sun's light, or only admitted here and there some straggling ray. From this mass of green suspended high above the earth, innumerable creepers and trailing plants hung down. Parasites, orchids, ferns depend from trunk and bough, interlacing with each other in fantastic forms, and turning in endless coils round the roots of the giant trees. Through such a tangled mass the traveller urges his way slowly and painfully. At every step he is tripped up, and must clear a path for himself with knife or tomahawk. He tramples under foot choice exotics, and ruthlessly thrusts aside or hews down creepers and ferns that would be the glory of an English hothouse. The air all the while strangely oppresses him, his temples throb, he perspires at every pore, he becomes impatient, and would fain push on more quickly. But he has not proceeded many steps before his foot catches in some 'supple-jack,' and he falls with violence to the ground. Thence, wearied and bruised, he rises, and proceeds with more cautious steps, until at length, with infinite labour and fatigue and loss of temper, he gains an open space. Such was my experience of a tropical forest. If I was enchanted on entering it I was somewhat less enchanted on leaving it. I had lost my way, was utterly exhausted by the heat and fatigue, and was, moreover, some hours late for breakfast. This latter misfortune, however, turned out in the sequel a positive gain. I received a hospitable invitation from the planter on whose estate the hotel was situated to breakfast with him, an invitation which my first experiences of a tropical forest rendered very acceptable.

CHAPTER IV.

Cotton-Growing in Fiji—A Plantation Breakfast—The Cotton-House—Labourers' Quarters—Sickness—Difficulties attending the Instruction of certain Islanders—Labourers at Work—Overseers—Tanna Men—Soloman Islanders—Erromango-men—Tokalaus—Ra-men—Fijian Labourers returning to their Homes.

WITH few exceptions, all who went to Fiji during the years 1870-1-2, went either to grow cotton or to be connected in some way with it. Fiji was emphatically a cotton-growing country until the commencement of 1873, when the cultivation of sugar began to attract the attention of capitalists.

To grow cotton successfully requires a great deal of attention and skill, together with a considerable extent of ground. Plantations, however, in Fiji, vary considerably in size, according to the amount of capital at the planter's command. Even the very best of them, in size and completeness, fall far short of those great estates which were once the glory of Virginia or South Carolina. Things in Fiji have always been on a much smaller scale. The largest plantation, at the time I speak of, was perhaps some 200 acres in extent, while the smallest contained but some ten or twelve acres, cultivated by a few Fijian labourers, aided by the proprietor himself. The estate on which I now found myself happened to be one of the most extensive and best conducted in the islands, and in describing it I shall introduce the reader to the pleasantest phase of plantation life. This plantation, then, extended over more than 150 acres of ground, all thickly covered with cotton-trees of the very best sea island variety. The mere number of acres fails to convey any idea of the money and time required to form such a plantation. Every acre has to be cleared of a dense forest such as has been described in the last chapter. Then the trees, when felled, have to be cut up and burned, the underwood to be removed, the ground hoed, and finally the cotton seed planted, and carefully tended for many months. All these processes involve much labour and expense, to say nothing of scientific knowledge ; and, unfortunately, many planters have gone to work without possessing either knowledge or money. Thus it has happened more than once in Fiji, that a plantation has been commenced, but only to be abandoned, and this after the planter had paid for his land, erected his house, and made good progress in clearing his ground.

Having premised thus much, I must now describe the routine of plantation life ; and, first of all, I will ask the reader to accompany me to the planter's house, or what, in Australia, would be called the 'head station.' Here we will enter ; and, after sharing the owner's hospitality, will go with him over his grounds, see his labourers at work, and find out what he thinks of cotton-growing as a means of making a fortune. His house is built of wood, like an American 'frame-house,' is one storey high, has an ample verandah all round it, and is roofed with galvanised iron. Now, everyone knows that iron is a conductor of heat, and therefore, it might be thought, the very worst material with which to roof houses in a tropical country. But it has been employed in Fiji solely because it affords a protection against fire. If the house were thatched in native fashion with reeds and cocoa-nut leaves, any malicious Fijian with an imaginary grievance might thrust an 'mbuka,' or fire-stick, into the roof, and destroy the house and its inmates. This has actually been done before on more than one occasion, and, consequently, most white men feel more secure under a roof of iron than under the more pleasant but treacherous thatch. The ground-floor, or rather the only floor, of the house is divided off into rooms, having doors opening towards the back and the front. They are constructed in this manner to facilitate thorough ventilation and coolness—for the two words are synonymous in the tropics. Entering the dining-room, I was introduced to the lady of the house, who gave me a cordial welcome, hospitality being a common virtue in new countries. There is no need to describe all the luxuries that were piled on that ample board—preserved meats from London, jams from Tasmania, curries made by the cunning hand of a Mauritius cook, native fish dressed in native fashion, roasted yams, baked taro, and many other Fijian delicacies. Everything was served up with an elegance that was the more charming from the savagery by which it was surrounded. During breakfast two black boys, dressed in red flannel, attended at table, while relays of savage men from far-off islands carried baskets of food to and fro between the kitchen and the house. During meal-time the doors were thrown open, and through them could be seen glimpses of forest trees and of fields of waving cotton, and beyond these again the line of breakers that marked the coral reef of Vuna. It seemed to me one of the prettiest and pleasantest spots in the world. If this is Fijian life and scenery, thought I, the more of it the better. My reflexions were cut short by the host proposing to take a ride over the plantation. A couple of horses were soon brought round, and we mounted. Close to the dwelling-house were several small buildings, all very much alike, made of reeds and roofed with thatch. These were the houses occupied by the white men employed on the plantation, such as the engineer, carpenter, overseer, and so forth. At some distance from these stood the cotton-house and ginning establishment. An eight horse-power engine brought from England supplied the motive power, while the 'ginns,' or machinery for separating the seed from the cotton, were tended by a number of little 'Tokalau' children, from eight to ten years old, who had come to Fiji with their parents. The cotton-house was built entirely of galvanised iron. The floor was smooth and polished, and scrupulously clean, and in many places covered to peculiar to itself. Nothing less than a long residence of years among the people would suffice to train the missionary for his work. But this continuous residence is a matter of the utmost difficulty. So innately ferocious and bloodthirsty are the natives, especially of the Soloman and New Hebrides groups, that any white man who would live among them must go armed, unless, indeed, his object be martyrdom. Otherwise, before he could possibly learn the languages and dialects of his congregation, he would, in mere self-defence, have to send so many souls of natives to Hades that the subsequent success of years might not suffice to compensate for their loss.

After visiting all the labour quarters we spurred our horses and soon reached the plantation proper. This was some half-mile from the dwelling-house. The road lay through what had once been the primeval forest. On every side were the dismembered trunks of great trees lying cracking and scorching in the midday sun, and ready to be set on fire the first windy day; among these, again, were stumps that had been uprooted, rocks that had been rolled away, and tangled masses of brushwood that had been cut down and now lay withering on the surface, or heaped up preparatory to being burned. On approaching the upper part of the plantation large groups of men might be seen busily employed at various kinds of work; some were on the outskirts of the cleared ground; others within the forest, where already their axes were laid at the root of many a tall tree. The islanders were all working cheerfully, but not with great skill or success. Indeed, it is not every man who can use an axe. Of all imported labourers, however, the Tanna men are the best for this particular work. They take to it kindly, and possess, moreover, great muscular development and powers of endurance. The axes which they use are of American manufacture, with handles of hickory, and especially designed for the roughest work. They will bear, as may be supposed, almost anything in reason, and sometimes indeed they are submitted to very trying tests. For instance, a lazy native tired of work will often deliberately strike his axe into a tree, and, pulling the handle sideways, break it off, in order that he may be obliged to remain idle while the axe is being mended. Under such circumstances, oftentimes repeated, it is perhaps scarcely to be wondered at if a white overseer occasionally loses his temper.

The majority of labourers at the time of my visit were employed in weeding the ground and preparing it for receiving cotton-seed. For this purpose they used knives about eighteen inches long, not unlike those which are to be seen in butchers' shops. Seated on the ground they cut the grass or small bushes which they then collected into heaps. Their work was very light, and, but for the intense heat of the sun, might have been performed quicker and better by a tenth part of the number of Europeans. But white labour in Fiji is too expensive to be used for such drudgery.

In Fiji white men are wont to work more with head than hands, and are valuable chiefly for their higher intelligence and administrative ability. Any white man who has had some experience in a plantation and can talk a smattering of the Fijian language is worth at least 50*l.* a year, with rations and a house. An overseer will get from 50*l.* to 150*l.* a year, according to his previous experience or the size of the plantation and the wealth of its owners. For the better class of appointments a person should have a thorough knowledge of cotton-growing, be a good accountant, and accustomed to manage natives. To such a man a share of the profits would generally be conceded, so that the position is one a good deal sought after.

Riding along the edge of the forest I watched the process of clearing with much interest. Here were a half-dozen of Tanna men with axes hard at work. They were felling an ivi-tree, the roots of which were of great size, and radiated in all directions from a central stem. Their work was very hard in that steaming atmosphere, but the men did not seem at all distressed. They were without exception the wildest-looking men, though not really the most ferocious, to be seen anywhere. They wore their hair long and twisted into minute plaits like those which may be seen in ancient Egyptian pictures. Of these plaits there could not have been less than two hundred on each head. Their ears were pierced, not with a minute hole for an earring, but with a large slit about an inch each way. The lobe of the ear was further dragged down by the weight of rings of tortoiseshell, or in some individuals by a plug of tobacco and a clay pipe. This, indeed, among many islanders is the favourite mode of carrying their pipes and tobacco or other very valuable articles. To all these Tanna men fancy names had been given by the overseer. There were Shakespeare, Bismarck, Napoleon, Jeff. Davis, and many others from the domain of literature or politics. One morning I happened to be present at roll-call on a plantation where the manager was a well-educated German, and the amount of brilliant names that passed before him on that occasion was truly surprising. First came Brasidas, quickly followed by Thucydides; then Schiller and General Jackson, Virgil and Cæsar, King William, and of course his *alter ipse* Bismarck. Nor were English worthies omitted, for there were Dr. Johnson, Byron, and Gladstone. More than one hundred names were required in all, so that the selection must have been a task of some little difficulty.

As we were watching the men at work the white overseer came up, and I was introduced to him. He was an Irishman, of about twenty-five years of age, whose home had been in strange lands ever since his earliest years. He was a short, dapper little man, with a merry twinkle in his eye and a determined look lurking about his mouth. He understood native character thoroughly, and took a great pride in his Tanna men, who formed, indeed, a sort of bodyguard for him.

It has often been remarked that these men attach themselves very readily to white men, for whose courage and superior knowledge they seem to have a profound admiration. In case of any *émeute* they are generally entrusted with firearms, and if properly led will face any foe. Occasionally, indeed, but very rarely, they have turned on their own employers; but when this has been the case there has been always some good reason for it. In one instance that came under my notice a Tanna man named 'Capitan' shot his master. But then the white man had been distinctly to blame, first of all in keeping the natives beyond the time specified in their agreements, and then in showing his revolver too freely when he did not intend to use it. Public opinion in Fiji in this instance took the part of the native, and his crime was punished as manslaughter instead of murder. The dress of these Tanna men cannot even be described to civilised ears. According to our notions it is more indecent than the absence of all clothing—but then fashion is as supreme in Tanna as it is on the Boulevards or in Regent Street. The services of Tanna men are invaluable in the procuring of labourers from other islands. They go in many cases as 'boats' crews,' and if well commanded neither bullets, poisoned arrows, nor hostile savages will deter them. If the days of gladiatorial combats should ever be renewed on earth they might fitly take the place of the Dacians and Gauls of Roman times. They are, it need scarcely be said, thoroughgoing savages—

cannibals to a man, and treacherous even to each other, which all savages are not. But they are essentially and above all physically brave, and their innate valour serves as a basis for that cordiality which generally exists between them and the white settlers. The Tanna men are curious feeders, if, indeed, a stronger word should not be used. Not only will they eat flesh of men and pigs, but also that of dogs, cats, rats, lizards, and flies. On one plantation I remember seeing a litter of puppies basking in the sun, which the Tanna men had been fattening for some weeks, and on which they proposed to have a feast on the ensuing Sabbath. They will sometimes catch a lizard as it wriggles away among the stones and while yet alive place it in their mouths. I never remember actually to have seen them do this, but have it on such good authority, both white and native, that the fact does not admit of doubt. In Samoa the more delicate and civilised natives, especially the women, look at these men with the greatest aversion and dread; and indeed no wonder, for they are 'unco' people enough when seen for the first time. Their women, I think, may claim the proud pre-eminence of being the ugliest in the world.

After this digression it is time to return to the labourers who were at work clearing away the forest. The presence of so many white men and their overseer is a sufficient reason why they should be more than usually diligent. As we watch them they ply their axes with increasing zeal, giving vent all the while to queer sounds, which sometimes rise to the dignity of yells. The chips fly in all directions, and at every stroke the tall tree visibly quivers. And now the brawny Napoleon deals an Homeric blow and the axe buries itself deep in the wood. But Napoleon in his haste forgets how to withdraw the treacherous tool, and, pulling the handle ever so little to one side, breaks it short off, while the head of the axe remains imbedded in the tree. His occupation is now gone, and the overseer bids him stand aside. The poor fellow obeys, quite crestfallen, and I wished from the bottom of my heart that I could then and there have repaired his error. But there was no time for this; Bismarck, Shakespeare, and Jeff. Davis have it now all their own way. They work with terrible energy till the perspiration pours down their dusky skins and the foam gathers on their lips; and now, after many well-dealt blows, the tree begins to totter. First a few ominous cracks are heard, then a shiver, as it were, runs through each giant limb, and the whole mass leans towards the sea. Now, Tanna men, is the moment for a few vigorous strokes! With loud cries they cut into the hard wood, and as the chips fly in all directions poor Napoleon receives rather a severe blow on the nose from one of these missiles. The old tree is all the while cracking and bending more and more, and at length with a loud crash comes to the ground. The dry branches leap high into the air, while many a trailing creeper and delicate orchid is crushed and buried in the ruin.

High above all the din rises a wild shout of exultation, and then the men sit down to rest after their labours. The overseer says a few words of praise to each, and introduces me all round as the 'Man of Death'—the Tannese periphrase for a doctor—and I shake hands with each doughty warrior, for war is in truth the real business of every man there. 'Big fellow tree that,' says Napoleon, who by this time has recovered his good humour, and is all the better for his enforced inactivity. There is no laziness about him, and after dinner he will ply a new axe with as much vigour, but it is to be hoped more discretion, than he did the old one. He is far too good a man to be allowed to remain idle, especially when there is so much clearing and other heavy work to be done on the plantation.

Having thus seen the Tanna men at work we shall do well to take a look at some of their fellow-labourers. First of all come the Soloman Islanders. They dwell apart in huts of their own, far away from the head station and the other labourers. They are a treacherous lot of men, both feared and disliked by their employers. Subsequently to the time of which I am writing, and when they were imported in greater numbers into Fiji, they committed some terrible outrages. Sometimes on dark and stormy nights they have been known to leave their huts, crawl stealthily down to the beach, and seizing any boat they could find, put her before the gale and make for the nearest land. Occasionally they have made a descent on some spot and carried off any luckless Fijians who might be there, and finally have killed and eaten them. About the time of which I am writing they sailed away in a large whale-boat, having captured three unfortunate Fijians who were tranquilly fishing on a coral reef and suspecting no evil. One of them they ate incontinently, the other two they killed and cut up into small pieces, which they pickled in a rough way with salt water, and carried with them for further use. Many of the Soloman Island labourers I had already met on board the ship during the voyage from Levuka, and they recognised me again, but the recognition they accorded me was forced and sullen, and did not, like that of the Tanna men, come with a good grace. Their country is a great archipelago of islands lying far away to the west and north of Fiji. It is a land of which little is known by whites, and what little is known of it is not to its advantage. It is unhealthy, and has not hitherto been productive of any articles of much commercial value. There is no difficulty, however, in getting there from Fiji. The trade-winds blowing strong and true will carry a ship more than fifty leagues a day to the westward. On the twelfth day out from Fiji, if the passage has been a quick one, the voyager will see dark masses of green foliage and tall cocoa-nut trees rising from out the waste of waters, and that evening may drop anchor off New Britain or New Ireland, or Bougainville Island. *Sed revocare gradum* becomes by-and-by the question. The wind is fresh and true as ever, and the long rollers tumbling in on the reef tell of strong breezes out at sea. But now wind and current and waves are all going the wrong way for the mariner bound eastward. There is no help for it, however, and a long beat to windward is inevitable. All that can be done is to ship a little extra ballast, to brace the yards sharp up, and to take advantage of every shift of wind during the tedious voyage back to Fiji. There are plenty of hands on board, or should be at any rate, in a labour-vessel. So the ship's head is put to it and she is allowed to 'thrash' her way back to Fiji. Some thirty days have come and gone and the voyage is not yet half over. The wind and sea are so heavy that little real progress is made. Meanwhile an eye must be kept on the natives who are on board. They have nothing to do now but hatch mischief, and already in their dull minds are vaguely wondering at the length of the voyage. At last the wind comes round a little. It is blowing very fresh, and the little brig leaps over and sometimes into the great waves. Every now and then as they strike her a mass of spray rushes over the cowering passengers. They have never in their lives kept the sea in such weather as this, and their best canoes would have sunk long ago. One by one they creep under the hatches and chatter by the hour, or sleep, or eat yams, or make spears and arrows for use on future occasions. Meanwhile, as the breeze freshens, the little vessel makes a terrible fuss, creaking and straining in every timber, and wetting everyone through and through. But the captain, however, knows what he is about; he served his time in a China tea-clipper, and his boast is that he will carry on with any man alive. He has, indeed, no certificate from the Board of Trade or any other Board, and is not on the whole a man ever likely to pass successfully a competitive examination. But for this sort of rough and dangerous work men are required rather than certificates; and this man has been tried before and never found wanting. Again, as evening approaches, the breeze gradually dies away. The sun sets in a fine weather sky, and the Southern Cross is seen a few degrees above the horizon. Next morning the breeze is back in its old quarter, that is, right ahead. Forty, fifty, sixty days have come and gone, and Fiji is once more in sight. The voyage in all has lasted four months, but has not been unsuccessful. There are seventy natives on board, for whose passage 10*l.* must be paid per head. Of this the captain will get 1*l.* and each seaman 2*s.* The second mate was wounded by a poisoned arrow as he was filling the ship's casks with water, and died within a few hours; so that the voyage has not been altogether uneventful. It was through some such voyage that these Soloman Islanders had just passed when I first saw them. They had, at any rate, been well fed, for they were fat and sleek, and their dark bodies smooth and shining. They did not, however, like work, and no wonder, for no one perhaps does at first—or at last for that matter. Quitting the Soloman Islanders, we come on a group of Erromango men. They are well-formed, but very black. They murdered their missionary a few years before—the Rev. W. Gordon. The sister of the man who dealt him the fatal blow with a tomahawk is below in the cotton-house, and will tell all about it by-and-by. She says that Mr. Gordon told the islanders that if they did not repent and become converted a pestilence would before long sweep them off from the face of the earth. That year, strangely enough, measles actually did come, and killed more than half the inhabitants. The old chiefs met; and remembering what the white man had told them, believed that he was punishing them for their hardness of heart, and resolved that he should die in his turn. They first killed his wife and child and then himself. This is the account given by those who were on the spot on the fatal day and witnessed the murder; but another version of the affair has been given in some quarters.

Close to the Erromango men are some Tokalans. They came from low-lying islands of sand near the Equator called the 'Radick Chain,' or 'Marshall's Group,' or sometimes the 'King's Mill Islands.' Cocoa-nuts are their principal food. They are passionately fond of alcohol in any form, and know how to make an intoxicating drink not unlike champagne from the young shoots of the cocoa-nut tree. They are a wild-looking set of men; their hair is long, and hangs like elf-rocks over their shoulders; their eyes are peculiarly large and handsome, and their teeth pearly white. Their skin is copper-coloured, and they belong to the lighter or Eastern race of the Pacific. They are very brave, and fight with knives in preference to any other weapons, and hence, being naturally pugnacious, their bodies are frequently strangely scarred and mutilated. Sometimes it is an ear that has been lopped off. Sometimes it is an eye that is missing, sometimes a finger or hand. The women fight side by side with the men, and adopt the same code of warfare. As a rule the Tokalans are friendly to the whites, and are found to be very good men for light work, such as cotton-picking. They have, however, neither the robust physique nor the uncouth manners of the Tanna men. They are not cannibals, and, indeed, their diet is limited to two articles of food, viz. fish (sometimes eaten raw) and cocoa-nuts. They are the only imported labourers who bring their women with them, and these, though sometimes very pretty, are, as a rule sadly deficient in moral virtue. They are, in fact, dreadfully naughty—far more so than any natives imported into Fiji. They are always well treated on plantations, and in return are good and trustworthy servants. On a plantation with which I am acquainted in Fiji a chief from the 'King's Mill Group' had settled with his family, but within a few months had sickened and died. On his deathbed he called the planter and solemnly made him a present of his children, who, he said, would work for him as long as he required. If the mother ever went away the children were to remain with their white protector. Then the father died, but I can answer for it that the adoptive father was faithful to the trust imposed upon him. I saw these little fellows running about the plantation happy and contented. They did not do any work, and were treated in all respects as white children might have been. The planter, who was a plain man, told me this himself, and added that he hoped never to lose sight of the orphans. As illustrating the haughty spirit and vindictive nature of these Tokalans, I may relate a tragedy which happened many hundreds of miles away from Fiji. A Tokalan chief had come to work on a plantation, bringing with him several wives. One of these he had presented to the overseer, and all her people had felt honoured by the white man's preference: just as the Jews had felt honoured by the promotion of Esther. But in time the white man grew tired of his dusky bride and bade her return to her former husband. This she refused to do, in spite of the entreaties of the chief, who warned her at length that if she continued to disobey him he would put her to death. She was deaf, however, to all warning; but one evening when returning from the cotton-field she chanced to meet her husband, who then and there cut off her head. He fled away into the bush, and was soon pursued by some of the inhabitants of the island. But pursuit came too late, for suicide had quickly followed murder. His body was afterwards found deep in the forest, unburied and uncared for.

Suicide is by no means uncommon among these people. Rather than face the sea of troubles that threatens them they prefer to die at once. One case of this came under my notice in the person of a patient of my own. He was slowly though surely recovering from an attack of dysentery. But one morning, when I went as usual to visit him, I found him hanging lifeless to one of the beams of his house. His fellows buried him without any solemnity, only requesting the 'white fellow carpenter to make one box.'

Besides those already mentioned there are other nationalities to be found among the labourers imported into Fiji, but they require no particular notice. There are, for instance, Banks' Islanders, some of whom had never seen a white man until the labour-ships visited them. They are willing workers, somewhat timid and shy at first, but capable of great improvement. There are Sandwich men, whose heritage of fragrant sandalwood has exposed them for years to the attacks of Tanna men, and occasionally even of the far-off Tongese. There are Niue men, the 'savage islanders' of Captain Cook, tattoed on the backs of their necks, and excellent men on board ship. Finally, there are two strange and solitary beings who have come from an unknown country and speak an unknown language. They were picked up by a passing vessel many hundreds of miles from any known land, floating in the same tiny canoe in which they had been blown out to sea. They had lived on shellfish and a few cocoa-nuts as best they could, and when found were but skin-and-bone. No one could understand what they said, and they have never named their country ; or if they have, the name does not correspond with that of any island on any chart. They are now fat and sleek, and as happy as the day is long. There is an entry in the ship's log of the latitude and longitude in which they were found, and this is probably all the clue they will ever have to their lost homes.

A totally different but equally important class of labour to the cotton-planter must now be mentioned. That spoken of hitherto has been imported from a distance. But there is besides this the native, or Fijian, as opposed to the foreign or imported labourer. On the east side of the great island of Viti Leon is a tract of coast-land some hundred miles or more in extent. The soil there is niggard and the landscape dreary and uninviting. There is no tropical vegetation, no sands fringed with cocoa-nut palms, no calm lagoon; nothing, in short, to cheer or stay the traveller. The coast is rugged and ironbound, affording no harbour even to the small craft that visit it occasionally from Levuka. So studded is the sea with reefs and rocks and shoals that the mariner can never sail except by daylight. Then, indeed, from the masthead he can generally discern the outlines of the coral rocks and the 'horses' heads' in sufficient time to avoid them. This coast is known in Fiji as 'the Ra,' or, where it trends away to the north, 'the Ba.' The land here is a mere narrow strip, running backwards at most a few miles, after which it is lost in a chain of lofty mountains. These mountain fastnesses have been from time immemorial the homes of a race of cannibals, who have never as yet embraced Christianity nor submitted themselves to the authority of Cacobau. They make frequent raids on the people of the coast, who are thus exposed to all the miseries of a predatory and never-ending warfare. It has been already shown that the country of the lowlanders is dreary and unproductive. The inhabitants are hemmed in on one side by the ocean, on the other by the mountains and the warlike tribes they contain. This state of things, continued through centuries, has left its mark on the race. Compared with Fijians from other parts of the group these lowlanders are a degraded and miserable set of men. With them the struggle for existence degenerates into a mere struggle for food. I have often seen them stalking along the seashore like gaunt spectres, searching with wolfish eyes among the rocks and stones for something to eat. But besides food these people stand in need of weapons to defend themselves against their cannibal neighbours. How to get these weapons was a problem which long exercised their minds, and which the white man at length solved satisfactorily. When cotton-growing began there was, of course, a great demand for labourers. The earlier settlers found on the Ra coast an ample supply of this. On the one hand was a half-starved race of men, lean with hunger and harassed by hereditary foes; on the other, fields white with goodly blossoms of cotton, but perishing for want of hands to gather them; hence an arrangement was soon effected. The planter agreed with the native chief to supply him with say ten muskets, with powder and bullets in proportion.

For such a gift the chief would lend the planter perhaps thirty young men for the space of a year. Each of these was to receive in goods the value of 3*l.* sterling, and be brought back at the planter's expense to his home. These goods were of course given and received at a value previously fixed by each party. The three pounds generally represented a musket, a flask of powder, twenty bullets, some tobacco, and a *sulu* (waist-cloth) or two. If these articles did not actually cost the white trader the sum for which they passed current, they at any rate represented a far greater value to the native, whose very existence depended on his being better armed than his opponents. After the bargain had been struck the chief used generally to send down to the village a message that so many men were required to go to work. A sort of conscription then took place, and in a very short space of time the thirty men marched down in Indian file to the beach, and amid a great deal of noise embarked on board the planter's vessel.

Here they were packed as closely as herrings, but this was a matter of small moment when the voyage was so short. Sometimes the planter would not be able to complete his complement of men at one place, and would have to visit several villages. I have known men thus occupied for more than a month, and finally obliged to return with perhaps not more than half a dozen men. As soon as the planter has obtained enough to satisfy his immediate wants he turns his face homewards. If he lives, as most probably he does, up to 'windward,' he will have a head-wind the whole way back; but by keeping in-shore, and going along quietly at night, when the land-breeze is blowing, and taking his chance of reefs and shoals, he may get back to his plantation in two or three days. During all this time the natives are generally fed by the planter, though theoretically, I believe, they are supposed to feed themselves. There is, of course, nothing worthy of note on such a voyage as this. The natives sleep all day and night, eat enormously, and smoke cigarettes of native tobacco. They use one another as pillows with the greatest good humour, and sometimes sing a monotonous chant that possesses little either of poetry or music. At last they arrive at their destination, where they meet other of their countrymen who have arrived before them. They soon build themselves a house of reeds, and within twenty-four hours after their arrival may be seen at work in the cotton-field. They are provided with long butchers' knives, and chop the grass and weeds in a lazy and unworkmanlike manner.

Most planters consider them an unsatisfactory lot of people, and would willingly pay 10*l.* more for the passage of Tanna men than be troubled with these lazy Fijians. However, all planters have not the requisite money, and hence are compelled to employ these inferior workmen. A planter dares not coerce these Fijians in any way, for then they would at once tell their chief that they were ill-treated, and would refuse to remain on the plantation. They would very likely steal their employer's boat, and with a fair wind return home on the first opportunity. Sometimes they will plunder and even occasionally threaten the planter with violence. If the latter be an American or Frenchman, he will defend himself with his revolver or as he may best think fit. If he be an Englishman his better plan will be to submit quietly ; for should he shoot or wound a native even in self-defence, he will most probably be 'deported' to Sydney by the next ship-of-war and tried for his life. Even if acquitted he will be a broken man, ruined in purse and in credit, his plantation overgrown with weeds, his cotton crop lost, and his soul embittered by what he feels to have been a cruel injustice. There is, fortunately, however, one method by which these Fijians may be kept somewhat in order. Their country is nominally subject to Cacobau, and they are therefore to a certain extent vassals of Bau. Hence the word of a Bau chief according to his rank generally carries more or less authority with it. Such a chief used to be found ever present in the person of Ratu Johnny, who used regularly to visit those plantations in Tavinni where Ra men were at work. A word from a planter would always procure the presence of this formidable personage. Before him the most loud-talking and rebellious Ra man would collapse as quickly and completely as did Thersites before Odysseus. Nor, if guilty, was his punishment very different from that of Homer's demagogue. Ratu Johnny or one of his henchmen would administer a sound flogging, or as many as were necessary, until the refractory workmen were thoroughly convinced of the injustice of their cause. After this they would work smoothly for a few months, till the re-appearance of the redoubtable Johnny would again proclaim that a hitch had occurred somewhere. After the year of their contract had expired the natives were, of course, returned to their own homes. The day on which they left the plantation was one of no little importance to them. On that day they received their wages for the past year. In most cases they were allowed to choose in what form they would take the money coming to them. As a rule all would gladly take the musket and bullets; but as several shillings then remained to be expended, there was room for varieties of taste. Some preferred the balance of their money in tobacco, others in percussion-caps, others in gaudy prints or ribbons, and by no means a few preferred a bottle of gin to everything else. When all the wages had been paid over there followed a season of infinite mirth and confusion. Guns would be fired in all directions, not loaded with ordinary charges, but half-filled with powder, on the top of which wet sand had been placed, to increase the noise of the explosion. The reports that some of the tough old Tower muskets made under this treatment more resembled the noise of cannons than of guns. Why they did not burst more frequently is difficult to understand. They were, however, of good metal, and many of them had been tried in their country's behalf. With many of these muskets the quaint brass fittings and flint locks bespoke a respectable antiquity. From the dates on the barrels many of them might have done good service in the Peninsular campaigns, or have been levelled against French Cuirassiers at Waterloo. When a sufficiency of powder had been expended the time had come to say good-bye to the friends left behind. Here the gin came into play, and caused such copious tears and such noisy and agonising adieus that a stranger might have thought the time-expired men were about to embark for a journey across the river Styx, and that the planter's vessel was nothing less than Charon's awful ferry-boat. In the midst of salvoes of musketry and hoarse shouts of 'Good-bye' to their comrades on shores the emancipated labourers are finally induced to go on board. The trade-wind is blowing fresh and fair; in a moment the excited natives have by main force lifted the anchor and set the sails, under the direction of a solitary white man. Their tears are dried now, their theatrical grief has quite subsided; they begin to eat voraciously of yams and cocoa-nuts, and one by one to drop off to sleep. Meanwhile the little craft has gained the open sea, where she glides along under a genial sky and over the blue waters, broken only by the curl of some breaker on hidden rock or sandbank. The Englishman who steers the boat and one native of Rohinal, or Savage Island, who keeps a look-out for dangers ahead, are the only persons awake on board. Meanwhile the little craft goes steadily on, and next day reaches the village which some of the passengers call their home. Here the same noisy scenes are repeated as at starting, but with these the captain or employer has nothing now to do. He goes down the coast ever further, dropping portions of his sable human freight at different places until at last he has landed it all. He is now prepared to take on board another set of labourers, but perhaps these are not so easily to be obtained as he would wish. It may require several weeks before he can get the number he requires, and at this work we will leave him; wishing him all the success that perseverance, energy, and diplomacy have a right to expect.

CHAPTER V.

Another Plantation—Salt Beef—Bachelor Planters—Starting a Cotton Plantation—Purchasing Land—Sources of Trouble with Natives—Advantages of Possessing an Entire Island—How to Procure Labourers—House-building—Native Servants—Sowing Cotton Seed—Feeding Labourers on a Plantation—Cotton Picking—Cotton Ginning—Uses of Sea Island Cotton—Cotton Growing as a Commercial Speculation—Elements of Uncertainty in it—Living on Credit—Commercial Morality—Death of a Planter—Omens—A Fijian *meke*—Night Air.

IN the commencement of the last chapter a plantation was described such, perhaps, as every plantation might be if the owners were capitalists. Were this the case no doubt planters would surround themselves in Fiji with the same luxury and comfort as in Ceylon or Virginia. But, unfortunately, very few planters in Fiji are capitalists, or have even enough money to keep up the most modest establishment. The plantation described in the last chapter had been formed by Sydney merchants. It had cost some 7,000*l*., and in the end had turned out a losing concern to the proprietors. And now it will be well to visit one of the poorer class of planters, and see how he has fared since he came to settle in Fiji. He is a man of middle age, and wears that peculiar tropical look which makes people appear much older than they really are. His house is small, and built of reeds and cocoa-nut leaves, like those of the natives about him. The floor is formed of gravel, while a screen of native manufacture roughly divides the whole house into two portions, which by courtesy may be called rooms. The roof or ceiling is as it was left by the native workmen, and has become a refuge for centipedes, spiders, cockroaches, and other vermin. To a wretched habitation like this the unfortunate planter, who has been for the most part delicately nurtured, has brought a wife and family. Few European ladies can stand the climate of Fiji, and this lady is no exception to the general rule. His children are probably all sick and irritable to the last degree; and no wonder, for, likely enough, they have never been exposed to a temperature night and day of 85° Fah., and consequently are suffering from 'prickly heat' and the so-called 'Fiji sores.' These sores are common to all new arrivals, and are most annoying while they last. In the moist hot climate of the islands any wound or abrasion, however slight, may refuse to heal, and, assuming an unhealthy character, may remain uncured for weeks or even months. There is, fortunately, little or no pain attending such sores. They are indolent if left alone, but if irritated by work or bad food are very liable to become unmanageable, and then a trip to a more temperate climate is the best remedy for them.

The planter and his family have no servants, except one Fiji woman, who is more trouble than she is worth, besides being a consummate thief. In addition to all this the food they are obliged to eat is of the coarsest and most unpalatable kind. Salt beef, as salt and tough as beef can be, that has been several years in cask, and has circumnavigated the globe; ship-biscuits swarming with weevils, a boiled taro or yam, and a few bananas are their usual fare. This coarse fare may not, perhaps, affect the planter himself, but it tells cruelly on his children. What with the sickly heat, the insufficient food, the mental anxiety, and the rough life generally, every member of the family is more or less an invalid.

At sunrise the planter leaves his house and commences work. For him there is no such luxury as an overseer, and indeed he has so few labourers that such an official would be a mere mockery. His labourers are reduced, from one cause or another, to about a dozen Tanna men; and having no immediate prospect of being able to pay even these men himself, he will have to hand them over to some more successful neighbour. His plantation, however, in spite of everything, looks well. There are some forty acres of cotton in full bearing, but the planter is at his wits' end to know how he can pick it. He has no men of his own, while his neighbours have not sufficient for themselves, and are, therefore, in no mood to lend. In this melancholy state of affairs he will, perhaps, endeavour to retrieve matters by his own exertions. He may work along with his Tanna men from early morning till towards evening under a burning sun, and returns home at length, weary in mind and body, only to find, perhaps, his wife attacked by fever, in addition to her other miseries, his children more sickly than ever, and a letter from the Levuka merchant informing him that one of his bills will fall due in a few days. Such is a truthful sketch of a phase of plantation life which I have seen more than once in Fiji. These hardships and disappointments are, of course, in some degree of the planter's own causing, for no man ought to undertake such a thing as cotton-growing without sufficient capital. Still, for all that, men are sometimes unduly sanguine, especially in new countries. Should they succeed they deserve the more credit; should they fail they deserve sympathy rather than ridicule or abuse.

Between the two extremes of the two kinds of plantations described above there are, of course, different degrees of comfort or discomfort. Generally a clever manager will make things fairly comfortable, and this is especially the case if the planter has had a little capital to commence with. One thousand pounds should be enough to start a fair plantation; that is, of course, with average luck as regards the seasons and the procuring of labour. Occasionally a man may have bad fortune, either through sickness, hurricanes, difficulty of procuring workmen, or other causes, such as to falsify the most careful calculations; but if a man has been ordinarily lucky, and has had sufficient money in his pocket to start with, plantation life should, as a rule, be pleasant enough. Such a man will be able to build himself a wooden house, and furnish it with some little regard to decency and comfort. The food, indeed, when I was at Fiji was always coarse and bad. Salt beef was the staple article of diet. This beef, it must be borne in mind, was not like the ordinary salt beef that might be used in an English household or served out to well-fed soldiers or sailors. The beef used in Fiji, in early days, had been in brine for many years. Some said it had once been in the Navy, and had been condemned. However this may be, I know in many cases it was in a very unwholesome and even disgusting state. 'Can you eat salt beef?' used to be a question often asked in Fiji. For myself, though I tried during two years, I could never learn the art.

As might be expected, food in such a condition, and in a climate like that of Fiji, proved to be very unwholesome. In a case which came under my notice a planter, who lived in a distant island, had come to Levuka expressly to purchase beef and other provisions for his plantation. On arrival home the cask was opened, and found too late to be in a bad condition; but there was, however, no help then. It had to be eaten somehow, and the result was an attack of dysentery, which nearly proved fatal. In addition to salt beef Australian meat could generally be obtained in Levuka at the time I write of. This was good as an occasional change, but many seemed to dislike it almost as much as they disliked the salt beef. No fresh meat was to be had save fowls and pork anywhere in Fiji out of the capital. Fowls, when they could be bought, were generally sold at from one to two shillings each. The vegetables principally in use were yams, taro, and pumpkins; and of fruits, the banana, orange, and cocoa-nut. Most of these latter grow plentifully in Fiji, but are rarely eaten by whites. They are considered a food more suitable for native stomachs, and to most whites become very distasteful after a short trial.

As regards the inner life of a planter little need be said. Few of the planters have either time or inclination for reading, even supposing they could procure books. There may be exceptions to this, but what I have stated above is the rule; indeed, a large plantation will occupy a man's whole time and thoughts, and he is fortunate if he can snatch a few weeks' holiday in the course of the year.

Let us look in on a bachelor planter and see how he enjoys life. We are sure of a hearty welcome, at any rate, for he is of a most hospitable turn, and ready to share the last morsel of beef or 'nobbler' of gin with friend or stranger. The planter whose home we are about to visit is a young man of some thirty years. He left England at the age of fifteen, and went to Queensland. After a few years of public school training, and with his education far from complete, he had been sent across the seas to farm sheep. Of course neither his parents nor friends generally had the slightest notion of what sheep-farming really meant. His mother, indeed, considered that his name, and the fact that he was a gentleman by birth, would somehow induce the Colonial authorities to present her son with a valuable run, ready fenced in and stocked with sheep of the best breeds. He received letters of introduction to the Governor of the country and other men in official positions, with an outfit of warm and heavy woollen clothes, and was packed off without any great regret on either side. On his arrival in Queensland he soon got into the ways of the place, learned to ride a buckjumper, found his letters of introduction were as useless as his warm clothes; discovered also that, as he had not a capital of some eight or ten thousand pounds, it was folly to attempt sheep-farming. Then for several years he wandered about the country on horseback, leading a thoroughly Bohemian life, doing odd jobs on stations; sometimes snubbed, but on the whole well received and fairly treated by the wealthy and self-made men whose houses he visited in search of employment. After some ten years of this work the rush to Fiji commenced, and soon the rumours of it reached the distant sheep station he was on. He followed the multitude, invested a very small capital in the purchase of a piece of land, and now behold him a tolerably happy and prosperous man. He has long ceased to look on England as his home, and has no wish to return to it. His Fiji house is his castle, and he is quite contented with it. As we enter his welcome is cordial and hearty. He bids us be seated, for though there is only one solitary chair in the house there are plenty of empty gin-cases, which are quite as good for all practical purposes. A bottle of square gin is soon produced; and as there are not enough of glasses the company drink out of teacups or pieces of cocoa-nut shell. Every man helps himself with tolerable liberality, for the weather is sultry and provocative of thirst. By-and-by dinner is brought up; it consists of a piece of salt beef, flanked by a plateful of yams, to which a fowl has been added. The fowls, by the way, on most plantations are as wild as partridges, and scattered all round the house in the cane-brakes, or further away in the forest. But this difficulty is soon overcome. A Fiji man grates a piece of cocoa-nut, and, placing it on the ground, utters a peculiar sound. In a few minutes the fowls come hastening in from all points, and begin to peck with might and main. Meanwhile a Fiji man has loaded a fowling-piece with a tremendous charge, and, for fear of missing his mark, has crept up stealthily to within a few yards of the doomed bird, which he straightway blows into space. The remains are picked up, and within half an hour are on the table. Meanwhile, it is worthy of notice that the dinner, in spite of the primitive cookery, turns out to be a success. The guests are all in good spirits, and have plenty to say for themselves. The planter has not heard any news from Levuka for a month, nor any from England for six. He does not care very much for English news, but is always interested in anything from Queensland, which he has gradually come to regard as his native land. All his friends are there, and some of the happiest days of his life have been spent on pleasant 'head stations.' And now dinner is over, and the guests sit in the verandah, and smoke pipes and drink gin-and-water, and philosophise on things in general. The host points to a retriever dog that crouches at his feet. This dog is old and cross, and might be considered useless, but its owner values it more than fine gold or precious stones. He tells us that that dog and one other possession are the only things he prizes much in this world. We ask him what that other is. He hesitates, and at last calls out 'Sulu mai!' when, presto! a pretty young creature suddenly appears from the interior of the mosquito-curtain and places herself by his side. This is Sulu, the light of his rough home and the companion that makes a hard lot at least endurable. Sulu is a Samoan native of some seventeen years old. Her complexion is but little darker than that of a Spanish or Italian woman. Her hair, long and wavy, and unfettered by any artificial headgear, streams wantonly over her graceful shoulders—

> Fa nove crespe l'aura al crin disciolto
> Che natura per se rincrespa in onde,
> Stassi l'avaro sguardo in se raccolto
> E i tesori d'amore e i suoi nasconde.

Her eyes, like those of all her countrywomen, are large and full, realising to one's mind the Boôpis of Homer, while, like Aminda, her dress, though concealing yet reveals the graces of her form. To this young girl the white man seems almost a godlike being. The light air and blue eyes that tell of his Northern descent are more beautiful to her than the swarthy features of her own people. His strength, his courage, his power generally, are greater than she has ever seen in the greatest chiefs of her own country. On his side her love does not go unreturned. Before he knew her his house was a dreary-enough place, rough, untidy, and uncomfortable. But since Sulu has been there much has been altered for the better, and home-life, in a word, rendered somewhat tolerable. She did not appear at table with his guests, because a coloured person is no more allowed in Fiji than in India or the Southern States of America to eat with a white man. Though the host himself might not particularly object to it his guests probably would, and, at any rate, it is not the custom of Fiji. It would be superfluous to enquire into or defend from a moral point of view the relations that exist between the planter and this Samoan woman, unless it were to glorify ourselves by a contemplation of our superior righteousness. After all the case stands somewhat as follows:—With infinite toil and pains, and after the lapse of some centuries, we in England have succeeded in developing a certain code of civilised morality in latitude 53 N. and amid the fogs and rain-clouds of an English climate. This done, we proceed to make one code a standard by which to judge people all over the world. We weigh them in a balance of our own construction, and then, without any misgivings, declare them to be found wanting. Some may think that a man situated in the peculiar circumstances we have described should be judged somewhat differently from one surrounded by the comforts and luxuries of civilisation and wealth. However, this is not the place to find arguments for or against a man in such a matter. I relate only what has come under my own personal observation, and can merely state that it would have been quite impossible in any account of Fijian life to have avoided a reference to the peculiar relations which, more or less, have always existed, and still exist, between whites and natives. It is, however, only fair to add that these relationships are not nearly so frequent as might be supposed, and, with the growth of a healthy public opinion, will become less frequent every year.

Having now given, or tried to give, some idea of what plantation life really is, I shall proceed to describe the process of starting a plantation. The first step is, of course, to procure the land. This is generally done by purchasing from the chief of the district a certain block or section which the planter has probably already determined would suit his purpose. To effect this purchase might seem a simple-enough matter, but not unfrequently it has been found to be both troublesome and difficult, and sometimes even impossible.

The planter must first of all make, as far as possible, certain that his estimate of the cotton-growing capabilities of any given portion of land are correct.

It frequently happens that land apparently fertile enough in itself is yet not suitable for cotton-growing. The best soil for cotton is said to be a light, friable one, and the best situation to be one with plenty of sunlight and well open to the sea-breeze. Without sunshine and fresh breezes Sea Island cotton will not grow to perfection, that is, the pods will be neither numerous nor large. The tree itself may all the while seem to flourish most luxuriantly, but it is only wood and not cotton. The land being chosen, the next step is to effect a purchase of it from the chief. But previously to this the planter must most carefully search for all persons who have a claim or think they have a claim to the ground in question. Land has very frequently been sold more than once by the same native to different individuals without their knowledge or consent. And hence, unless every precaution be taken as regards the title, infinite confusion will afterwards result. Nor is it always possible to find the important chief when he is wanted to conclude the bargain. He may be gone on some warlike expedition to a distant part of the group, he may be busy drinking kava or gin, or finally he may choose to keep a white man waiting weeks or months, just to show his own importance. The most vexatious delays to the planter occur from all these and similar causes, and may result in the loss of many valuable weeks or months at a most important season of the year.

As to the price of land it varies a good deal in different parts of the group. In the best districts of Tavinni it has been known to go as high as thirty shillings an acre, though perhaps an average of one pound an acre would more nearly represent its general value. Land close to the seashore is more expensive than that in the interior of the country. In many cases thickly-timbered land is highly prized, because, although the labour of clearing is greater, the soil is almost certain to be highly productive. Some land is also covered with valuable groves of cocoa-nut trees, which form a source of income immediately available to the purchaser; or perhaps land may contain wild yams in abundance or produce bread-fruit, or other things, all of which can be utilised as food for the labourers on the future plantation, whereby an important saving may be effected. Occasionally, in old times, land instead of money used to be given by a chief in return for work performed. Thus a land surveyor once received as much as 600 acres of first-rate land in payment for professional services, and this land he afterwards sold for more than one pound an acre. Grants of land, too, were sometimes made by a powerful chief to his favourites; and in this way, many of the earlier plantations in Fiji were started. Occasionally a whole island can be purchased, and when such is the case it is best for all parties. There are innumerable small islands scattered among larger ones in the Fiji group, especially towards the north-eastern portion of it. These generally contain several square miles of arable land, and are well supplied with cocoa-nuts, bread-fruit, bananas, oranges, and other tropical productions. The value of such islands is now well known, and probably no island of any size could be purchased now for less than from 3,000*l.* to 5,000*l.* The advantages of possessing an island are, that there are no natives to rob or otherwise annoy the planter, as they are always removed at the time of sale; that no fencing is required; that there are ample supplies of food, and other facilities for keeping stock, such as sheep, horses, fowls; and, finally, that the soil and climate of such islands have been found by experience best suited to the growth of the finest varieties of Sea Island cotton. Occasionally a subordinate chief will oppose the sale of a certain piece of land, and then the white man must pay him a further amount, unless, indeed, the leading chief is sufficiently powerful to overrule the claim.

Supposing, however, that a planter has obtained the land of his choice, his next step will be to procure labourers to work it. This he may do in two ways, namely, either by 'purchasing,' that is, paying the passage-money of certain Tanna or other emigrants to Levuka, or by sending a vessel down the coast, and procuring Ra labour. If he has money at his command the former of these two plans is much the more preferable; if he has not, he must of necessity adopt the latter. Frequently a Levuka merchant will provide him with a certain number of men at a fixed charge per head. This money need not always be paid in cash, but can be written down as a debt secured on a future cotton-crop. In this way a planter may find himself in debt before even beginning work. At the same time that he is effecting arrangements for a supply of labour with this agent in Levuka, the planter will have also entered into a contract with the Fijians in his immediate neighbourhood to construct him a dwelling-house. A contract of this sort the natives will generally undertake with great readiness, and perform with sufficient punctuality. The white man addresses himself in the matter exclusively to the chief of the village, who then provides the necessary men and materials and receives all the payments. The natives begin their task by first clearing the ground; they next raise a square heap of stones on the site of the future dwelling, and make the surface even with sand or shingle.

In many cases this preliminary work is dispensed with, but a house is always drier and more healthy for being elevated some height above the surface of the ground. The next step is to drive in several posts, generally three on each side, and two at each end. These form the frame on which the future walls are to be built. This done, some natives more skilful than their fellows place in position the beams for the roof. 'The ridge-pole,' as it is generally called, is the most important of these, for on it will fall the task of resisting hurricanes or other violence. The ridge-pole is not unfrequently the entire trunk of a cocoa-nut tree, which is generally quite long enough to extend between the gables of an ordinary house. Having thus got the framework together the rest of the work is comparatively easy. It consists in placing smaller posts between the large ones, and then twisting reeds between the smaller ones, somewhat in the manner of a basket. These reeds are all tied with cocoa-nut fibre to the main posts, and thus not a nail need be used in the construction of an ordinary native house. As soon as the walls and roof are finished the contract is considered to have been performed. The planter must provide himself with doors, windows, and furniture generally, for such luxuries are never seen in Fijian houses. The doors and windows can be purchased ready-made in Levuka, into which place they have been imported from San Francisco or New York. Where natives are prowling about, a good door and a good lock are not among the least important requisites for a planter's house. As to other furniture he may practically please himself. Many men are content with boxes or empty gin-cases for chairs, with a few planks of wood for a table, and with a supply of mats laid on some bamboos for a bed. One essential, however, for sound sleep is a curtain large enough to surround the bed on all sides, and to rest on the floor; otherwise the mosquitoes will render sleep impossible.

A kitchen is always built at some little distance from the house, and consists of a few posts driven into the ground and roughly covered in with cocoa-nut leaves. In most cases the furniture of the kitchen is as simple as that of the house. A large pot to boil salt beef and yams, and a few stones to form a native oven, are all that some planters allow themselves. Occasionally, however, the cooking apparatus is more elaborate, and in a very few cases a 'range,' perfect according to English ideas, may be met with. As to cups, saucers, and glasses, if they could be procured of iron or triple brass so much the better. Nothing short of this would ensure their preservation from native stupidity and carelessness. Many of the native servants, arguing from a knowledge of their own wares, consider cups and plates to be merely shells which the white men find in the seas that surround 'Sydney' or 'London.' They are mightily astonished at the brittleness of these 'shells' in hot water, and at the planter's wrath when they are broken. However, it must be allowed that, considering all things, native servants learn their duties with tolerable quickness, and become eventually good cooks and butlers.

But long before such can be said to be the case the planter will have fairly commenced work. His men will have arrived from Levuka, or his own ship will have come in from the New Hebrides or Soloman Islands, or, finally, his Ra men will have been sent up from Viti Leon by their chief. His house will have been finished, and will have cost him from one to two pounds sterling per fathom of six feet, for such is the native mode of reckoning, learned, no doubt, from the first white sailors who visited the group. Fortunately for the planter, it matters not what the height or breadth of his house be, as it is only the length he pays for. Thus a building 36 feet long would cost some six pounds sterling; or, if any extra timber or workmanship had been used at the owner's request, the price might be somewhat higher. The windows, doors, and other necessaries might safely be put down at the same price as the house, and thus it might be said that a house such as has been described might be taken possession of for about twelve pounds sterling. The chief would probably accept goods in part payment, and hence, as regards the planter, the actual cost might by this means be somewhat further reduced.

Having got his land, house, and a few labourers together—twenty imported foreigners, we will suppose, and the same number of Ra men—the planter may commence work in earnest. Thus far, supposing he has purchased 100 acres of land, his disbursements will have amounted to at least 400*l.* He has now to provide his natives with tools, which, however, consist only of American axes and long knives. The axes he gives to the Tanna men, and sets them to cut down the heavier timber. The knives he puts into the hands of the Fiji men, and orders them to clear away the long grasses or brushwood with which the ground is encumbered. This kind of work requires a good deal of time and labour, and there must of necessity be so many interruptions to it that even with forty good labourers the second year will have passed before the whole plantation is in full bearing. But no planter waits until the whole extent of the ground has been cleared before he begins planting his cotton. So soon as a few acres, say ten, are ready he employs a portion of his men in planting them with seed. In many districts, on the removal of the forest and brushwood the surface of the soil is found to be as clear of weeds as if it had been newly turned over. This is due to the fact that the tropical vegetation which it used to support was so dense as to shut out the sunlight, and so render all vegetable life impossible. As soon, however, as the rank growth has been removed from the surface the soil below is found to be wonderfully productive. The planter, if wise, will plant his seed with his own hands, or otherwise it will not be sown with regularity or neatness. The mode of planting is simple enough. A hole is made with a stick in the ground, half a dozen seeds placed in it, and the hole filled up. A mark is then placed over the spot, in case the seed should not germinate. Four feet further on another similar hole is made, another mark placed over it, and so on until all the cleared ground has been gone over. When the sowing has been finished the labourers return to the work of clearing another portion of the plantation, coming back, however, to the cotton-trees as soon as they have grown a few inches in height.

Meanwhile the forty labourers have to be fed, and how this is to be done is frequently a knotty problem for the planter to solve. Sometimes there may be sufficient food in the shape of cocoa-nuts, wild yams (*tivolis*), bread-fruit, or bananas in the forest to keep the wolf from the door. In that case one man in every ten will be told off to find this food and cook it for his fellows. There is no need to see that this individual works well, for if he does not his hungry comrades will themselves take his case into consideration. More frequently, however, the planter is obliged, especially during the so-called winter months, to purchase yams or other food. This is a heavy item of expense, especially where many labourers are employed, and sadly reduces the calculated profits. Sometimes, however, it is impossible even to buy food. In such cases half or perhaps the whole of the labourers on a plantation will be taken from the cotton and sent out to get food as best they can. Many Polynesians seem to have an instinctive knowledge of the places where the wild yam is to be found; though it may be hidden many inches below the surface, they will root after it as cleverly as the pigs in Perigord are said to root after truffles. There need be no anxiety felt lest the labourers should not find enough to eat, for they are thoroughly accustomed to this work in their own country, and Fiji is more fertile than most oceanic islands. After many months of continuous labour, many disappointments, and much anxiety, the planter at length may have the satisfaction of seeing his lands day by day becoming white with the pods and blossoms that are to win him wealth and independence.

His cotton is now ready for picking, and this to him is the busiest time of all the year. If the weather is unpropitious at this critical moment, if his men are too few in number, or lazy or insubordinate, all his money, time, and anxiety will count for nothing. We will suppose, however, that his cotton-crop is a good one, that his trees have arrived at maturity, and have escaped the treacherous worm, the hurricanes, and the many other dangers to which they have been exposed during the period of their growth.

This is indeed supposing a great deal, and there are few practical men in Fiji who would not tell you it is supposing far too much. There are yet, however, many other dangers to be confronted. At the moment when the cotton is being picked from the trees rain may fall in torrents, saturating the opening pods, discolouring them, and thereby reducing their value one-half. Again, the cotton may ripen so quickly over a large extent of ground that the labourers may not be able to keep pace with the prolific yield of the plants, and thus again a very large percentage of the crop may be lost. The next step is to dry the cotton, and this the heat of the sun will generally do in about twelve hours. It is then carried into the cotton-house, the weight carefully noted down, and the name of each individual picker and the amount he has picked registered. At the end of the week these amounts will be added up, and the man who has worked hardest, or at any rate most successfully, will receive a clay pipe and tobacco, or perhaps a boar's tusk, the prize most coveted of all others.

The cotton may now be said to be ready for ginning, and for this purpose will probably be sent to a neighbouring plantation where a steam-engine is at work. The ginning consists of separating the seeds from the cotton-wool, and this is done very completely and quickly by some machinery made specially for Sea Island cotton. After ginning the cotton, if really good, comes from the machine in long, silky masses, very different from its dingy appearance in the pods. It is then collected and pressed into bales, which are generally purchased by some merchant in Levuka, deep in whose books the planter is tolerably certain to be by this time. From Levuka the bales are shipped to Sydney, where they are subjected to such enormous pressure that the cotton already pressed loses further three-fourths of its bulk. In this state it is put on board one of the Australian clippers and conveyed to London, whence it is forwarded to various parts of England and Europe.

Such cotton as Fiji produces is far too valuable to be used for ordinary purposes. It is to the common cotton what a chronometer is to an eight-day clock. While American or Bombay cotton may be worth from sixpence to ninepence a pound, as much as five shillings has been obtained for an unusually good sample of Sea Island grown in Fiji. The special use of the Fijian cotton is to mix with silk. For this purpose it is bought largely by French and Italians, and is then transformed by the looms of Lyons and Milan into those gorgeous textures that excite the cupidity of all civilised women.

And now a word as to the pecuniary position in which the planter will find himself after all the labour and expense he has occurred. Will he probably gain or lose by his attempt to grow crops? This is the important question. The answer cannot be given categorically, for many elements of uncertainty will always enter into it, some of which may now be discussed.

At the commencement of cotton-growing in Fiji the most exaggerated notions were current as to its profits. Nothing in truth could look on paper a more captivating or secure speculation. To begin with, the land could be bought at a cheap rate, and if the country improved, as everyone said it must, would become in time exceedingly valuable. Then labourers were so cheap—only three pounds a year per man, and three men were said to be sufficient to look after two acres. More important, however, than all else was the well-known fact that the cotton-tree was one of the most prolific of plants, both in the quantity and the frequency of its yield. Three crops a year were what the sanguine planter confidently anticipated, and indeed would often count upon, as though they were already picked and stored in his house. No very accurate statistics as to the amount of cotton produced per acre or the expense of its production have ever been obtainable in Fiji, few planters caring to trouble their heads with such calculations. It used to be said that twenty pounds sterling per acre might be considered about a fair net profit, and nothing was more easy than to show on paper that such a result was not only probable but well-nigh certain. The expenses of 100 acres planted were roughly estimated at some 200*l.* a year, thus leaving a margin of profit on which the earlier planter hoped to be able to retire after five years of work.

How miserably all such expectations were falsified it is almost unnecessary to remark. Some of the causes, however, may be pointed out which tended to dash such bright hopes and make so many men bitterly rue the day when they embarked their fortunes in Fiji. At the very commencement there were land troubles to be encountered. After the planter had paid his money and was about to begin clearing, some wretched 'claimant' would turn up, with some alleged priority of title or some indefinite grievance about payment or what not. Sometimes it would be a white man, in which case arbitration or an armed defence or a tame surrender of rights were the only possible courses open. More generally, however, all the trouble would be caused by some petty chief, who considered himself hardly used in the matter of the sale of the land, and would try to extort more money from the planter by threats of violence. In such a conjuncture the planter, especially if French or American, would generally know how to defend himself. But if, unfortunately for himself, he happened to be a British subject, he could only fall back on the superior chief from whom the land had been purchased and request him to be good enough to keep his rebellious vassal in order; or, with still less chance of redress, refer his case to the British Consulate. The Consul would hear his statements and promise to lay them before the captain of the first ship-of-war that should come into Levuka. He could, of course, do no more, and with this the planter would have to rest satisfied. When the promised vessel did at length arrive of course the captain had received no instructions in the matter; and if he entered into it at all was pretty certain to side with the native chief, who not only was a chief, and hence *ex ipso facto* much better than a mere planter, but was also perhaps an ally of the missionaries, and even backed by their influence.

Supposing that these troubles have been safely tided over, and the land eventually acquired, the next source of loss arises from the difficulty of procuring labourers. The whole theory of cotton-growing proceeds on the assumption of a plentiful supply of cheap labour. Hence the rationale of the employment of slaves in America and other countries in its cultivation. As regards the labour traffic generally the subject will be considered hereafter more in detail; but for the present it will be enough to say that the planters' requirements in the matter of labour were very frequently not fulfilled, and this from a variety of causes. At one time there would be no natives in Levuka disengaged, at another time the labour-ships bound from the New Hebrides or Soloman Islands would be kept back by head-winds or bad weather; at another the workmen actually on the plantation would desert or refuse to work without the slightest warning. Again, there would always be a considerable percentage of labourers sick, to say nothing of those who were shamming, or of the women and children and old people, who could not be expected, even under favourable circumstances, to do a proper day's work. Many of the new hands, who now for the first time in their existence saw a white man, and learned what work really meant, were so stupid and obstinate as to be of scarcely any use for some months, during which valuable time was being lost, at perhaps the most critical season of the year. By-and-by the planter would see with dismay that the first twelve months of his plantation life were actually gone, and that instead of being out of the storekeeper's books he was deeper in them than ever. Perhaps, however, he had had capital of his own, in which case he would now begin to perceive clearly enough that cotton-growing was a matter of considerable expense and doubtful profit. After nine months, supposing he had commenced planting at a suitable time of year, say March, he ought to have a little cotton ready for picking. And now it is time to speak of some of those peculiar difficulties and dangers which surround a Sea Island cotton-crop, and to which the dangers and difficulties that surround other crops are by comparison insignificant.

First of all, as to Sea Island cotton and what it really is. All cotton used in common has probably been derived from some one wild species, just as all the varieties of pigeons have descended from one common parent, supposed by some to be the blue or the rock pigeon. In the same manner Sea Island cotton is a variety of the cotton-plant produced from other plants by careful selection through a number of years. This selection was first practised in some of the small islands that lie off the coast of Georgia and Florida, and the cotton from the place where it was first produced was called 'Sea Island.' If examined carefully this cotton will be seen to differ from the ordinary or Egyptian in some important respects. For instance, the tree on which it grows is smaller than the Egyptian cotton-tree, the leaves are of a different shape and size, and the seeds are separate within the pod, instead of being agglomerated together.

As regards the cotton itself, the most unskilful eye can at once detect a difference in the length and appearance of the 'staple,' as it is called. The Egyptian is short and of a dull white; Sea Island is long and silky, and in fact from its appearance might be called 'vegetable silk.' It is the length and glossy whiteness of fibre that give to Sea Island cotton its high commercial value. Nearly all these qualities, however, have been artificially produced, and depend for their continued existence on a careful and systematic cultivation.

It is well known that artificially-produced varieties, whether in animals or plants, have a strong tendency to revert to the type of their ancestry. Hence there is a continual struggle on the planter's part to prevent his dearly-prized Sea Island variety from reproducing in successive generations the gross leaves, the thick wood, and the short staple of its low-born parent. To guard effectually against this untoward result he must pick by hand and examine every seed before committing it to the ground. Any seeds that are found agglomerated together or too large in size or not black enough in colour must be promptly cast away. But after all, from even the most carefully picked seed there will spring up a certain number of trees that will recur to the Egyptian type and lose many of the characteristics of the pure Sea Island. These trees must be destroyed as soon as noticed, otherwise insects will convey the pollen from their blossoms over the whole plantation, inoculating the best trees, and thereby injuring not only the growing crop of cotton but also the next year's harvest of seed. By care this tendency can generally be checked, but there are no lack of other difficulties in the background. No sooner has the cotton appeared above-ground and put forth tender shoots and leaves than they are attacked by a worm. This animal is to the cotton-planter what *oidium* is to the vine-grower. It soon, if allowed to go unchecked, eats its way into the central stalk of the leaf, destroys the circulation of sap, and so quickly kills it. To resist these subtle attacks the young plants must be watched and the insects brushed off daily, and all the dead and decayed leaves removed. As the plant approaches maturity the dangers that gather round it are even more difficult to guard against. For example, too much sun will ripen the pods before they have attained their full size; too much rain will ruin their colour and destroy their value. With the greatest care and skill a large percentage of pods will always be lost at picking-time, chiefly from this latter cause. It happens, too, that the weather in Fiji is generally wet from December until March, and during these months the heaviest crop of cotton will frequently be produced. Even in settled weather a sudden shower will often break over a district, and before anything can be done in the way of protection will severely damage the cotton that is spread out to dry. Then there are other dangers to be encountered in the various processes of ginning, of packing, and of transit from the island where it was grown to Levuka. It has happened sometimes that a large crop, when safely housed and ready for exportation, has been set on fire by a revengeful native; but this has not been a very frequent occurrence. Besides all these sources of loss there must be mentioned the hurricanes that devastate Fiji at intervals of a few years. When one of these tempests comes upon the luckless planter his position is indeed pitiable. Not only is his cotton damaged, but his trees are actually uprooted from the ground, and carried perhaps into the sea or some neighbouring river. His dwelling-house, kitchen, labourers' quarters, and cotton-house may all be levelled to the ground in the space of a few hours, and his boat broken in pieces, while he perhaps congratulates himself that he has escaped with his life. It must not be supposed that these dangers and difficulties are merely potential, and may or may not happen. On the contrary, the records of cotton-planting in Fiji will afford numerous proofs, if proofs be needed, that the above account of the risks of cotton-growing is by no means fanciful or exaggerated.

When, however, to all the above is added the expense of living on credit and working with borrowed capital, as many planters are compelled to do, it is easy to understand how cotton-growing in Fiji has not paid as was expected. The earlier planters committed numerous errors owing to their want of technical knowledge and experience in this peculiar industry. Some of these errors were such as might have been amended, while others were irretrievable. Many whites started with insufficient capital in the first instance, and consequently from the commencement of their work were obliged to borrow at high rates. They expected, of course, to clear themselves in a year or two; but instead of this it was found that the cotton in many cases scarcely paid for the working expenses. Every bale of cotton, as it was produced, had to be shipped to the merchant at Levuka, with whom the planter kept an open account. The value of the cotton was placed to his credit, and seldom sufficed to clear off old scores. Then he had to borrow afresh to pay his labourers, borrow more to procure fresh ones, and borrow still more to pay interest on the existing debt. On the top of all these money difficulties would come some disastrous hurricane that would level to the ground his cotton-trees, his houses, and his hopes in indiscriminate ruin. Nevertheless, in spite of all these drawbacks it is difficult to understand how, with a sufficiency of capital to start with and tolerable prudence and skill on the planter's part, cotton-growing in Fiji should not be a paying speculation. As soon as the labour traffic shall have been organised on a proper basis, as soon as a bank and insurance office shall have been established in Levuka, and thorough business connexions formed with other countries, there will be no reason why cotton or sugar growing should not yield ample returns. Till then, however, the greatest caution must be exercised in the investment of money, or disappointment and loss to the speculator will certainly be the result.

I have spoken about the expenses of living on credit, and have now a word to say in regard to those storekeepers who at one time used to advance money and goods on credit to the planters. These men were no common usurers or mere greedy money-lenders. They were enterprising men, and in most cases themselves large planters. There being no recognised Government in Fiji, there was no such thing as legal security for money lent, or possibility of recovering the same by any legal process. Thus the strange sight was continually afforded of money advanced without security, and of a man's word being taken instead of his bond. Very seldom indeed, at least in early years, was the confidence thus reposed wilfully abused. But at length, about the year 1871, the number of planters had so increased throughout Fiji that some other system was found to be necessary for the protection of all parties, and hence one reason for the formation of a Government. Up to the end of 1871, however, the storekeepers of Levuka had been obliged, in order to carry on their business, to advance both money and goods to planters, and accept a bare acknowledgment of the debt as security. As might be supposed, in several cases they incurred heavy losses. But after all this system, though apparently so insecure, was not really so. Most of the storekeepers knew exactly the class of men they had to deal with, and knew that if they could possibly pay their debts they would undoubtedly do so. Such vulgar methods as repudiation or intentional compromise were seldom or ever thought of on either side. Nor, indeed, would such methods in any way have bettered an unprincipled debtor. In a small place like Fiji every man's business was pretty well known.

If it could be shown that a planter would not pay his 'storekeeper' in Levuka when able to do so, another merchant would, most assuredly, refuse to give him credit. As a consequence of this he might find himself unable to pay his labourers, or to provide himself with food, anywhere short of Sydney. But to trade with the sharp business communities of Sydney or Melbourne required either ready money or substantial security; and hence dishonesty in Fiji came in most cases to be a suicidal policy. Still a knowledge of this fact need not change our estimate of those early traders who boldly ventured on such perilous enterprises in a country about which so little was known. Had it not been for the energy and capacity of men like F. and W. Hennings, Fiji would never have so quickly and so thoroughly become an English community. They and men like them were the channels through which capital flowed into a new field from the old and wealthy communities of Australia and New Zealand. If their ventures succeed in their lifetime the profits should justly be large, as their conceptions and labours have already been. Should they not, however, ultimately be successful, such pioneers of progress, at any rate, deserve a meed of praise for the good work they began.

It was now some weeks since my arrival at Tavinni, but I still continued the guest of the planter whose acquaintance I had made on the voyage from Levuka. Over him, poor fellow, a change only too common among Europeans in Fiji was rapidly passing. Dysentery, that foe dreaded by all white men in tropical countries, had laid a heavy hand upon him, and day by day was slowly but surely compassing his death. Anxiety of mind during a harassing and exciting fortnight in Levuka, followed by the trying voyage from Levuka to Tavinni, had changed a slight sickness into a mortal one. Some Fiji natives who visited him on the last day of his life prophesied that he would die about the turn of the tide, which at the time of their visit was coming in. In this case, as in many others which subsequently came under my notice, their words proved true. Some hours after this it was 'high water,' and scarcely had the tide begun to ebb from the reef when poor W—— died. That persons apparently do die in Fiji more often at the time of 'high' or 'low water' is a phenomenon which has been frequently remarked and commented on. There is probably some truth in it, and it may possibly be due to certain atmospheric changes occurring about those times. In England, in the same way, every hospital nurse will tell you that more deaths occur in her wards between midnight and four o'clock in the morning than at any other time in the twenty-four hours. Natives and whites in Fiji further allege that when a certain fly of the 'blue-bottle' species hovers round the couch of a sick man his end is not far off. To the sick man who knows this the buzz of this loathsome fly becomes at once a sound of terrible import. Some mysterious and unerring instinct has seemingly prompted it to settle on the bodies of dying men, and thus to their fading intellects it comes as a messenger from beyond the grave, as a herald of approaching doom. Such notions are no doubt absurd and unscientific; but nevertheless they are firmly held by the Fijians, and by not a few whites who have lived for any length of time in the islands.

The same day on which W—— died his body was laid reverently at the foot of an old ivi-tree. In this spot a grave had been made by his Tanna men, and round it assembled the few settlers which the district contained. The scene was an impressive one. At one end of the open grave stood the fellow-planters and personal friends of the deceased, and facing these a motley crowd of swarthy, wild-looking men, brought together from many a far-off island of ocean. On one side was a tropical forest, with its heavy masses of foliage hanging listlessly in the sultry air; on the other the Pacific Ocean, ever chafing and fretting against those coral reefs which severed the island from the outside world which lay beyond them.

According to the usual custom in Fiji all plantation work was suspended on the day of the funeral. The labourers, freed from their daily tasks, soon spread themselves in all directions, each in search of his own particular form of amusement. The Tanna men strayed into the bush to look for wild yams or insects, or, in short, whatever they could by any possibility eat. The Tokalans, more intent on social joys, wandered up and down the coast, visiting their countrymen and regaling themselves with the milk of young cocoa-nuts. The islanders from Banks' Group speared fish or fired arrows at them as they darted in and out among the tufts of coral. The Fiji men made small fires, on which they roasted yams and land-crabs and discussed all the gossip of the group. As the shades of evening crept on, the coral reef became dotted here and there with lights; canoes with torches in their bows flitted noiselessly over the glassy surface of the lagoon, while the merry laugh of the crews that manned them was borne landwards by the evening breeze, and, as a few of us sat under the verandah of the planter's house, fell somewhat discordantly on our ears.

About half a mile from where we sat some Fijians had lit a fire on a point of land, and were now about to perform a *meke*, or native dance. Forming a circle, each man grasped his neighbour's hand, and then altogether uttered a loud shout. At first their movements were tame enough, but they quickly became fast and furious. Each man strove to outdo his fellows in the strangeness of the contortions or the grotesqueness of the attitudes into which he would twist his body; and although each seemed to work legs, arms, and body solely on his own account, it soon became evident that even the wildest movements were more or less concerted and bore a relation to the rest of the dance. There was a Coryphæus whose gestures and motions every dancer strove to follow and imitate. The ruddy glare of the fire burning brightly rested on each moving figure in turn and made it stand out clearly and well-defined amid the surrounding gloom. At intervals a sudden blaze leaping up would reveal to view the swarthy, wild-looking men as they circled in the mazes of their giddy dance, and the fitful light would quiver and play on the muscles and sinews and brawny arms of the dancers while they brandished their spears in the air or wielded ponderous war-clubs. With faces bedaubed with soot and naked bodies smeared with oil and ochre, the uncertain glare of the fire the while illuminating now their features, now their bodies, they appeared strange and unearthly beings, such as might fitly bear their part in some wild Walpurgis Night or fill a niche in the 'Inferno' of Dante. By-and-by the fire sank down, and in the gloom that succeeded you could scarcely distinguish the half-human forms as they moved restlessly to and fro amid the sombre stems of the forest. The burden, too, of the women's voices was borne on the breeze as in dreary cadence they sang for the dancers, and with these notes too came mingled the harsher sounds of bamboo drums. The ruddy flames leap up once more, and this time the women can be seen as they bend forward over the fire and sway their wrinkled bodies to and fro, pausing in their dreary movements only to heap on fresh fuel. After a brief pause the wild revelry is once again at its height. The men, in a frenzy of fierce excitement, career round the fire, bending at one moment to the earth as if in flight, at the next brandishing club and spear in all the insolence of victory, chanting all the while a wild war-song, which swells ever louder and louder, and masters at length even the Corybantian din of the rude drums. The orgie ended, the light dies out as quickly as it flashed forth, and once more the weird old hags and the painted warriors and their wild measure are suddenly lost to view, wrapt in the profound night of the forest around. The revels are ended, but only for a short space. They will be renewed again, not finally to cease until the moon sinks behind those distant hills. Then the furious Bacchanals will gladly snatch some hour or two of feverish rest, for they know that the stern reality of the cotton-field awaits them at the earliest dawn of to-morrow.

While the savages were enjoying their hours of mirth, a few of us whites still lingered on the verandah in a more sober and thoughtful frame of mind. Our conversation was of him who had so lately sat there with us; and as we thought of his early death we conned over all the chances and risks to which the settler in Fiji is peculiarly exposed—risks to fortune from capricious winds or untimely rains, to health from hard fare and a treacherous climate, to life from the hostile and ever-present savage. Thus musing we sat far into the evening, till the cold land-breeze began to blow down from the central ranges and a heavy dew to settle on everything around. This of all others is the moment of the day most dangerous to health in Fiji. The freshness of the evening air is not health-giving, as in England, but treacherous, and sometimes even deadly, and cannot be too carefully guarded against by all who desire to avoid attacks of rheumatism or fever. As a rule, indeed, the climate of Fiji is healthy enough; but for all that it is never safe to expose oneself carelessly to the breeze that blows off the land after sunset.

CHAPTER VI.

A Fiji Canoe Voyage—Scenery along the Coast—Shipwreck—Old Hands—A Deserted Plantation—Dangers of Canoe-travelling—Arrive at Wairiki—A Native Teacher.

NEXT morning I awoke with a slight touch of fever; and this not passing off immediately, I determined to remove some thirteen miles higher up the coast to a large native town, once the capital of the island. After some little delay, owing to not being able to obtain any means of conveyance, I fortunately made the acquaintance of a planter who was about to proceed to the same place, and accordingly we agreed to travel together. On such journeys in Fiji it is usual to procure a white man's boat if possible, but occasionally the traveller must be contented with a native canoe. These canoes, except in the case of the large war-canoes, are simply trees hollowed out and sharpened at both ends. They are kept on their keels by means of outriggers connected to the sides by a framework of wood. As may be imagined, such crafts are very liable to upset, especially when the *cama*, or outrigger, becomes submerged; it then loses its buoyancy and leverage, and becomes a source of weakness instead of strength.

The canoe on which our fortunes were embarked on this occasion was about twenty-five feet long by one broad. The outrigger was some four feet distant from the body of the canoe, and the connecting framework was covered over with a few rough boards. On these my companion had piled his freight, consisting of some tea, a large package of sugar, several knives for his labourers, some tobacco, and other plantation stores. The crew consisted of two Fijians, who were provided with paddles, and were supposed to do all the hard work. These paddles were in shape not unlike teaspoons, and in length about three feet. When we were all on board and the cargo had been safely shipped, it was impossible not to see that the canoe was very unseaworthy. Her enormous length and narrow beam did not promise much safety in rough weather; while the sides were not more than a few inches above water. Add to this that there was a very sensible leak in the bottom, which necessitated the use of a large baler every few minutes. However, I comforted myself with the thought that my fellow-voyager knew the customs of the country much better than I did, and had besides a valuable cargo at stake. If an accident should happen, I had at most to dread a wet jacket or perhaps a shark.

The canoe lay at a little distance from the shore, and the Fiji men offered their backs to carry us on board. This custom is always adopted towards those to whom special respect is intended; it is, in fact, a delicate compliment conveyed by deeds rather than words. It cannot, however, be recommended as a mode of locomotion to anyone wearing a decent coat, for native backs are always smeared with cocoa-nut oil, some of which is certain to adhere to the traveller's garments. As soon as we were safely on board, the canoe was pushed into deep water, and the natives, jumping in after us, began to ply their paddles with a zeal which evidently could not last long. Indeed, in a very short time they grew tired of the short, quick stroke, and exchanged it for a slower one. Every now and then they would make a spurt, and send the canoe through the water for a few minutes at great speed; but after this they would cease altogether and light a cigarette or eat a yam or commence a conversation. Such is the mode in which work of every kind is done among the Fijians, and to every remonstrance that was made our men returned the usual answer, '*Malua vaka leilai*' ('Wait a little').

The scenery as we worked our way slowly up the coast was thoroughly Fijian. At one moment we were skirting a belt of low flat land, dotted here and there with the homesteads of planters, and already in many places white with early cotton-blossoms. Behind the belt of low-lying ground rose a central mountain, which formed, as it were, the backbone of the island. Its slopes were clothed with vegetation of varied form and hue, while its summits were scorched and brown and barren, and in many places lost in a zone of clouds. Advancing further the coast became more bold in character. Our canoe was now gliding past a wall of solid rock, against which the waves rose and fell gently—for the trade-wind in its daily journey had not yet come thus far. And now, peering cautiously over the side of the canoe, we could see through the clear water the bottom, some forty feet below. There the tufts of coral, with branching stems and embryo leaves, formed as it were a miniature forest, while round their bases were clustered in rich profusion delicate algæ and odd-looking shellfish; while fish many-coloured as the rainbow darted to and fro within that fairy abode. Some of these fish were bright blue, others, like those in the 'Arabian Nights,' orange or black; others, again, striped alternately with black and white. Here, indeed, was an aquarium on a truly gigantic scale. But beautiful as are all these forms of marine life, their beauty is borrowed in part from the element by which they are surrounded. Seen when the tide is out a coral reef is shorn not of half but of all its charms. The shapely trunk and spreading branches of the coral-tree become mere sharp and vulgar points of rock which pierce the feet of the unwary naturalist; the seaweeds lie flat and dull, the shellfish are dingy and commonplace, while the gay-coloured fish are no longer to be seen, for they have followed the retreating waters seawards.

As our progress up the coast continued the scenery again became changed in character. We crossed a deep and narrow bay, fringed by dark masses of trap-rock, and overshadowed by dense and somewhat gloomy foliage. How a vegetation so profuse could thrive on soil so uncongenial seemed at first sight difficult to understand, until a nearer approach revealed little patches of rich loam, hidden away in crevices of the rock, which in many places was so smooth and bare that the hardiest creeper could scarcely cling to it. Behind this rocky barrier the mountain rose sheer and abrupt, while its steep slopes were covered with underwood and trees of many varieties. There, for example, was the ever-present cocoa-nut palm, the bread-fruit, the *dilo*, that yields a costly gum; the *nokonoko*, or iron-wood, well suited for war-clubs; the *daku*, or Kauri pine of New Zealand; and the *vaivai*, which will neither crack nor warp in the hottest weather. Were you to stand, indeed, on shore, under the shadow of these lofty trees you would see but little, for the stifling air and sombre twilight of the tropical forest would be all round you. At a little distance from the shore such, however, is not the case. Here you can distinguish the various forms of leaf and bough, from the deep ripe tints of the older growths to the more delicate green of the young leaves, which seem struggling upwards towards the light and heat of the sun. At intervals, through some chance opening, you catch a glimpse of white stems innumerable, which like great pillars bear up the leafy dome; while orchids and ferns and delicate mosses cling to every branch, and tangled creepers hang in festoons from tree to tree, or trail in rope-like masses on the ground. So sheer is that mountain-side and so deep that bay, that the sun's rays seldom disperse the solemn gloom that rests on its shore. Save for a few hours after sunrise trees and ferns and creepers alike all live in a dim twilight. Beneath their dark shadow all is rank and decaying. On all sides the ground is thickly strewn with a chaos of dead forms, with leaves and fruits and fallen timber. When a tree falls it quickly becomes enveloped with moss or fungus or other parasite plants. Then worms and ants in countless swarms infest its bark and win their way into its solid texture, so that soon it lies hollowed and worm-eaten, and fast crumbling to dust. Fruits or dead bodies that chance to fall on that rank soil quickly become seething and festering masses, instinct with loathsome shapes. So swiftly, indeed, do the swarms of insects seize on their prey that they might almost seem to have sprung fully formed from the earth, but all the time they owe their being to the hot breath of the tropics, which quickly brings life out of death, and metamorphoses all matter with a rapidity unknown in other climates.

But soon we had crossed this deep bay, and were now coasting along a rock-bound shore. Far above us on the mountain-sides could be seen great masses of foliage, but for all that the trees were small and stood apart, and the forest generally seemed younger. Asking for an explanation of these changed appearances, I was told that all the hillside had once been occupied by a busy population, and that it was no long time ago since it was occupied by villages and homesteads and plantations. Whence, then, the present desolation? It was the result, and indeed a measure, of the decay of the Fijian race—a decay brought about by many different agencies, all tending in the same direction, and all likely to end in the total extinction of the race.[1]

Hitherto the sea we had been skimming over in the canoe had been glassy calm, and save for the long, heavy roll that rose and fell as regularly as a pendulum we might have been on some inland lake. Though only ten o'clock, the morning was intensely hot. The land-breeze had died away some hours ago, and the trade-wind had not yet come down from the Straits of Somo-Somo. But now it might be seen gradually approaching from the eastward in the form of a dark line on the water, feeble and ill-defined at first, but soon at every moment increasing in power. With it came numerous little waves which washed playfully against the low sides of the canoe. This no one at first minded, and the men, refreshed at intervals by a glass of gin-and-water, paddled bravely on. Soon, however, the full strength of the breeze came down upon us, while, the 'sea' grew short and high, and the waves began to break into the canoe with a somewhat angry sound. We baled as fast as

[1] See further on this subject a series of papers by the Author in the 'New South Wales Medical Gazette,' May–July 1873.

we could, while the natives paddled with might and main. But all efforts were useless, for our vessel was destined to be filled, and indeed anyone might easily have foreseen that such would be the case. We were a good mile from the shore, between two headlands, and it seemed probable that we should have to swim most of the distance, running the gauntlet of innumerable sharks. In these desperate circumstances the canoe was put before wind and sea; and so judiciously did the natives manage her, that we succeeded at length in gaining the shore, without any worse damage than wet clothes and the loss of a portion of the cargo. Once on land there was no help but to remain there till the wind died away, which it did not do until sunset.

The spot where the canoe had been beached was called in Fijian 'Matana,' which being interpreted means 'The Eyes.' It had formerly belonged to a white man, by name Beddoes, who had died shortly before my arrival in the group. He had lived many years in the islands, and belonged to that class of men known as 'old hands.' It is a class the members of which are every day becoming fewer, for the conditions under which such men could exist are every day passing away. Beddoes had come originally to Fiji at a time when to settle there was emphatically to take one's life in one's hand. He must have been a man of uncommon personal strength and daring, for long after his death the most extravagant stories were current about his exploits. He had managed to overawe the common natives by brute force, and had gained over the chiefs by his skill as a worker of metals. He had won upon the heart of the great lord of Tavinni by the skill with which he had furbished up his wretched old muskets and cast for him a fresh supply of leaden bullets. He had in his time given innumerable gifts of gin or of rum, and had not been above helping to drink them with the chiefs. On occasion, too, he had been ever ready to stand by his native protector when some 'cute trader was trying to drive a bargain harder than usual. For these and similar services Beddoes and his contemporaries had received payment in houses and slaves and broad lands, few of which they had succeeded in keeping for long. Most of these men spent their lives in riot and dissipation, unchecked by any social restraints, and harassed by no misgivings about the future. In most islands of the South Pacific probably since the buccaneering days of Drake and Tasman white men have at intervals settled, and lived and died savages in all but colour. Representatives of the 'old beach-comber' are to be found not only in Fiji but in Tonga, Samoa, Rotumah, and many other out-of-the-way islands.

Most of these men came, in the first instance, either as deserters from ships-of-war or from whaleships. Sometimes, however, they came as shipwrecked sailors or runaway convicts, while one individual whom I met in Rotumah told me he had been left there forty years before by a rascally captain, just as the prototype of Robinson Crusoe is said to have been left on Juan Fernandez. At any rate, in whatever way these men first became domiciled in these places, they bear in character and subsequent conduct a startling resemblance to each other. In all cases they have passed a stormy youth and middle age, while the declining years of their lives have generally been devoted to gin or 'kava.' Many of these men had fortunes within their grasp more than once. One well-known character of this sort in Fiji is or was 'Brown Boots.' At one time he owned some of the richest and fairest portions of Tavinni—lands that to-day might have been worth to him many thousands of pounds, had they not been parted with long ago for a few bottles of gin or staked on the turn of a card. 'Brown Boots' himself is in far from affluent circumstances now. The struggle for life in Fiji is greater than it was in the good old times, and poor Boots's strength and spirits are not what they were some thirty years ago. About this man the most extravagant stories are current—as to how he got his name from a pair of untanned sea-boots that a Yankee captain entrusted to his care, and which were never returned; how when no other pilot could be obtained he has taken a ship through an intricate channel, though all the time so helplessly drunk that two men had to steady him as he stood aloft on the fore-yard; how he was laid out for dead and about to be buried; how he was saved from being eaten by a word casually spoken. Poor Brown Boots! thy life hath been a stormy one, and yet thou art not a bad fellow, but truly thine own worst enemy!

With the changed times that have of late come over Fiji, and indeed the South Pacific generally, such men of course find their positions sadly changed. Their occupations are gone as completely as that of Othello ever was. They are no longer the only men who can build a boat or cooper a cask or mend a musket, and accordingly have fallen much in native estimation. The evening of their lives is a gloomy one. Hustled aside by younger comrades, looked on as useless, and, indeed, not particularly respectable, they are forced in many cases to fall back on the hospitality of Fijians, who now show them but scant courtesy; nay, it is well if they do not openly sneer at their poverty and forlorn condition. Yet, though the 'old hands' have sadly fallen away in these latter days, it is only fair to remember that many of them in their youth must have been men of a daring character, and possessed of a certain amount of ability. Had this not been the case they must have perished long ago, as so many others did at the very commencement of their careers. Some of the tales they can tell now about old times, past for ever, are very grim indeed, and show that men who could live through such scenes must have borne themselves bravely and well. Drink and unbridled savage licence of manners and morals dragged them down; but we can scarcely wonder at their yielding to some temptations which even now prove too strong for many of the whites settled in Fiji.

During my compulsory visit to Matana I took the opportunity of walking over the deserted plantation, and could not but be struck with the amazing fertility of the soil. The cotton-trees, though untended, were nevertheless covered with white pods, and labourers only were required to gather in a rich harvest. All over the plantation sugar-cane and tobacco were growing wild side by side with the cotton; while there was no lack of bananas, paw-paws, pine-apples, cocoa-nuts, and other tropical productions. But the place was utterly neglected, and, indeed, at this very time was actually in search of an owner.

Towards evening the breeze began to fall light, and the sea to become calm once more. The moon rose about 9 o'clock, and, with the first glimpse of its friendly orb we started on our way. From here to Wairiki was some eight miles, and we expected to accomplish the distance in two hours. When about half-way we met a large double canoe, with a fire brightly burning on each side. The crew were lustily blowing conches, which in the still air sounded as loud as fog-horns on the Banks of Newfoundland. These natives were carrying turtle to the chief, and they and their vessel were to a certain extent privileged. In passing such a canoe as this the rule is to allow her to keep to seaward of you—you passing between her and the shore. Our natives either forgot this or did not act on it till the last moment. Then, indeed, they ran right across the bows of the King's vessel, which very nearly passed over us. We escaped once more, but only by a very narrow margin; and, on the whole, the excitement of having first sank and then been run down was too great to be pleasant.

The more a man sees of canoe-travelling the more is he convinced that it is extremely dangerous and unsatisfactory. Canoes are treacherous things, even in native hands. They are poor vessels in a seaway, are difficult to manage under sail, are not particularly fast, and, moreover, are extremely liable to upset. It is, or was, no uncommon thing to hear almost every week of some white man having been capsized out of his canoe and losing either his life or all the property he had on board. It sometimes happens that a canoe is blown out to sea, either from the mast breaking or from the crew being too weak to propel her with their paddles against an offshore wind. In such a desperate case the best plan is to steer right before the wind, and pick up the first land met with. I have seen a canoe thus blown away from the Friendly Islands, with a large number of passengers on board, reach Fiji after a voyage of three weeks, when all hopes of her safety had been abandoned. In old times a canoe thus blown out to sea was considered a present from the gods to the people to whom she came, and all her luckless passengers were, as a matter of duty, killed and eaten. They were said 'to have salt water in their eyes,' and as such were doomed irrevocably to be clubbed first and then cast into the oven.

Wairiki was reached without further adventure, and obedient natives soon carried us ashore. It was past midnight when we arrived, and it seemed at first probable that we should have to 'camp out,' for every house in the village was either full of people or else locked up. In this conjuncture my companion fortunately bethought him of a 'native teacher' who lived close to where our canoe had been hauled up. This man belonged to a class of men unknown before the advent of missionaries. He occupied a leading position in the community, and yet was a native of low birth. He had been chosen by the Wesleyans as a 'lay reader' on account of a natural gift for preaching, and on account, too, of his zeal and piety. Many of the native teachers are from Tonga, and perform no small share of the real hard work of the missionary's so-called 'labours.' As a class they are no doubt useful to the Wesleyans, but to most whites appear conceited and puffed up, and possessed of but little humility of spirit. However, this worthy man was far superior to many others whom I have met. His house, like all in Fiji, was built of reeds, but inside was better furnished than such places usually are. He soon supplied us with clean cool mats and a mosquito-curtain of native cloth large enough to cover a family. A leather valise, which had kept me company in many a long ride through the Queensland bush, served for a pillow, and thus equipped I soon fell asleep, not to awake until the morning sun came pouring in through the narrow doorway.

Next morning our host provided us with towels, and we went to bathe before breakfast. But, alas! what a change from the sparkling waters of the Levuka river to that wretched brook at Wairiki! In one spot, indeed, some philanthropic man had essayed to make a dam with earth and small stones. This he had partially succeeded in doing, and had created a shallow pool, more, perhaps, to the advantage of sundry pigs than of his fellow-men. But such as it was we were obliged to be contented with it. For the benefit, however, of future travellers it may be mentioned that there is a much better bathing-place some distance from the village, where the luxury of a bath can be thoroughly enjoyed, and where the scenery fully compensates for the length of the necessary walk.

Returning to the house of the 'teacher' we found him busy preparing breakfast. His wife was a pretty, graceful woman, of Fijian extraction, but fairer and better-looking than the average of her countrywomen. Neither he nor his wife could tell their own ages or that of any of their children. To Fijians the lapse of time is only made known by the approach of age or infirmity. Until these unwelcome reminders come upon them they are content to let the years roll on unheeded, or at most marked by the advent of a yam crop or a new moon. But as the number of moons increase somewhat quickly, the count is soon lost, and thus it comes to pass that scarcely any native can tell his own age. Such a fact speaks volumes for the easy, uneventful, and therefore (if we set aside the Aristotelian definition) possibly happy tenor of life in the far-off sunny islands of the Pacific.

After breakfast my friend started once more in his canoe to go further up the coast, while I proceeded to take a look at the village which was to be my head-quarters for the next few months.

CHAPTER VII.

Wairiki—Tiu Cakou's House—Monotony of Savage Life—Tappa-making—Tiu Koominooa—Ethics of Trading with Savages—British and American Subjects—Hotel at Wairiki—Two Residents.

WAIRIKI in 1872 was the largest native town in the island of Tavinni. It had long been really, though was now only nominally, the capital, for 'Tiu Cakou' (pronounced Thakou), 'Lord of the Reefs,' seldom honoured it with his presence. It was a vague, straggling kind of place, divided into two unequal parts by a sluggish stream. On the banks of this were always to be seen women either washing clothes or making *tappa*; while in its turbid waters pigs, ducks, and children disported themselves at leisure. Its normal condition was anything but pleasant or wholesome, though such considerations were of little moment to the inhabitants. Crossing this stream the traveller found himself fairly in the native town. That large house on the left is the residence of *Yadi* (pronounced Yandi—lady) *Mela*, Tiu Cakou's queen; that one on the right, of *Ratu* (Fr., master) *Quilo* (flag), his brother. That imposing-looking edifice between the two, rising up like the mosque of an Eastern village, is the palace of the great king himself. It is a fine effort of Fijian architecture, and is worth looking at closely. Although more than one hundred feet in length and forty in breadth it is divided into only three large rooms. These are separated from each other by partitions some twelve feet in height, formed of split canes. As you enter the house by a low door placed at the end of the largest room your eye can travel through each succeeding room till, through the open windows of the last, you see the village stretching away to the eastward, and finally lose it in the trees and brushwood of the forest around it.

The sides of this house are formed, as usual in Fiji, of reeds fastened securely together by cords of *sinnet*, or cocoa-nut fibre. The reeds are then attached to large posts placed at intervals of a few yards. These posts are made of a peculiarly hard and oily wood, somewhat like teak, able to resist the attacks of white ants and other vermin. The tradition runs, whether truly or not, that the posts in this house were driven into the ground through the bodies of slain men; and seeing that the house was built in old cannibal times, there is nothing improbable in the story. The roof was an elaborate structure. It depended for strength and solidity on the 'ridgepole,' which, indeed, is to a Fijian house what the keel is to a ship. It is, in fact, its most important part, and the backbone of the whole structure. In this instance it was formed of stems of cocoa-nut trees, jointed together with great neatness, and covered with 'sinnet.'[1] On this central beam were laid bamboos, and the whole framework was then covered over for a thickness of several inches with reeds and leaves until perfectly watertight. A roof so constructed is, perhaps, the very best that could be devised for a Fijian climate. The only objections that can be raised against it are, first, the danger of fire; and, second, its liability to harbour tarantulas, scorpions, rats, lizards, and other vermin. The first of these, except in the case of a cotton-house surrounded by malicious natives, is more imaginary than real; the second can easily be guarded against by the use of an inside lining of calico placed over the beams from one end of the house to the other. There were, properly speaking, no ceilings in Tiu Cakou's palace. From the ground-floor to the roof it was quite empty, and thereby it gained enormously in comfort. During the hottest months its interior was always cool, and through its open doors and unglazed windows the land-breeze or the sea-breeze, according to the time of day, could wander at leisure. In addition to other ornaments each end of the ridge-pole and some portions of the sides of the house were adorned with white shells (*ovum ovulum*), to show that they belonged to a great chief. Similar shells are also used, and for a like purpose, on canoes and other property. To the Fijian mind these convey the same notion as the letters V.R. or a 'broad arrow' does to an Englishman.

[1] Fine cord made of the fibre that surrounds the cocoa-nut.

On entering the first and largest room the contrast between the lofty proportions of the exterior of the house and its mean and even squalid furniture was very striking. The floor was covered with a large native mat. In many places this was ragged and torn, and allowed the dry leaves and reeds on which it rested to be seen through. Two or three half-naked children, in charge of an old one-eyed woman, rolled about the floor; while some Fijians sat in one corner endeavouring with more or less success to talk and eat yams at the same moment. There was a fireplace at one end of the room—a large open one, like those that may yet be seen in English country houses of the date of Queen Anne or the first George. A fire of logs of the bread-fruit tree was burning brightly, and over it was suspended an enormous iron pot full of yams. At this moment a loud knock was heard at the low wooden door, and immediately afterwards a pig entered. He seemed to know the place well, and at once, without let or hindrance, directed his steps towards the saucepans and other utensils piled up in the corner. The further end of this same room was occupied by several beds, composed of mats, and having large mosquito-curtains suspended over them. These beds were not only for the regular dwellers in the house, but also for any chance-comer who might stand in need of its hospitality. Beyond this first room was another, floored with boards, and furnished in a much more civilised manner. This was occupied by Mr. H——, secretary to Tiu Cakou. He was an American by birth, and, like so many other white settlers, had first visited Fiji on a whaling cruise. It was his first voyage to sea, and had been a fairly successful one. The vessel was homeward-bound from the summer whaling-station, that vast waste of waters that lie to the south of Cape Horn. In passing through the Fiji group, then but little known, the ship struck on a coral reef, and quickly went to pieces. H—— was one of the very few who escaped, and it was, as he used to be fond of saying, by the 'skin of his teeth.' After being wrecked he lived ashore among the natives, learned their language, and finally married a half-caste girl, whose father, a white man, had been killed in some native feud. After a while he acquired lands and other property, and eventually became secretary to the chief of the district. He was one of those men who could put his hand to almost anything, from coopering a cask or mending a musket to writing an official letter to the captain of a ship-of-war, which is considered the severest test of a man's diplomatic powers in Fiji. His duties were those of a secretary, interpreter, and collector of customs combined. In exchange for the work thus performed he was provided by the chief with a large house, with the work of so many men annually, and with a certain sum of money, which was, I believe, often in arrear. So much for a brief sketch of a man the course of whose whole life and fortunes were changed by one accident. Besides Mr. H—— many other white men held official positions under chiefs. In the old times such appointments were much more valuable than they are now, and much more important. They now confer few of the privileges they used to do formerly, while the chances of receiving large tracts of land or other enormous payments for services rendered are very remote indeed. In fact, many whites do not now care to accept such appointments, for they entail a great deal of unpleasant duty without any corresponding gains.

The labour of constructing a large house such as has been described in Fiji is indeed immense. The native carpenter has no planks ready-sawn and to his hand that he can lay on as if he were building a wooden house. Each individual reed has to be carefully adjusted and placed side by side with its fellow. It has then to be secured in its place, and this so thoroughly that neither wind, rain, nor sunlight can penetrate between the two. Most of the larger pieces of timber are encircled with coil after coil of cocoanut fibre, all twisted by hand, while many of the smaller beams and posts are ornamented with elaborate devices of the same material. This house of Tiu Cakou's had been built entirely by compulsory labour, so that its cost cannot be accurately estimated. But if the workmen were paid wages at all approaching what they would expect to receive from a white man, many hundreds of pounds sterling would not suffice, and this without including the price of the materials.

After living a short time at Wairiki I began to

make the acquaintance of many of the villagers, and to gain some insight into Fijian inner life. Were I asked what was the most salient characteristic of savage life I should reply, its monotony. The Fiji man rises at the same hour every day, eats the same food, cooks it in the same manner, occupies his time with the same employments, and goes to rest at the same hour. The climate is much the same all the year round, except during the rainy season, when it is a little warmer, while there is not perhaps twenty minutes' difference between the length of the longest and shortest day. Add to all this that there is little communication between the various villages, that the native mind is slow of apprehension, and cares little for novelty; that there are no public events of any importance transpiring, and if there were, that there are no means of discussing them, and you have the essential groundwork of a very uninteresting state of society. The women find 'fit occupation for all their time in tending their offspring. In addition, however, to this they are expected to make *tappa*, or native cloth, the universal and only covering of Fijian men and women before English calicoes became cheap and plentiful. Even now the use of this tappa is very extensive, especially among the poorer people. Its mode of preparation is simple enough, although requiring a good deal of time. It is somewhat as follows:—The bark of the *malo*, or paper mulberry, is stripped off, care being taken that the several strips shall be as long as possible. It is then rolled up and allowed to soak some time in water. By this means the outer bark or epidermis can be easily scraped off, and this is generally done with a bivalve shell somewhat like a cockle. The *massi*, as it is now called, is laid upon a large flat block of hard wood, and pounded unmercifully with grooved mallets. One strip of *massi* is generally placed on the top of another, and by repeated blows the two are welded together until they become one piece. By this hammering process they become also wider than before, a two-inch strip being beaten out into one of eighteen inches, while at the same time the length is considerably shortened. The whole strip is then dried, and is ready for use, but generally several of these pieces are joined together with a paste made of arrowroot. This done, they are spread out to dry and bleach, and at this stage a good idea of the size of these pieces of native cloth can be obtained. I have seen many such exceeding thirty yards in length, and Mr. Calvert in his work mentions having seen one of 180 yards. At Wairiki, indeed, there is or was an enormous bale of this tappa, originally intended as a present to Cacobau. Judging from appearances this might easily have extended half a mile in length had it been spread out. As it was it formed a solid mass of some thirty feet long by ten broad, and about eight deep. After the gift had been presented it was found impossible to convey it to Levuka entire. No ordinary vessel could have taken it on deck, nor would it have passed through the hatchway of any vessel. Accordingly it was allowed to remain where it was, and a shed was built over it to protect it from the weather. Tappa is generally worn white, and is preferred thus for head-dresses. A chief will often wrap many yards of it round his head somewhat in the manner in which a surgeon would put on the old-fashioned 'capitulum' bandage. No one but chiefs are allowed to wear a head-dress of tappa, which, according to the caprice or conceit of the wearer, may be raised to an almost unlimited height. When well-made such a head-dress bears some resemblance in shape to a Parsee's hat.

Tappa is often dyed brown, and occasionally even ornamented with elaborate patterns. The dye used is obtained from a plant called *lauci*, the botanical name for which is, I believe, *aleurites triloba*. The process of printing the patterns recalls the old days of the wooden types of Guttenburg, or the early efforts of our own Caxton. Without entering into too minute a description of these blocks it may be stated that the surface of the wood is covered, according to the intended pattern, with small pieces of bamboo and cocoa-nut leaf. These raised portions are then smeared over with the dye and the cloth pressed down upon them. When this process has been completed there still remains a large margin of untouched cloth. This is now dyed black instead of brown, while the block hitherto used gives place to patterns cut out of banana-leaves. The larger pieces of dyed tappa are mostly used for mosquito curtains.

But though they afford a sufficient protection against insects, they are too warm, and shut out not only the mosquitoes but also the fresh air. Fiji women make use of strips of slit bamboo in cutting the wet cloth, and these wooden knives answer this purpose better than the best steel. The noise of tappa-making, especially when a large number of women are at work together, is very great. The sound, however, is a cheery one, and reminds the traveller of a ship-building yard in England. Tappa-making is *tabu*, or 'forbidden,' in the town where a chief lives, for fear of disturbing the great man's slumbers. This simple fact may serve as an illustration of the despotic kind of rule under which Fijians in common with most Western Polynesians live. I have heard of an unfortunate man who was killed on the spot because his merry but indiscreet laughter had disturbed the noontide repose of his chief. It is no uncommon thing for white men calling on a chief for business purposes to have to wait hours for an audience, until the chief chooses to say that he is awake. In such a case no native would be bold enough to disturb him, as his head might pay the forfeit of such presumption.

About this time there was on a visit at Wairiki a well-known and once celebrated chieftain. He was called Koominoa, was father of Yadi Mela, Queen of Cakadrovi, and was hereditary ruler of the island of Koro. At the time I first made his acquaintance he was an old man of some seventy years, tall and thin, and feeble. His skin hung in great wrinkles on his attenuated frame, his hair was white and closely cropped, and his face had a weird, hungry look about it that was not pleasant to contemplate. In his youth he had been a great warrior, and, it must be added, a great cannibal. It is said that on one occasion he killed six hundred persons on the island of Rabi (Rambi), because, having caught two turtles, they had sent him only one. The turtle is a royal fish throughout Fiji, and for a *kaisee* or common man to eat one was to incur the punishment of death, and such until lately was the recognised penalty in the Fijian code. It was probably, however, a rare occurrence at any period of Fijian history to devastate a whole island on such trivial grounds, while, of course, at the present day such a proceeding would be wholly impossible. It so happened that I had brought a 'chimney-pot' hat from Sydney, the only one, probably, to be found in the whole Fiji group. To this piece of headgear old Koominoa took a huge fancy. In his eyes it far surpassed the most skilful efforts of native hatters. He begged for it piteously, pleading his poverty, his advanced age, and the affection he had always shown to white men. But finding entreaty useless, he at length offered to purchase it, and, as he had no money, I consented to be paid in kind, and agreed to accept two large pigs, equal in value to about five pounds sterling. He at once, as soon as the bargain was concluded, placed the hat upon his head, and called out to one of his attendants to bring him a looking-glass. Then, standing up to his full height, he surveyed himself complacently for several minutes, muttering all the while expressions of approval. His appearance was irresistibly comic. His tall, gaunt figure was almost destitute of clothing, his face was lit up by a half-smile, half-leer; his lustreless eyes were fixed with delight on the glass, while high above all the hat, sadly crumpled, and brushed the wrong way, completed the strange figure. When this scene had lasted long enough the hat was removed, to be kept safely until paid for, and for greater security was deposited in the house of the King's brother. But the old man begged so earnestly that he might be allowed to wear it at the missionary services the next Sunday that I granted his request. No sooner, however, had he got possession of the hat than, taking advantage of a fair wind, he sailed away in his canoe to Koro, and I never saw him again. This little incident affords an instance of the duplicity and short-sighted cunning that characterises most Fijians in their intercourse with Europeans. Anything given on credit to a native generally means a free gift, and a few pence gained at the moment by some silly act of dishonesty is more valued by most Fijians than a good name or large legitimate profits. Experience has unfortunately shown that it is quite impossible to repose any confidence in the average Fijiman in money matters, except in a few very rare cases. The white settler has or had until lately no legal means of redress, for a native was seldom worth the trouble of suing, except in the case of some powerful chief. Sometimes a Fijian may be induced to work off a debt, that is, pledge himself to labour for so many days until the money he owes is represented by an equivalent sum due to him for his work. At first sight this plan might seem equally advantageous to the planter and the native, but it is not found to be so in practice, simply because the native will not keep his word. In the case of a chief who owes money the plan is more promising, as the chief will readily enough send some of his unfortunate vassals to work for him; nor does he care how much they may suffer in his service, or how much he may pay in this form to gratify any particular whim.

And here a few words may be permitted on the ethics of native trading. In dealings with savages, Fijian or otherwise, the intrinsic value of any article to the manufacturer is no measure of the value that the native may place upon it. The value of anything to a native is in direct proportion to its actual utility to himself or to the difficulty he would experience in procuring it. These principles are, indeed, much the same as those which regulate prices in all communities, but somehow their logical application to savages would seem to have been overlooked in some quarters. Many excellent and well-meaning persons might think it a shameful abuse of knowledge and power, if not indeed an actual moral wrong, to sell to an islander a musket which cost eight shillings for as many pounds. But it is evident that this musket may prove of such vast service to the islander who buys it as to be to him almost priceless. On its possession may depend his life, his property, his liberty, in a word, all that makes existence worth having. Again, to manufacture such an article would be quite beyond the power of any number of natives working for an unlimited time. Hence, so far as the native is concerned, no amount of labour or the products of labour would be sufficient to procure him a musket. Again, many objects, such as beads, rings, pipes, or coloured ribbons, are to the savage exactly what precious stones are to us. His eye sees in them objects of peculiar beauty and rare occurrence, and they accordingly possess for him a fictitious value. That a plain man with a cunning machine working in some back street of Birmingham or Coventry can produce such things at will does not lessen their value in the eyes of the South Sea Islander. No skill or power that he could bring to bear would be equal to producing such results. Accordingly, whether a man sell all that he has in order to buy a pearl of great price, or whether a savage gives away tons of cocoa-nut oil or blocks of sandal-wood, or even his wife, for a few beads or an old musket, the principles involved are identical. Civilised persons do not feel surprised when they hear of a connoisseur paying a fabulous price for a group by Canova or a painting by Vandyke. To some men, however, all sculpture and all pictures are much the same, and would be represented by a very trifling sum of money indeed. It is the same with savages. At one island you may get quantities of cocoa-nut oil representing many pounds sterling for your beads or old iron, at another group a few degrees east or west the same articles may be valueless. But here, on the other hand, the natives will insist on purchasing your muskets or hatchets or printed calicoes at apparently absurd rates. At the present day, however, in most of the Pacific groups all trading is more or less overdone. The wealth of the natives is small and strictly limited in kind, and the profits to be realised are after all not large, when the danger to life and property from the treachery of natives, bad charts, hurricanes, and other dangers is taken into account. Besides, most groups and islands, however remote and savage, can number one or more white traders among their permanent inhabitants, and they are always ready to buy native produce. Such men must live literally, rifle in hand, in the midst of constant danger and excitement. Their profits are large, but unfortunately, on the principle *vos non vobis*. The Sydney or Melbourne house which has sent these fearless traders down to their island with a small stock in trade generally manages to absorb all the returns, save a mere nominal percentage.

It will thus be seen that what many well-meaning but misinformed persons have stated about island trading can hardly be borne out by facts. It is still said that natives are 'cheated' and 'imposed upon' by white-men. Missionaries, as a rule, have not been slow in taking up the same cry. In their case this is scarcely to be wondered at, as the advent of the trader destroys much of their influence, and nearly all that portion of their income represented by the vague term 'offering.' But so far as my experience goes I believe the average South Sea Islander is habitually cautious and canny to a degree, and will never pay a fraction more than he thinks the wares are worth to himself. But, on the other hand, the case of the trader has perhaps scarcely received the consideration and sympathy due to it. It is a strange fact, but nevertheless it is a fact, that while England as a nation glories in the wide range of her commerce, she not unfrequently spurns the men who are daily extending it in new countries. She enjoys the fruits of such men's labours and yet calls the men themselves 'adventurers,' and treats them in many cases as if they were pirates, slavers, or rank malefactors. That such is the feeling of England, at any rate in official circles, is well known in many a far-off land. It is a melancholy fact that Englishmen throughout the South Pacific generally can be ill-treated and all but slain with impunity. The captains of the vessels-of-war who visit these islands are either unable or unwilling to do much in the way of protection or redress. A Frenchman or American living ashore among natives is universally respected and feared, and the advent of a gunboat or frigate belonging to either of those nations strikes terror into the hearts of native wrong-doers. But such is not the case when an English ship is descried in the offing. The natives have been taught by experience the dislike which the

PROTECTION OF ENGLISH SETTLERS. 157

English have to help their own countrymen or to punish an adversary apparently weak, and have not been slow to better the teaching.

In Fiji the *prestige* of the British flag was sadly impaired by the unfortunate Rewa expedition, where, from motives of mistaken leniency, shells were fired *over* the natives instead of *at* them. In the end the boats of the expedition were obliged to retire with the loss of several men killed and wounded, while free passages were generously offered by the Commodore to the unlucky settlers whose lives were no longer safe. It is well known that numbers of English in Levuka call themselves American subjects, merely in order to obtain the better protection which that country, rightly or not, is supposed to extend to her citizens. A remarkable instance of this fact came under my notice in Fiji. A large landowner actually left the group for some time and resided in the United States, in order to qualify for American citizenship, and thus to vindicate certain rights of ownership which had been grossly violated by the chief of the district in which his property lay. He had in vain appealed to a succession of ships-of-war, and as a last resource had changed his nationality. This decisive step promised to be successful, for on the last occasion on which I met him he informed me that a vessel-of-war would be despatched from San Francisco to Levuka with the express object of enquiring into his claims. It is humiliating to have to write thus; but it is well to tell the truth, even when there is no likelihood of its being believed.

Wairiki can, or could, boast of one hotel, and to this I betook myself. It will be sufficient to say that it possessed a strong family likeness to the hotel at Vuna; and indeed, out of Levuka, all hotels were much the same in Fiji. The proprietors of this particular hostelry did not dread competition, for there is no other house within miles where any food can be procured. At the moment of my arrival dinner was announced. I remember we had as fish a piece of porpoise. Gentle reader, have you ever eaten porpoise? If not, I hope you may never be called on to do so. The flesh is in texture like a very fine sponge, and in taste like cod-liver oil. Ugh! it haunted the palate for long afterwards, and rendered one suspicious of even such choice dainties as parrot-fish or turtle. The porpoise was flanked by the inevitable salt beef, unpalatable and unwholesome, as usual, while yams and bananas completed the *menu*. I mention this partly because, with the exception of the porpoise, it was the dinner of three hundred and sixty days out of the year, but chiefly to disabuse persons of a very prevalent notion that the Fiji Islands are abodes of comfort and luxury. The former of these two words should certainly not be mentioned within the confines of the group, while, as regards the latter, scenery and vegetation are indeed luxurious enough, but the food—*i.e.* such food as a white man can live on continuously—is insufficient and bad. This is one of the chief drawbacks to Fiji as a place of residence for women and children or delicate persons. No doubt this state of things will be remedied in time; but as it is, anyone who wants to live comfortably in Fiji must import the bulk of his food from New Zealand or Australia, a distance of two thousand miles.

But if the dinner was bad the excellence of the company compensated for it to a great extent. There were two men at table both of whom were characters in their own ways, though differing widely from each other. One of them was named *Ratu Quilo*, and was the brother of Tui Cakou, chief of Cakadrovi. He was, perhaps, one of the most polite, polished, and subtle Fijians to be met with in the whole extent of the islands, and, let me add, politically one of the most dangerous of men. He was generally credited with passing his time in hatching plots and abortive conspiracies against his brother, who, in turn, pardoned him as often as he sinned. Quilo was a very large and powerfully-built man, his forehead ample, and his head fairly symmetrical, though there was a decided deficiency where phrenologists are accustomed to place the moral qualities. His eyes were bright and intelligent, and, on the whole, he would have passed in any country as a good-looking man. Strangely enough in the Egyptian Museum at Boulak, Cairo, there is a wooden figure which, in outline of face and figure, exactly resembles him, and is said to be some four thousand years old. At the time I first made Quilo's acquaintance he was past middle age; and in spite of his fine head and manly form he was reported to be a coward. It was said that he had run away during more than one battle, and was much better as an *intriguant* than a warrior. He had long ago abandoned such evil practices as polygamy and cannibalism, and now with all the docility of a catechumen listened to the teachings of the missionaries. Some there were, indeed, who used to insinuate that this docility was part of a deep-laid political plan. His brother, the ruling chief, was notoriously immoral and stiff-necked, and there were not wanting men to suggest that Quilo was anxious to enlist missionary influence in the development of certain ambitious schemes of his own. However, very little if anything of all this was known positively, for he was far too clever a politician to take many persons into his confidence. All such surmises time will prove or disprove; meanwhile it will be strange if Quilo's name does not by-and-by become better known to Englishmen in connexion with Fijian politics.

Opposite to Ratu Quilo sat a man whose name is familiar to every resident in Taviuni. Dr. B—— had at one time been a surgeon in the British Navy, but had quitted the service to develope a pet scheme of his own. This was nothing less than to grow coffee in the Island of Madagascar. After many rebuffs and some five years of incessant labour he had succeeded in getting his project favourably considered by the late Emperor Napoleon III. He could show letters from the Emperor and other influential persons, and from his own account success seemed to have been all but within his grasp. But the scheme ultimately broke down, and in the bitterness of disappointment Dr. B—— sailed for the Australian colonies. From thence he drifted to Fiji, indifferent as to what fate might have in store for him. His urbanity and good-nature were proof against every annoyance, nor did it seem possible to put him out of temper. His store of learning was ample and varied, and his tastes those of a studious recluse. He was, in fact, the very last man that should have gone to a new and rough place like Fiji. But, after all, he was only one of a large number of curious characters who, like waifs and strays on the ocean of life, had drifted somehow or another to those distant shores. Poor fellow! from a worldly point of view his life had not been a success; but this probably was no fault of his. All who would rightly understand what are those 'shallows' that men drift into when they do not take the tide in their affairs that leads to fortune should visit some of the queer, out-of-the-way places of the earth. Unlucky men who have thus drifted into shallows are to be met with on Australian gold-diggings, on distant sheep-stations far away in the 'back-country,' on Pacific islands, in quiet Continental villages; but, meet them where you will, their histories have been all more or less the same. The demon of failure has set its seal upon all they have attempted through life. Such men may at times have been mocked by a little delusive success, but the final result was never for a moment doubtful. Yet many such men are free from all degrading vices, and possessed apparently of considerable ability and energy of character. B—— was of the number of these. The stars really seemed to have cast a baleful light on his life, and to have entered into some hostile conjunction at his nativity. On one occasion B—— received a gift of a thousand acres of land from a grateful patient. His friends thought at length that luck had turned in his favour. Not so, however. Scarcely had the ground passed into his possession when the hitherto quiet natives became unruly, committed numerous outrages, and soon succeeded in giving that part of the country so bad a name that it became a matter of difficulty to sell an acre in the district. But B—— had become so thoroughly resigned to his bad luck that this extra slice did not in the least disturb his equanimity. Provided he had plenty of books to read, he cared apparently but little what adversity or prosperity befell him. It is, perhaps, rare to meet a man so thoroughly schooled into being a philosopher by mere force of circumstances. He told me that the process had been a very gradual one, that he had been conscious of its existence, and that he now considered it complete, in which latter statement all who had the pleasure of his acquaintance would probably agree.

CHAPTER VIII.

Tropical Rain—The Fijian Language—Professional Poisoners—Medical Science in Fiji—Fijian Idiosyncrasies—The 'Mat Fever'—French Missionaries.

AMONG other objects which I had proposed to myself in visiting Wairiki was to find a vessel direct to Vauna Levu, 'the big land,' which lay only a few miles away across the Straits of Somo-Somo. But week after week slipped by and there seemed little hope of accomplishing my purpose; for although the Straits might have been crossed easily enough, a hundred miles of rough, broken country would still have intervened between me and Mbua, my destination. Vessels, indeed, were somewhat scarce at this particular season of the year. It was now the middle of the 'hurricane months,' or rainy season, and wise men went to sea as little as possible. The winds, too, were very variable. The regular 'trades' had ceased to blow, and instead of them fierce squalls alternating with wearisome calms swept all smaller craft from the sea. The weather was hot, oppressive, and unwholesome, and the frequent showers that hung about the horizon or broke over the island were heavier than any rain ever seen out of the tropics. In some of these down-pours it was as though the windows of heaven had been opened. The rain descended in torrents rather than in streams. But fortunately a shower like this would give timely notice of its approach. First of all came a cold blast of wind, then the loud patter of heavy drops on the broad-leaved banana-trees would be heard, and in a moment or two, if a friendly shelter had not been already gained, you might imagine that an unusually powerful shower-bath was playing on your head. The natives, in spite of their well-oiled backs and scanty clothing, carefully avoid such rain as this, which experience has taught them is fraught with danger to their health.

Seeing there was no immediate chance of getting away from Wairiki I accepted a mosquito-curtain and a mat in Tiu Cakou's large house. Most of my time was now passed among the natives, whose appearance, customs, and habits of life possessed as yet all the charm of novelty. While this novelty lasts on either side the Fijians are rather an engaging people; but they soon tire of a white man, and he in turn soon tires of their filthy habits and deceitful ways. Savages, in fact, are not interesting people, and those who are obliged to live among them quickly find this out. However, as my lot had been cast among them for a time, at any rate it seemed wise to study their modes of thought and action, and learn as much of their inner life as possible. To do this it was necessary to gain some knowledge of their language. I could obtain no books, although I afterwards found that there was a grammar and good dictionary published by the missionaries. The plan of learning the language I adopted was simple enough, and I am inclined to think it is better than a library full of grammars and dictionaries, if you want to gain a colloquial knowledge of any language in a short time. I asked a friend to translate me the phrase 'What is that?' in Fiji. 'A cava ogo,' pronounced 'Athava ongo.' Then, using this as a key, I plied all natives with incessant questions, regardless of time or place. Pointing to the nearest house, I would say 'A cava ogo?' Answer, '*Vali*,' a house; to a fowl, answer '*Toa*;' to a pig, answer '*Vuaka*,' and so on, till in a very few days I had learned the names of most of the common objects around me. The verbs and pronouns had to be picked up by ear, but even so the process was not a very tedious one. Everyone who has studied a few languages knows how small a vocabulary will suffice for our ordinary conversation or a day's work. Such is more especially the case in a language like Fijian, which possesses no written literature. But here the paucity and even insufficiency of the vocabulary is an unexpected but real source of difficulty, on account of the vast number of meanings which the same word must necessarily have. Take for instance, the word 'matana,' meaning primarily, perhaps, 'a point;' then the eyes, and then by an easy transition the face, and then the front of anything. In addition to this, however, it means a particular spot whence anything issues, as *mata in wai*, a spring of water, also 'a spear-point,' also one of a number of small things, as a 'drop.' It is also used as a preposition, meaning in front of, and finally forms more than sixty compound words.[1] All this is puzzling to a learner, who generally loses the thread of the discourse he is listening to, and, owing to the numerous and various meanings of the words employed, has little chance of recovering it.

The Fijian language belongs to the family known to philologists as the Turanian. It possesses many words in common with the Samoan, Tongan, Rotuman, Savage Island, and other Pacific dialects. But, on the other hand, many of its words in commonest use have little or no apparent connexion with those used in other groups. Fijian is probably a composite language, and has borrowed both words and roots from widely-different sources. On the whole, however, it assimilates more closely to the tongue of Eastern than of Western Polynesia. Even within the small compass of single islands more than one form of the language is often found. In some places these differences may be sufficient to constitute a dialect, in others a mere *patois*. Thus, between the polished and courtly language of Bau and the language of the mountaineers of Viti Levu there is as much difference as between the *Platt Deutsch* of Hamburg and the classical German of the school of Weimar, or between the dialects of Lombardy and the Italian of Manzoni. In many cases the

[1] See Hazlewood's 'Fijian Dictionary,' *sub voce*.

differences are not so striking. Thus, the language of the Cakadrovi province, including Vauna Levu, Tavinni, Rabi, and other islands, differs from that of Bau chiefly in the omission of all K sounds. For instance, a Levuka man would call a pig *vuaka*, whereas a Wairiki man would say *vuaa*, or perhaps alter it still farther into *puaa* ; *vinaka*, ' good,' becomes *vinaa*, and so on. I becomes J, as Viti becomes Fiji, in the eastern islands of the group, where Tongan influence has been felt ; and so on through various dialectic changes. Bau is the Athens of Fiji, and the dialect there spoken has now became the classical dialect of the whole group. In it all translations and official documents are written, and it will probably soon supersede all other forms of the language, except among the lowest orders of the people.

Fijian is neither a rich nor a flexible language. Its vocabulary, as we have seen, is strictly limited, while its grammar contains neither genders, case-endings, nor conjugations properly so called. Its pronouns are unwieldy and complicated, consisting of no fewer than four numbers. The language itself is as yet in an undeveloped state. Like the Greek of Homer, it abounds in numerous particles and redundancies, which would soon disappear were it more cultivated. It possesses, of course, nothing approaching a national literature. Its prose compositions are all translations of religious works, executed by missionaries, with the aid of native Pundits. As the works of foreigners these can have but little hold on the people at large, nor is it to be supposed they will ever to any great extent affect their modes of thought. The folklore of Fiji is neither particularly copious nor interesting, and what there was of it forty years of missionary teaching has pretty well abolished. There is no reason to suppose that the Fijian language, any more than the race which speaks it, is destined to a long life. It will soon be a language as thoroughly dead and forgotten as that of the Incas or the Tasmanians, with the exception, perhaps, of a few fragments rescued by the exertions of foreign philologists.

Having acquired some power of expressing myself in their language, I lived a good deal among the natives. I thus had ample opportunity of learning Fiji politics, and of finding out what the average native thought of the great movement which was bringing so many white settlers to the islands. The prevailing notion in the native mind undoubtedly was that most of these whites had been obliged to leave their own country on account of a famine, and that they had come to Fiji in search of food. As *matai-nimate*, or 'man of death,' I was everywhere welcome. A case of surgical instruments was examined with curiosity not unmixed with awe. Many natives probably considered me in the same light as one of their own *matai*, who with the practice of medicine generally unite that of professional poisoning. The flora of Fiji is rich in many poisonous plants; but the knowledge of them is kept a profound secret, and confined to a few families. The men who possess such tremendous knowledge are, as might be supposed, universally feared and respected. They form at once faithful body-guards to a chief and swift and terrible messengers of his vengeance. They may be seen, perhaps, lounging in the neighbourhood of some village one day and disappear the next. Soon afterwards the chief or other high head droops and dies with unusual symptoms and strange suddenness. No enquiries are made, no questions asked, but perhaps within a week or so the dead man's wife joins the harem of the superior chief. Then men's tongues may be loosed for awhile; but prudent persons generally say little on such occasions, for fear of a like mishap coming upon themselves.

Intercourse with the natives afforded many opportunities of gaining some knowledge of the system of medicine practised amongst them. Surgery, as a science, cannot be said to exist in Fiji; most Fijians prefer death any day to undergoing a severe operation. The natives as a rule are healthy, but of a decidedly weaker constitution than the average European. The popular notion that savages have a greater power of repair in their system and greater constitutional strength than civilised men does not seem to be borne out by facts. The Fijians are liable to almost the same diseases as the white residents in the group, and of the two races the native suffers the more severely. Dysentery is quite as fatal to Fijians as to whites, though perhaps, owing to differences of food and other causes, somewhat more common among the latter. Many natives died a few years ago from an epidemic of influenza, which travelled from east to west, following the course of the trade-winds. During the prevalence of this epidemic a good opportunity was afforded of witnessing that peculiar form of despondency which frequently seizes on natives without any apparent or adequate cause. It is a common saying that a Fijian will frighten himself to death; and there is more or less of truth in it. Natives, in some extreme instances, have been known to lie down on their mats and resolutely refuse to get up or take any nourishment until they actually did die. Every physician knows that occasionally patients will declare that they will not recover; and in some diseases, as typhus-fever, this depression of spirits augurs ill for the result. But among Fijians mental despondency seems to arise more from superstition than from bodily weakness. It is said that apparently healthy natives have literally been frightened to death by hearing prophecies that they would not live longer than a certain specified time; but such extreme cases are perhaps somewhat doubtful. Most Fijians, when old, suffer a good deal from rheumatic pains, and to cure these they cut themselves with knives or fragments of glass, or by means of small pieces of smouldering tappa burn the skin over the affected part. This last method of cure is identical with the use of the *moxa*, at one time a fashionable mode of treatment with English physicians.

Among the appliances which I had brought down

to Fiji from Sydney were a scarifier and stethoscope. The former of these gave unbounded satisfaction. Nothing was considered more witty by those in the secret than to place this apparently harmless instrument on the back of some unsuspecting native and touch the spring. In an instant twelve lancets would plunge into the swarthy flesh. Then would follow a long-drawn cry, scarcely audible amidst peals of laughter from the bystanders. As soon as the native had recovered from the alarm consequent on the suddenness of this attack he would ask to have the application repeated perhaps some five or six times. The reason of this request was not very evident at first, but I found by-and-by that the operation was considered a wholesome one, and also that the regularity of the marks left on the skin was much admired. I have known a native come several times to have these marks cut on his arm, and on one occasion, on the Ra coast, I succeeded in procuring an opportune supply of food by means of this instrument. It was at a time of great scarcity, and the natives, who had not enough for themselves, refused to sell any food. In this difficulty I bethought me of the scarifier, and by the simple expedient of exacting a taro-root from each person who wished to be operated on succeeded in collecting enough supplies to complete the journey.

Second in importance to the scarifier *sed longo intervallo* came the stethoscope. At first this instrument was a complete mystery to the natives. They could not make out whence the sounds came that they heard through it, nor did they like to allow anyone to listen to their breathing. One chief would on no account allow his chest to be examined. On my asking for a reason he informed me that he feared lest some one would tell him he was ill and would die, which he thought would be a most serious if not fatal assertion. If a native consents to undergo any operation he will generally bear it with exemplary firmness, evincing no sign of suffering or weakness. But his consent is rarely gained to any such proceedings, and as a rule natives prefer death to the pain of an operation. Fiji produces many valuable drugs, some of which deserve to be better known. The inhabitants are perhaps the most skilful herbalists in the South Pacific, and the cures they sometimes succeed in making are well worthy of attention. They are also accomplished poisoners and abortion-mongers. The latter they practise in various ways, and by means of a variety of medicines, none of which are, however, absolutely new to science.

For the first few months of residence a native village is a tiresome place. But after a time a man becomes accustomed to doing nothing. The enforced idleness that was so irksome at first becomes by-and-by rather the reverse. The climate at one period of the year makes all work a nuisance, and absolute quietude almost a necessity. The monotony, too, of savage life is so complete and profound that as it were it neutralises itself. There is so little to mark the lapse of time, that it passes away noiselessly and swiftly, and in the end the sum of all impressions left on the mind is decidedly pleasant. For most whites in Fiji the day begins at sunrise, when, quitting mat and mosquito-curtain, they make for the nearest river. Then comes breakfast, a meal of little importance, and generally consisting of native fruits, yams, and tea. About this time of day most new arrivals, especially during the hurricane-months, feel weary and exhausted. They contract the disease known as 'mat fever,' and are never so comfortable or so much at ease as when lying down, book in hand, within the shadow of an ample mosquito-net. Towards the close of the day the air becomes less oppressive, the appetite returns, and after another bath comes dinner or tea, according to individual tastes. The evening is generally the pleasantest portion of the whole twenty-four hours. This is the time for native games and dances, for cool breezes and pleasant reunions, at many a hospitable planter's house. But the evening is soon over, and long before ten o'clock most of the white population scattered through Fiji, with the exception of a few restless spirits in Levuka, have gone to bed. During the cool months of the year, which correspond to our summer months, a healthy man feels as vigorous as ever. The 'mat fever,' if resisted, is soon cured, and in a new country like Fiji such an anomaly as an idle man ought not to exist.

At Wairiki the native population was nominally Christian. They had all *loto'ed*, that is, professed a desire to become Christian, and some had even been baptised. There were, however, a large number that always hovered between Roman Catholicism and Wesleyanism, and probably a still larger number who were at heart heathens. Two French priests, under the jurisdiction of the Bishop of Typasa *in partibus*, tended this mission zealously and skilfully. Their establishment was on a much smaller scale than that of the Wesleyans, and showed what men really in earnest could sometimes effect with the most inadequate means and under most unpromising circumstances. These missionaries belonged to the society of 'Marists,' which resembles, in some of its most praiseworthy features, the Society of Jesus, but is without the political bias of the latter. They had commenced their labours by building their own house, and had shown the natives that they were not merely theologians, but also skilful *matai*, or carpenters, a trade which all Fijians hold in high respect. The house was built of wood, one story high, and encircled by a large verandah. The inside was as plain as the outside. In the sitting-room was a tolerable library, composed of the most Ultramontane theological works, interspersed with a few of a more readable nature. On each side of this were the apartments of the priests, scantily furnished, and hung round with the same agonising prints of saints and martyrs that are so common in France and Italy. The house was built in the centre of a plot of ground, some few acres in extent, which had been cleared and planted with cotton by the priests themselves, aided by the voluntary service of a few converts. By dint of much labour and some engineering skill a stream of water had been conducted through bamboo pipes from a spring that lay far up the mountain. This water was always cool and pure, and not only irrigated their moderate plantation, but afforded an unfailing shower-bath in hot weather. And thus, in this quiet retreat, these pious men passed their days, supporting themselves by their own labours, and devoting their lives to the instruction of the natives around them.

Setting aside all considerations of the value of missionary enterprise in general, it is impossible not to respect such single-mindedness and self-denying devotion as these priests exhibited in their lives. French religious societies are not so wealthy as English, nor has the French missionary in Fiji as easy and comfortable an existence as his English colleague. For a considerable time after the Franco-German war all the usual sources of missionary income were cut off. The priests were during this period obliged to support themselves by the labour of their own hands almost entirely. This they did bravely and well, devoting at the same time all their spare hours to visiting the sick, teaching native children, instructing former converts, and gaining fresh ones. In this, perhaps, they were not quite as successful as the Wesleyans. Strange as it may seem, capital is as necessary in missionary enterprise as in more purely commercial undertakings. This the French priests could not command, and no amount of zeal, energy, or ability could make up for the lack of it. Without money you cannot have missionaries, native teachers, schools, or churches; but further, without these you cannot have converts; and, to complete the syllogism, without money you cannot make converts. This is the plain truth, and there is no use disguising it. As regards the natives themselves the Roman Catholic ritual seems better suited to their peculiar mental constitution than does the Wesleyan. Its doctrines are presented in a less abstract form, its ceremonies are more numerous and interesting, its vestments are more gorgeous, its canons exact an equal amount of self-denial, and afford a greater opportunity for display. After all, however, grave doubts as to its utility exist in the minds of many who have witnessed missionary work in the South Sea Islands. There is a fatal slipperiness about the Fijian character which renders all impressions evanescent. Any novelty is quickly taken up, to be as quickly cast aside when it has ceased to be novel. To make such converts as will stand the test of persecution, of neglect, and of poverty for religion's sake you must have stronger stuff than the average Fiji man. To convert such people is like ploughing the sea—your labour is quickly done, but it leaves no record behind it. As Mr. Buckle remarks in his 'History of Civilisation,' the higher and more abstract doctrines of Christianity are beyond the comprehension of an uneducated and almost irrational savage. Of the truth of this fact I have myself seen many illustrations. A Fijiman will listen coldly while the missionary expounds the Athanasian Creed, or the doctrine of faith and works, but will be all eagerness and attention, when he is shown a picture of doubting Thomas, or of the Last Supper, or when he hears the bell tinkling in the sacrifice of the Mass. The advent of missionaries marked an epoch in the history of the South Sea Islands, as much as the advent of Christianity did in the history of the West, or the advent of Mahomet in the history of the East. In all three, to compare great things with small, there exists a certain parallelism. The early missionaries to Tonga and Fiji found opposed to them a worn-out religion, a mere set of forms, from which all vitality had departed, and which had lost all hold on the people. Such was the case in the Roman world in the time of Augustus; and such too was the case in Arabia. So is now the case in Fiji. A number of natives are ever ready to change one form of Christianity for another, and that without any sufficient reason. Did the priest offend them last Sunday, next Sunday they will attend the Wesleyan service; did the Wesleyan minister fail to please them, they will without a moment's hesitation go to Confession and attend mass. With such people the work of an earnest missionary is indeed disheartening. After some twenty years of strenuous exertions the priests are forced to confess that the results have not been satisfactory. With the Wesleyans the state of matters is much the same. This statement will probably be received with derision in some quarters. I can, however, only speak from what I have seen myself; and in spite of numerous congregations, large schools, and long lists of 'offerings,' I do not hesitate to say that Christianity has no sensible hold on the people of Fiji. The improvement that has taken place in their social condition of late years is to be attributed in great measure to the increase of trade and commerce, in a word to the influence of white civilisation in the group. In one respect it would seem that the Roman Catholic missionaries act more judiciously than the Protestant. While the Wesleyans aim at making their converts theologians, the priests aim at doing this and at civilising them besides. Of the conduct of the various sects of professing Christians towards one another, of their jealousies, their strifes and their mutual invectives, nothing need now be said. The whole subject of Christian missions in the South Seas and their influence on the inhabitants of the various groups is a very large one, and desires careful attention. To say on the one hand that Christianity and missionary zeal have done nothing for the natives of Fiji, is to state what cannot be borne out by facts. On the other hand to attribute to missions and to them alone the improved state of the Islands of late years is manifestly absurd. But to repeat what has been already said, no man, however little he may esteem missionary work in the abstract, can deny a meed of praise and respect to these honest Frenchmen who have devoted themselves with so much zeal to the conversion of the heathen. They approach somewhat the type of the ideal missionary apostle, working among the heathen, and yet supporting themselves by honest labour. They apparently, of modern missionaries, have inherited most of the spirit of St. Francis Xavier or Vincent de Paul. If their success is not now as great as in the days of the pioneer missionaries, it is because the times rather than the men themselves are changed.

CHAPTER IX.

Voyage to Ngalena—Fijian Girls—House Building for a Chief—Tiu Cakou—A Fijian Dinner—Kava Making and Drinking—How a Chief transacts Business—An American Planter—Fijian Half-castes—The Land Question—Position of Englishmen in Fiji.

Tiu Cakou, Lord of the Reefs, and Chief of Cakandrovi, was, after Cakobau, perhaps the greatest man in Fiji. So much land did he possess, and so powerful was he, that it behoved every white man to make his acquaintance and strive to gain his good-will. He was generally supposed to reside at Wairiki, but had of late quite deserted this locality, on account, as was said, of the importunities of the white settlers. Be this as it may, he had certainly left his former capital and had betaken himself to a place called Ngalena, some thirty miles higher up the coast. He had lately married his hundred and eighty-third wife, and this, coupled with the fact that Ngalena was, from some cause or other, free from mosquitos, had induced him to make it a temporary residence. Here, therefore, I and several other whites, who were anxious to settle some important matters, waited upon him.

Borrowing a whale-boat, we started a little after

sunrise. The company consisted of some four white men and half a dozen Fijians, a few of whom were furnished with oars. The majority, however, preferred to work their paddles, which they did later on when the breeze died away. Taking advantage of a light air off shore, we coasted along close to the land. Although pretty well accustomed to Fijian scenery by this time, and not in a particularly transcendental mood, I could not but notice the variety and beauty of the landscape. We were now on the 'windward' side of Tavinni, where for countless ages the trade-winds have carried all manner of seeds, and deposited all their moisture on a virgin soil. The struggle for existence is here intense. With the exception, perhaps, of Ceylon, it might be difficult to find any ground so thickly covered with vegetation as is the eastern portion of Tavinni. The country for miles inland is a vast garden of rare fertility and beauty. In some parts it is thickly covered with groves of cocoa-nut trees that yield the largest nuts and the best of oil; in others it is more open, and the sun can penetrate to the soil beneath. In such spots a dense undergrowth has sprung up, composed of the croton-oil plant, the castor-oil, arrowroot, ginger, turmeric, capsicum, and now and then a root of the kava (*piper methysticum*), from which the native drink *agona* is made. In some spots the vegetation is so thick that the cocoa-nut trees overhang the water; but generally a strip of bright sand intervenes between the land and the sea. Our voyage was like the pleasantest of picnics, with the further addition of an element of excitement. We were really sailing over a comparatively unknown sea, and about to visit a barbarian chief. As the day wore on, the land-breeze was exchanged for the trade-wind. The natives plied their paddles bravely, singing songs which in heathen times had done duty for hymns, and might even now be supposed to exercise some influence on the breeze. The priest, who was on board, discusssed the state of Europe generally and the position of parties in England. He shared the belief, in common with so many of his order, that England was at heart Catholic, and that the Ritualistic movement was but the beginning of a widespread revival in favour of Romanism. The Fiji men, with the exception of one, who kept a look-out for rocks, when not paddling, were busy eating yams, smoking cigarettes, or lying asleep on the bottom of the boat. Just as the sun touched the horizon we were abreast of Ngalena, and a few minutes afterwards lay at anchor in a still and secluded bay, on the shores of which Tiu Cakou had fixed his residence.

The anchor once down, everyone prepared to go ashore, the native crew lending their broad shoulders for the purpose. As we were carried up towards the beach, we found an admiring crowd drawn up to receive us. Among this crowd was nearly the whole female population of the village. Now Fiji women are not as a rule pretty, or even passably good-looking. The young girls are, however, graceful and timid, their figures almost perfect, and their dress, when they do not wear European clothes, becoming, if somewhat fantastic. On this occasion they mustered in great force. Trusting to the friendly shades of evening which had already settled down on sea and land, they cared little what they wore. Indeed, their dress was of the scantiest, and eked out now and then by a red flower in the hair, or a necklace of berries, or a bit of some green creeper twined round their waists. As usual I was described as the 'man of death,' and straightway became a person of some importance. On approaching the village, which lay at a little distance from the shore, a tremendous noise was heard, composed of the shouts of men, the shrill voices of women, and what sounded like blows of cyclopean hammers. All this proceeded from some two hundred natives, who, late as it was, were still at work building a house for their chief. They had already cleared away the bush, and while some were laying the stone foundations, others were driving in the posts, and others, again, carrying materials from the neighbouring forest. All was bustle and excitement, every man making as much noise and probably doing as little work as he conveniently could. On a small scale the whole scene recalled Virgil's description of what Æneas saw at the building of Queen Dido's city, and possibly the two conditions of society were not very dissimilar.

Our arrival had at once been made known to Tiu Cakou; but, as though he scented business afar off, he had returned an answer which in Fiji is equivalent to 'Not at home.' We were informed that the chief was asleep, while an official of the Court added that there was little chance of his awaking that day. Meanwhile we were shown into a large native house, hung round with muskets, rifles, cutlasses, Fiji mats, mosquito-curtains, and other valuables. After waiting here some two hours, we saw unmistakeable signs of a feast being prepared. A large pig had been killed, fowls were being shot all round us or chased by Fijians armed with sticks; while fish, cocoa-nuts, taro, yams, and sugar-canes were brought in in large quantities from the 'bush' and laid on the ground.

While speculating as to what all these preparations might mean, Tiu Cakou was suddenly announced. His slumbers were concluded, and he was curious to see who the whites were that had penetrated his seclusion at Ngalena. The chief's appearance was decidedly prepossessing. He was over six feet in height, and well proportioned; his figure was graceful and all his movements were instinct with ease and dignity. His features were open and regular, and his complexion swarthy, but not so dark as that of most Fijians. He had an Oriental look that was far from unpleasing, and this appearance was further heightened by the ample folds of white tappa which encircled his body and trailed on the ground. He carried himself proudly among his Fijian subjects, who, crouching low, did not dare to stand upright in his presence. In a word Tiu Cakou looked every inch a chief, and, as one of those 'nature's nobles,' might have despised hereditary distinctions. The superior physical development and intelligence of the chiefs in Fiji as compared with the common people is very remarkable, so remarkable, indeed, as at once to attract the attention of a stranger. It is generally possible to single out the chiefs from any crowd of inferior natives by their stalwart figures and lighter complexions. All this is probably to be explained by good feeding and the absence of harassing work for many successive generations, rather than to any virtues or qualities inherent in their blood.

Tiu Cakou is in many respects a man far superior to the ordinary run of Fijians, and if his life should be prolonged will probably yet fill a page in Fijian history. He is very brave and fond of danger and excitement. His capacity is perhaps scarcely equal to his valour, and if one may judge by appearances, he seems somewhat devoid of ambition. He has never been tainted with the vice of cannibalism, and boasts, what is no empty boast in the mouth of a Fiji chieftain, that he does not know the taste of human flesh. On the other hand, however, some very ugly stories are current about him, and probably from a civilised standpoint of morality many of the actions of his life would not bear a rigid scrutiny. Tiu Cakou was alternately a Wesleyan and a Roman Catholic as the mood came upon him, and at this particular time when I first saw him was inclined towards Catholicism. The French priests exercised a good deal of influence o er him, and in their presence he was docile and courteous. Although he had nominally abandoned heathenism, he had not been able to bring himself to abandon polygamy. He had been married 183 times, and was still not too old to marry again. His first and chief wife was a daughter of old Tiu Koominooa, and still lived in a large house at Wairiki, surrounded by her maidens and enjoying all the honours of royalty. His latest bride was a half-caste Tongese, a woman of great personal charms and considerable mental ability. She was not long in acquiring an influence over the chief which she did not scruple to use for the advantage of her countrymen, to the great disgust of many Fijians. In virtue of his lineage Tiu Cakou could marry whomsoever he pleased. If on a journey he stayed at any village he would straightway marry some maiden of the place, and from that moment the poor girl's life might be said to be blighted. She could never marry anyone else, unless, indeed, the chief chose to give her away as a gift. If she was unfaithful to the memory of her lord, and that was all she could claim of him, death was her punishment. Her mouth was tatooed at the corners, she received a daily allowance of food, was called the 'chief's wife,' and with this empty title her cup of earthly bliss was supposed to be full.

Tiu Cakou was a thorough libertine, nor was he

always scrupulous as to how he chose his victims. Some of the stories told about him recall King David in his worst moments. In spite of the social and legal status which the chief's wives possess, their fate is very much to be pitied. They are condemned to lead a life of practical celibacy under a penalty of death, and have little to look forward to in the future. Occasionally one of these women may be given as a present to some favourite; but this is a piece of good fortune which falls to the lot of few. As a rule they hang about their native towns leading a weary, listless life, until some fortunate accident or death itself removes them from the scene.

Had Tiu Cakou been educated under more favourable influences, he might have become a man of more note. As it is, his opportunities have been few, and he has never had any but the smallest field for the display of genius or ambition. He is, or was until lately, the slave of two fatal vices—libertinism and drunkenness. Of the former, enough has been already said; of the latter there is not much to say. In his youth he learned intemperate habits from sailors and dissolute whites who then lived on the islands, and at an early age had become an habitual drinker. He used to take enormous quantities of raw gin, and when under the influence of this cared little what he did or said. At the time I first made his acquaintance he had temporarily abandoned gin and had taken to kava. Subsequently I met him at Levuka, where, flushed and excited with drink, he had come, under the guidance of the wily Maafu, to barter his kingdom away to Cacobau and the knot of whites who formed the so-called 'government'

But on the occasion of this my first visit Tiu Cakou was affability and sobriety itself. He shook hands with us all, instead of rubbing his nose against ours after Fiji fashion, and bade us welcome to Ngalena. By this time dinner was ready, and he ordered it to be spread on the ground. All then sat down in a circle, each guest being provided with a plate, a fork, and a banana leaf. Knives were dispensed with, except by some of us who fell back on our penknives. The meal, which was a good sample of a Fijian dinner of ceremony, commenced with soup. This was made of fish, cocoa-nut milk, and a variety of herbs all boiled together. Its flavour was very good, and if naturalised in England it might become popular, that is, if merit had anything to do with such a result. After soup came, naturally enough, fish. It was a parrot fish, not unlike a turbot in shape and flavour, save that its scales were blue and that it had the bill of a parrot instead of the teeth of a fish. It is well known in the Mediterranean, and therefore need not be further described. After the fish came the *pièce de resistance*, which was nothing more nor less than an entire pig of large size roasted whole. It was carried in from the oven by two men who bent under their burden, not because of its weight, but out of compliment to the chief who had provided such a splendid animal. These men laid it down in the centre of the circle as we sat, and at once began to dismember it with their great knives. They fell to work with a zeal and *empressement* that showed how much the work was to their taste. First of all the legs were severed from the body, and then the head, and then huge slices were taken from the ribs and back and handed to us wrapped up in a banana leaf. The flesh of the animal was almost untouched by the fire, and the uncongealed blood still ran from the open veins. This I learned afterwards was done with a purpose. In such a climate as Fiji meat cannot be preserved without salt for any length of time, and salt the natives will not use. Consequently they fall back on repeated cooking, and by this means are enabled to keep meat fresh for some two or three days. The portion cut off at the commencement of the feast would next day be placed in the oven to be more thoroughly baked. Along with the fish and pork came yams and taro. It is difficult to describe the taste of these vegetables, suffice it to say that the former is not unlike a very dry potato, whilst the latter is also like a potato, but more moist and starchy. Neither is in flavour equal to a potato, although on this point there may possibly be differences of opinion. As soon as all was finished, the banana leaves which had served for plates were taken away, the mats rolled up, the floor swept, while the announcement was made by a loud clapping of hands that the chief had ended his repast. This was the important and anxiously expected moment for all the women and hangers-on about the place. This was a signal that their turn had now come, and certainly they did not require a second bidding. On our side we were somewhat wearied with sitting cross-legged so long, but were now able to lie at full length on the floor and smoke *seleucas* of native tobacco. About eight o'clock the chief wished us good-night, and left the house, but not until a bowl of kava had been prepared. How this was done will now be shown.

Long before dinner was ended some young men and girls might have been noticed cutting into small pieces a root not unlike that of a dahlia. This was nothing more nor less than the celebrated *kava* or *yagona* (pronounced angona) of all voyagers from the time of Captain Cook onwards. This plant is known to botanists under the name of *piper methysticum*, while kava is an extract prepared from its roots by a somewhat peculiar process. The root having been cut into pieces of a convenient size was ready for chewing. This necessary evil was ushered in with certain preliminaries which were somewhat reassuring. In the first place the persons chosen to discharge this office were young lads and girls; they carefully rinsed their hands and mouths with water, though their pearly teeth seemed scarcely to require such a formality. Then having individually selected a piece of the root they commenced to munch it slowly and solemnly. The word 'chewing' gives but a poor idea of the process; it more resembles ruminating had such a thing been possible with human animals. Then when the root had been reduced to a pulp it was placed in a wooden bowl and water poured upon it. Next, one of the young maidens, having once again rinsed her hands, plunged them into the bowl, and deftly spreading over the contents a wisp of *rori*, sank it to the bottom of the bowl, and brought up in its meshes innumerable small portions of the kava wood. This process she repeated several times, until at length the liquid was thoroughly strained, when it was fit for drinking. It was next, with more or less formalities and ceremonies, ladled out into cocoa-nut shells and handed round to the company. The chief drank first, and then the guests in order of merit, or in our case, as we happened to be sitting. No sooner had Tiu Cakou finished his draught than there was a great clapping of hands and loud cries of *maca, maca* ('it is empty, it is empty'). The same cry was repeated after each white man had drunk, though they were very far from being so loud or so hearty as in the case of the chief.

Some persons even in Fiji profess to be very much horrified at the mode in which kava is prepared, and will scarcely condescend to taste it. Individuals so squeamish that they cannot conform to the harmless and historical custom of drinking a bowl of kava with a chief had better keep away from the South Sea Islands. The mode of its preparation is certainly a little disconcerting at first; but this cannot be avoided. Some persons imagine that kava can be prepared by grating the dry root into cold water; but such stuff compared to real kava is like gooseberry wine to champagne, or Rosolio to Lafitte. It is not in fact to be mentioned in the same breath, as any old kava drinker will tell you. The taste of kava is at first very disagreeable. It has been likened to magnesia, or to weak soap suds, and perhaps no white man ever relished his first draught of it. But when the liquid has been once swallowed, the disagreeable taste gives place to a pungent and pleasant sensation that lingers for a long time on the palate, while a sense of comfort and contentment gradually steals over the whole frame. In this soothing power, just as in the case of tobacco or opium, lies the secret of kava. It possesses, too, like gin, whisky, and most other spirits, some volatile oil, that imparts to it its peculiar flavour and much of its influence over its votaries. If a man has once succeeded in drinking a bowl of kava with real pleasure, his fate is sealed. Every year of his residence in Fiji will probably make him a more confirmed kava-drinker, and unless he is endowed with a certain amount of strength of mind he will become a slave to the habit. Kava-drinking is probably more difficult to break off than either drinking of alcohol or excessive smoking; but perhaps it is not so destructive to health as either of these habits. How I learned to drink kava is probably how most men have learned to drink it. I had often taken a bowl with chiefs, and on other occasions, and each time seemed to dislike the nauseous mixture more and more. At length, one unusually hot day, after a long and tiresome walk through the 'bush,' I approached a native village, and knew by the aromatic odour which the wind carried towards me that kava was being 'brewed.' I was so thirsty that I could have drunk almost anything, and gladly accepted the bowl that was offered. No sooner was it swallowed than I felt at once refreshed: fatigue and lassitude gave place to comfort and repose. From that moment I was in danger of becoming a kava-drinker. As it was, I preferred it to beer, champagne, or any other liquid with which the white palate is wont to stimulate itself. Kava can probably be drunk with pleasure only in a hot climate. I have frequently heard the remark made in Fiji, 'The weather is too cold for kava to-day;' and anyone who analyses his own sensations will find that he looks for this drink more in hot than in cold weather.

Kava is essentially the national drink of Western Polynesia. It is to the Fijiman what opium is to the Chinese, bang to the Indian, fermented milk to the inhabitant of Central Asia, or whisky to the Scotchman. It supplies that mysterious craving common to all nations, and founded apparently on some physiological necessity—that craving for intoxicating or stupefying drink in one form or another. Kava resembles opium in many points, as in its soothing power, and in the hold it gains over those who have once become addicted to it. By the Fijian, and by many whites, it is endowed with almost every virtue, 'curative, preventive, and comforting under misfortune.' There can be no doubt that its effects on the human body are very peculiar, and would probably well repay a thorough scientific investigation. Its therapeutic qualities have, perhaps, never been properly tested. Persons in Fiji credit it with being a better blood-purifier than sarsaparilla, and with having the power to ward off diarrhœa, dysentery, and fever. If taken in moderation, it seems to be a kind of mere tonic; if taken in excess, it causes nausea, headache, and partial paralysis of the muscular system. It produces a lethargic state of the sensibility, but without the excitement or consequent coma of alcohol. In Rotumah the natives make a more powerful kind of *agona*, whether from some difference in the root itself or from a difference in the mode of its preparation. Here the bad effects of an excessive dose of kava can be studied with facility, for the natives consider it the height of wit to intoxicate sailors who land on their island. I have seen men thus drugged who could neither stand nor walk, and had to be carried on board the vessel; and, indeed, was myself on one occasion nearly the victim of a practical joke of this kind. The evil results of excessive kava-drinking are abundantly manifest in the persons of old topers. Their eyes become bleared, their bodies scaly, their hands tremble; while they themselves are haunted by a perpetual craving for their favourite drink, which, by a kind of Nemesis, they are unable to prepare for themselves. It is a humiliating sight to see some old white man, degraded by years of indulgence in this habit, going from one native house to another, and begging from the churlish inmates a bowl of the kava they are making. As likely as not they will refuse his request, and tell him to go to his own countrymen, who, however, know him as an 'old hand,' and are generally more pleased at his absence than his company.

By the time our party broke up the natives had long been in bed. The chief had provided large mosquito-curtains for us, and indeed had done everything he could to make us comfortable, for Tiu Cakou was not deficient in the virtue of hospitality. The night passed away quietly, and next morning we all were up before sunrise, in hope of being able to make an early start. But such was not possible. Tiu Cakou would not see anyone or transact any business till mid-day. At length he sent word to say he was ready, and would hear what the white men had to say. Each man had some favour to ask or some business to settle relative to land or cotton, or native depredations, or Fijian labourers. I was one of the first to enter, and was introduced in due form. Tiu Cakou was seated upon the ground cross-legged, having before him a large box, on the lid of which he was counting out a number of gold coins. His secretary, a white man, sat by him, also on the ground, and translated our conversation. The chief was good enough to appoint me his physician, to give me a certain portion of land, with a house already built upon it, and to promise to build me another as soon as possible. After a few more words we parted with mutual expressions of esteem on both sides. Scarcely, however, was my audience ended than the chief grew quite tired of business. He, therefore, abruptly refused every other petitioner, scarcely taking the trouble even to hear what he had to say, and, accompanied by a few followers, marched off into the bush, leaving the white men to settle matters as best they could. For my part I could not be ill-pleased at the success of my venture, and already in expectation saw myself a successful planter. The others, however, were not a little disappointed and annoyed at the capricious behaviour of the chief, particularly as he had acted in the same way on more than one previous occasion. Their propositions had been fair and business-like ones, and for the interest of both the parties concerned. But everything had been rendered impossible because Tiu Cakou had chosen to get out of temper. His conduct on this occasion affords a fair instance of one source of difficulty in buying land in Fiji, namely, to get your proposals even listened to by the chief. The whole history of the purchase of land by whites in Fiji teaches that the white man has been imposed upon by the native as thoroughly, and probably as often, as the native has been by the white man. Indeed, considering the difficulty of buying land, the uncertainty of tenure, the unsettled state of the country, and, finally, the price as compared with that of first-rate agricultural land in New Zealand or Australia, it has always seemed marvellous that planters in Fiji cared to pay as much for their plantations as they did.

As soon as Tiu Cakou's temper was known further stay at Ngalena was of course useless, and consequently the whale-boat was got under weigh as quickly as possible. In spite of every effort, however, we did not make more than some fifteen miles before nightfall, and justly considered ourselves fortunate in being able to reach the house of an American, who gave us a hearty welcome. This gentleman was the largest planter—that is, had more acres under cotton than anyone else in Fiji. He had arrived in the islands some twenty years ago, with few worldly possessions, but by a fortunate accident (nothing less than saving a chief's life) had obtained a grant of a small island. Here he cultivated cocoa-nuts, from which he made oil, and gradually saved a sufficient sum of money to purchase land in larger quantities. At the time of the 'rush' to Fiji, from 1865 to 1870, he was enabled to dispose of this at a good profit, and to commence cotton-growing on his own account. He had now over two hundred imported labourers at work, among whom might have been found representatives of every labour-producing group in the South Pacific. In fact, his men formed an ethnological collection; but this was perhaps their smallest virtue in the eyes of their employer. In addition to these two hundred there were some fifty Fijians from the Ra coast, fat, lazy, insubordinate fellows, whose work scarcely paid for the food they ate. All these men were housed and fed on the plantation. The principal article of their diet was yams; but occasionally taro, sweet potatoes, and rice were served out.

As our boat approached the shore, all these two hundred and fifty men could be seen pulling together on a chain, with which they were hauling a small vessel up on to the beach. At a critical moment their efforts broke the stout chain, and the dusky mass of humanity fell backwards in wild confusion. Strange oaths, cries of pain, of surprise, of encouragement, were at once uttered in some score or more languages, and in the midst of this babel we landed, and were at once invited up to the house. No second bidding was required, and we were soon seated round the planter's hospitable table. His wife was a half-caste Fijian; hence all his children were quadroons. It is very rare to see a Fijian quadroon, and in this instance the admixture of native blood seemed to have been anything but a disadvantage. If quadroons, however, are rare, half-castes are common enough. There are colonies of them in various parts of the group; for instance, at Levuka, the Rewa river, and on Vauna Levu. As a rule they follow the occupation of sailors in small craft, and in fine weather do well enough. As a class they bear an indifferent character; and while the men are neither particularly brave nor intelligent, the women are not over-virtuous or good-looking. It is a fact worth noticing that there is a strong tendency among half-castes and others with a less amount of Fijian blood in their veins to recur to the type of the less civilised parent. This may, perhaps, be to some extent the effect of early training, for, as, an almost invariable rule, the mother and not the father belongs to the darker race. It is not probable that the half-castes will increase much in the future. On the contrary, with advancing civilisation and the increase in the number of white women resident in the group, mixed marriages will gradually become fewer as the state of society which encouraged them passes away.

Making an early start next morning, Wairiki was reached without further adventure. There I took possession of the house given to me by Tiu Cakou, but found it was in such a dilapidated condition as to require more repairs than it was worth. As usual, too, in Fiji a dispute arose as to the ownership. The house and ground were both claimed on behalf of a merchant in Sydney, who, it was said, purchased them some ten years before; and although his claim might fairly be considered to have lapsed, it was none the less annoying to be involved in a dispute of such a nature. Until this question could be settled, it was manifestly useless to make improvements. After a good deal of trouble and delay I succeeded in obtaining a second interview with Tiu Cakou, who had himself given me the ground. But, unfortunately, on this occasion he was in a worse temper than ever, and was so far from helping me, that he repented of his former liberality, and decided that the land was not given at all, but only lent, and could neither be sold nor leased. Under these altered conditions I refused to accept the gift, which, indeed, would have been quite useless.

Until Fiji is united under one central authority it is vain to expect that the buying or selling of land will ever be conducted without disputes and misunderstandings on both sides. The land question has been the most fruitful cause of bloodshed between whites and natives from America to New Zealand, and from the days of Penn to our own times. It would seem as though no treaties, however clear and just, could command respect for any length of time. A sort of fatality apparently attends all land-dealings between the different races; the result in almost all cases has been that both parties consider themselves wronged, and prefer to fight rather than to yield tamely what they consider as their rights. In Fiji, at any rate, it cannot be said that the natives have been imposed upon or defrauded. In most cases the whites have paid more for their lands than could fairly be considered the market value; yet the natives are far from satisfied. The truth is, that no uncivilised men can or will reason out in their minds the consequences of alienating large tracts of country. Collectively they do not understand what they have done until they begin to feel pinched by hunger or cramped for room; but as soon as the land has been fenced in, the cocoa-nut trees cut down, and the bananas and yams cleared away to make room for cotton or sugar, then they begin to perceive the effects of their rashness, and of course to regret it. In many instances in Fiji planters would have been only too glad to restore the land to the original owners, if they in turn would only restore the actual money that had been paid over to them. This, of course, they could not do; and hence the beginning of sorrows.

The natives trespass on the white man's ground, steal his fowls or cocoa-nuts or yams; the planter defends himself as best he can, and ultimately in some angry moment blood is shed. The result is that many settlers become ruined men, while some lose their lives, and the natives are driven off for a time. Meanwhile these natives will probably have found earnest and eloquent friends in England who will plead their cause from many platforms, and will refuse to allow that a 'poor native' can do any wrong. The unhappy Englishman who has ventured to defend his rights will come in for no small share of contumely and abuse. Nay, it will be well, indeed, if a ship-of-war flying his country's flag does not try him by court-martial or carry him many miles away before a jury of prejudiced men. If he should escape this ordeal, is it very much to be wondered at if he forthwith changes his nationality and seeks under the Stars and Stripes that protection which he has failed to find under the Unionjack? Disguise it how we will, the fact remains that the position of Englishmen in Fiji is very far from satisfactory. Peace Society doctrines may be well enough in Birmingham or Manchester, but are held in little esteem by those savage and warlike races with whom Englishmen in various parts of the world must come in contact. It is a poor policy that compels a man to return a spear-wound with a moral platitude, or the ruin of his homestead and the blighting of his career with offers of arbitration. Of course England could not undertake an Abyssinian war or Ashantee expedition to right every distressed British subject; but surely she might hope to do in this respect as the Americans or French, or even the Germans with their embryo navy. As a matter of fact England does not protect her subjects in many parts of the world anything like so successfully as the nations above-mentioned. One reason for this is, perhaps, to be found in the instructions issued to captains of vessels-of-war; another is the knowledge which those officers possess that any severe measures adopted towards natives would be certain to be followed by an agitation in England, confined, perhaps, to one or two small circles, but not the less annoying for all that. The whole matter is a sore subject with many Englishmen who reside abroad, in Fiji and elsewhere, and perhaps this is not the place to discuss it. Those, however, of my readers who have witnessed the surprise and dismay of Englishmen on learning for the first time that, though their countrymen were ready to punish they would not protect them, and who further learned that their statement of foul wrongs and prayers for redress was only to be noticed as a 'literary curiosity,' will excuse this digression.[1] Our forefathers, indeed, did not look on 'Jenkins' ear' as a mere curiosity, pathological or otherwise, and yet its exact condition after being wrenched off by the Spaniard might have been of some scientific interest, especially to a certain large class of dilettante philosophers who treat of matters about which they have had no opportunities of gaining any real knowledge.

[1] See on this subject the 'Fiji Gazette' of October 25, 1871, where the captain of a ship-of-war is stated to have said that he would regard a certain petition as a 'literary curiosity.'

CHAPTER X.

A Hurricane—Its Effects at Wairiki; on the Group generally—Increased Demand for Native Labourers—A Labour-vessel—Ocean Islands—Tanna Boatmen—A Perilous Voyage—Straits of Somo-Somo—Leave Fiji for Rotumah.

WHILE I was busying myself about land, and as yet doubtful whether to become a cotton-planter or not, an event occurred which quickly decided me in the negative. This was nothing less than a hurricane; and as every settler in Fiji will probably have to experience one of these tempests during his residence in the group, I shall make no apology for describing the one I witnessed.

During the whole of the month of March 187—the weather had been unusually calm and sultry even for Fiji. At length, one day towards the end of the month, the wind set in from the unusual quarter of north-west. It began with fitful squalls accompanied by showers, but gradually settled down into a steady gale. The sky meanwhile became overcast. A dense pall of black clouds spread gradually over it from the north, while frequent thunder growled ominously in the distance. All night long the wind blew violently, and next morning the weather looked more threatening than ever. The barometer meanwhile fell very low; but all this was only the prelude before the curtain rose. As yet nothing more than a severe gale was blowing, before which any Australian or China clipper would have made a capital day's run. Every hour, however, the weather became worse. The sky was covered with clouds that drove along fiercely, and came so near the surface of the earth as apparently to touch the tops of the trees. Every object was enveloped in a moving mass of rain and mist. The rain poured down in torrents, flooding the lowlands, and transforming the little mountain-streams into rivers. All communication was soon cut off between the two portions of Wairiki. Having been away from the hotel at the commencement of the storm, I was not able to get back to it for several days. During this time I was dependent on the hospitality of Mr. Hoyle, Tiu Cakou's secretary. His house, as has been stated, was a very large and strong one, and had already borne the brunt of more than one hurricane. After sunset on the second day from the commencement of the gale the weather became suddenly much worse. The night was intensely dark, but its darkness was broken every moment by flashes of lightning of appalling vividness. Though every chink and loophole had been carefully closed, yet as we sat round the table the uncanny glare of the forked lightning was painfully distinct. Stepping for a moment outside the shelter of the house, I witnessed the strife of the elements in its full intensity. The sight was one which perhaps is rarely if ever witnessed beyond the limits of the tropics. The horizon seemed literally on fire, so quickly and vividly did the flashes of lightning succeed each other. At one moment, darting from the sky, they would plunge swiftly into the sea, now white with driving foam; at another, quivering in the air, they would linger for a moment before the eye and then be lost in the surrounding gloom. The colour of each successive flash was never the same. Some of the flashes would emit a pale pure light, others a lurid red; others, again, would be so blue and ghastly that you might deem they had come directly from the nethermost region. The glare never for a moment died out of the sky. Peal upon peal of thunder followed fast and loud, while the flashes of lightning as they darted across the welkin showed broad-leaved bananas all drooping and torn, the ground covered with water, and trees and houses bare and ruined. The scene, indeed, was unearthly in its intensity. It rather resembled some passage in the history of a condemned spirit or the portentous season that ushered in the birth of Glendower.

On regaining the friendly shelter of the house I found the company seated at the table; and as the bottle passed merrily round tales were told of perils and hairbreadth escapes on just such a night among the coral reefs and cannibal islands of the Pacific Ocean. Nearly every man in the company could tell some story of dangers escaped or adventures encountered which if met with in a novel would be condemned as improbable. One story told by an old Greybeard was somewhat as follows:—Many years ago, when a white man was yet an object of wonder and curiosity in Fiji, this old man, then young, had settled in the group and married a native wife. He, with his wife and family, was one day fishing, when a sudden squall came upon them. Their utmost exertions could not propel the canoe against the wind that had suddenly sprung up, and they were compelled to let it drift before the gale, which was fast blowing them out to sea. One after another each familiar object and island was passed in headlong career. At length, when at the extreme point of the group, and apparently doomed, the wind shifted a little, and they succeeded in reaching one of the Yassowa islands, that lie to the south of Fiji. No sooner, however, had they gained the land than the inhospitable natives straightway seized upon them, and declaring that 'salt water was in their eyes,' prepared to slay and eat them. The first victim was the youngest child. A ruthless Fijiman seized it by the feet and dashed its head against a tree. The mother in a frenzy of grief called to her husband, '*Matai* (F., carpenter), look what they have done to the child!' That one word acted as a talisman to save the lives of all. The fire had been kindled, the oven was already hot, and husband and wife lay bound, waiting for the fatal blow from a club. But the chief's quick ear had caught the word unintentionally spoken, and turning to the

Englishman, he enquired if he was indeed a *matai*. 'Yes' was the answer. 'Then,' said the chief, 'if you will mend my musket I will spare your life.' The man was soon released, mended without much difficulty the stock of the old weapon, became the chief's prime favourite, accumulated property, and was still alive, though very old, to tell the story.

Another of our company told how he had been homeward-bound, some twenty years before, from a long whaling voyage in the Southern Ocean. Day after day, as with the Ancient Mariner, a fierce fair wind had followed the ship for many a league, and the icy blasts that career round Cape Horn had been changed for the bright skies and perennial summer of the Coral Islands. But the mariners sailed the sea at a treacherous time of the year. A hurricane caught them off the Fijis and blew sail after sail away from the ill-fated vessel. Then the captain ran his ship before it under bare poles, and night settled down upon them still running their fearful race with death. The lightning-flashes showed all things clearly enough, and among other gruesome sights the mariners beheld a reef on which the breakers thundered and broke with a force no human work could resist. In a moment a huge wave had lifted the ship high in air, and the next dashed her to pieces on the rocks beneath. But the same wave that hurled the ship upon the reef carried one man over it. He immediately found himself in smooth water; and striking out boldly, reached the shore. Upon this island the natives were of a friendly disposition, and moreover the stranger was protected by an old Frenchman who lived on it. This old man had once served in the armies of the great Napoleon, but after the battle of Waterloo had quitted France for ever. He had wandered far and wide, until fate and declining strength had caused him to settle finally in Fiji. There he had married, and had one daughter, who, as might be expected, fell in love with the shipwrecked sailor. The restless old man was slain shortly afterwards in a contest with some natives from another island, and after his death his child married the man whom the ocean on that stormy night had sent her.

With us the thunder had by this time rolled away in the distance, and the wind almost completely died away. Indeed, after the commotion of the elements that had just been witnessed it seemed as though some breathing space was but natural. Yet those who knew what hurricanes were held this to be a bad omen. The calm was ominous of something to come worse than anything yet experienced. However, the company present was composed of men pretty well inured to dangers, and whose nerves were not easily discomposed; besides which, sufficient unto the hour was the evil thereof. Accordingly, after a few more stories, one by one each man retired to his mosquito screen and soon dropped asleep. After what seemed a short interval, however, I was aroused by an unusual noise. The house presented a strange spectacle. All the men were up and walking about, while the women and children were collected in the centre of the room crying bitterly with fear. Among the group were several Fijians who had abandoned their own houses, whose strength they doubted. To say that the wind was now blowing strongly would give not the faintest idea of the terrific tempest which had suddenly burst upon us. The noise of the wind was not like that of an ordinary gale, but more resembled what might be produced by a great body of water in rapid motion. The air seemed, in fact, to be a concrete moving mass, that overbore and levelled everything it met in its course. The house groaned and shook in every post and beam. The strong ridge-pole bent and cracked as though it must quickly break. The massive uprights swayed to and fro in the ground; while from the roof overhead quantities of dust, broken reeds, dead spiders, scorpions, and such like rubbish, fell down and increased our misgivings. The wind was now at its height, and the only question was whether it or the house would last the longest. The noise of the tempest was so great that you could scarcely hear your own voice; and indeed no one seemed particularly anxious to speak. All hope was now centred in that stout ridge-pole which ran from one end of the house to the other, and held gables and roof and sides firmly together. Whether it would stand the tremendous strain much longer, no one cared to enquire particularly; but at any rate a few hours or minutes would show. Packing up some valuables in as small a compass as possible, I seated myself near the door, which was now barricaded with mats and pieces of timber, to prevent its being blown in, and waited patiently for the end. I had not very long to wait, for towards morning the wind fell rapidly, and in a few hours was blowing only a moderate gale.

No pen could describe the scene of havoc and ruin that the village of Wairiki presented on the morrow. The ground was strewn with bread-fruit, cocoa-nuts, broken boughs of trees, and fragments of houses. The grass, the banana trees, and all smaller vegetation, were beaten down, and covered with water, mud, and *débris* of every kind. Many bread-fruit trees were blown down, others were stripped of leaves and blossom, and would not recover the effects of that night for years to come. The cocoa-nut trees were in as bad a plight. In some cases their tops had been twisted off bodily, in others every leaf and nut had been torn away, and the stems of the trees alone remained, planted like tall pillars in the ground. A few houses were standing, but most of these were so strained and damaged, and inclined so much to one side, as to be quite useless. The unfortunate owners were wandering about disconsolate among the ruins, picking up unripe cocoa-nuts, or begging a meal from their more fortunate neighbours. As the day wore on, however, the sun came out brightly, and men's spirits rose with the improved prospect. In Fiji, living is not the same weary struggle for existence as in England. There was no need to open a subscription list for the sufferers in Wairiki. No matter how forlorn and destitute a man might seem in the morning, there was no reason why he might not have a comfortable meal and a substantial roof over his head before evening. In a few days the village was as blythe and merry as ever; and, save for the shattered walls and broken trees, there were no vestiges to be seen of the fierce tempest that had so lately swept over the country.

After some time, when it had become possible to compare reports from distant parts of the group, it became abundantly evident that Wairiki had not come in for its full share. The centre of the hurricane had actually been at some considerable distance, and Wairiki had been only on the outskirts. From Levuka doleful accounts were received. Many of the houses had been blown down; many more unroofed; vessels had been wrecked in the harbour; and all kinds of property had been more or less damaged by rain and wind. Even more sad was the long list of vessels and lives lost in Fijian waters. At first it was hoped that many missing vessels would be heard of; but as day after day passed by without bringing any tidings, hope at length died out. Near the island of Koro, bales and boxes and loose spars were drifting about for many days; and although men knew a wreck had taken place, no one could name the vessel. At length, some six months afterwards, it was proved to have been an American brig, bound from Samoa to San Francisco. All hands had undoubtedly perished on that wild night. At Macuata, on the north-west of

Vauna Levu, the hurricane had been felt in its full intensity. Among other strange feats, it had lifted a small vessel from off the beach, and had blown it into a native village. In many outlying districts the planters had lost well-nigh all they possessed. Their houses had been blown down, their provisions damaged, their domestic animals killed or carried out to sea, their cotton crop irretrievably ruined. In some parts of the group the country presented an appearance as though a fire had passed over it. The grass and brushwood appeared scorched, and eventually withered away; while the leafless trees were scarcely able for weeks to put forth a green shoot, so severely had they been dealt with. These appearances were probably to be accounted for in part by the enormous quantities of salt water that must have been carried inland, in the shape of spray, by the force of the wind. As to the cotton crop, it was destroyed more or less completely throughout the whole of Fiji. Not merely were the blossoms and pods torn away, but the plants themselves in many cases were blown completely out of the ground, and piled in remote corners of the plantations. For all this there could be no remedy. The unlucky planter could only sow fresh seed, and wait a year for the returns which he had expected to receive in a month. The whole white community in Fiji continued to feel the disastrous consequences of this hurricane long after its immediate effects had passed away. During the next twelve months the islands were to all intents and purposes bankrupt, and men lived as best they could, buoyed up by hopes of better times. The calamity which they had sustained had been an universal one, and admitted of no alleviation. Many a planter who had heretofore struggled manfully with his load of debt was by this latest disaster hopelessly overweighted. Many a bold and speculative man, who had embarked large sums in cotton, now saw his money lost, and himself compelled, like others, to live on credit. The country, however, was young and vigorous, and next season things looked as promising as ever. But by that time fresh disasters had occurred, which proved to the full as potent as any hurricane in arresting the development of Fiji. As these, however, were political rather than natural, and depended on the caprice of men rather than that of the elements, they will more fitly be considered hereafter.

As not only the hurricane itself, but the so-called 'hurricane months,' during which such a catastrophe was alone possible had now passed, shipping resumed once more its wonted activity. Scarcely a week passed without the arrival of some large vessel from Australia or New Zealand, freighted with passengers and wares; while every little bay and creek sent forth some smaller craft to carry on the trade between one island and another. About this time, too, the demand for imported labourers increased largely. The development of the cotton industry had been more rapid than could have been expected, and thus the supply of labourers that had been hitherto sufficient was so no longer. This demand was created partly by the formation of new plantations, and partly by the fact that most planters began to see that it was cheaper to import natives from western Polynesia rather than employ Fijians, though the latter did not cost one-third as much as the former.

It so happened about this time that a planter near Wairiki was fitting out a small vessel to get labour for his plantation. This vessel might be taken as a specimen, though a somewhat small one, of Fiji labour-vessels in general. Though small, she was thoroughly seaworthy, and in her general appearance not unlike those hardy little pilot-boats that 'lie off and on,' in foul weather and in fair, at the mouths of the Thames or Mersey. Her size was twenty-two tons 'register,' and, according to the regulations then in force at the British consulate, would allow of her carrying some thirty labourers from any part of the South Pacific. She was not fitted up in any very elaborate manner. A loose sail spread over the ballast and an empty hold was sufficient accommodation for the passengers, who, thus housed, were better off than in many of their own villages. The whites on board consisted of five hands, and in addition to these two savage island boys were carried to cook and make themselves generally useful. The vessel was soon ready for sea, but at the very moment of her departure a hitch characteristic of Fiji occurred. The late captain had left the vessel somewhat suddenly, and no one had been found to fill his place. There were, indeed, plenty of men ready to 'sail' the vessel, but not one to navigate her. As showing the curious state of affairs in Levuka at this time, it may be stated that scarcely a captain who commanded a vessel in the 'island trade' held a certificate of competency. A man's own statements as to his abilities were accepted, and few questions asked. Unable to find a professional navigator, the owner of the vessel offered me the appointment. My knowledge of navigation was not, indeed, very profound; but seeing that I could 'take the sun' and use a chart, it was better than none at all. At the last moment, however, a man appeared, in whose favour I gladly yielded my claim. Furthermore, as certain abuses had already occurred in the 'labour trade,' I took the precaution of getting a written document from the owner, stating that I was merely a passenger on board, and had nothing whatever to do, either directly or indirectly, with the ship or cargo.

My object in undertaking the voyage was to gain some knowledge of the labour traffic by personal experience, and also to visit some of those remote islands of ocean which, lying far out of the track of all ordinary commerce, are only visited at rare intervals by a ship of war or some erratic whaler. Many of these small islands are hundreds of miles from any land, and some of them are not larger than Middlesex or Rutlandshire. Such microcosms nevertheless often contain inhabitants peculiar to themselves, and differing from other islanders in appearance, language, manners, and customs. How such isolated communities have managed to hold together so long; how intermarriage within such a small area have not caused the race to degenerate or die out; how, if the population has been increasing, the surplus has been got rid of from time to time; how the fauna and flora resemble or differ from other groups and islands, were all questions which I hoped this voyage would throw some light upon. It was intended that Rotumah should first be visited, then Tanna and other islands of the New Hebrides group, then Banks' Island and the Admiralty group generally, and that we should return to Fiji by way of the Loyalty Islands, supposing sufficient labourers had not been already obtained. The vessel was provisioned for a long voyage, and carried a cargo composed of knives, hatchets, printed calicoes, beads, muskets, gunpowder, scrap iron, tobacco, Jew's harps, and other things known to be highly esteemed by the inhabitants of certain islands. In such a voyage it was, of course, necessary to be well protected against violence or treachery. Each man, therefore, had a revolver and breech-loading rifle, while a number of muskets were put aside for some natives who were expected to join at Tanna. The inhabitants of this island are excellent boatmen, and are frequently employed by white men in this capacity. Their office is generally to row the boat towards the shore, while the captain or mate trades with the islanders and explains to them his terms. In case of an attack being made by the natives almost everything depends on the steadiness and courage of the boatmen. Should they lose their presence of mind, the death of the whole party will probably be the result, as has been shown by more than one catastrophe.

When all preparations had been completed, we crossed over from Wairiki to the neighbouring island of Vauna Levu, or 'the Big Land,' to take in provisions and water. The distance was only some twelve miles across, and yet it nearly proved fatal. A strong tide was setting down the narrow Strait of Somo Somo, and just as we were in the full strength of it the wind fell light, and soon died away altogether. The calm became every moment more profound, and we soon found that we were drifting bodily on to a reef, upon which, even at the distance of six miles, we could hear the roar of the breakers. The tide was running at least four miles an hour, and thus we had but an hour and a-half until our fate would be sealed one way or the other. We had no small boat on board, nor any materials wherewith to construct a raft. Our only hope lay in being able to anchor; but that seemed almost impossible, as the water, except on the reef itself, was too deep for any ordinary chain to reach the bottom. Accordingly, nothing could be done save to let the vessel drift nearer and nearer, until in the immediate vicinity of the reef the water became shallow enough to allow the anchor to bite. Meanwhile we were approaching the reef apace, and could already see with unpleasant distinctness the great waves as they rose and fell, and broke with a sullen roar on the rocks beneath. Amid the calm of that still evening their roaring seemed like a death-knell. From where we lay becalmed we could hear the sounds of human voices and the lowing of kine, and yet we were hopelessly cut off, perhaps for ever, from the land that lay so near. But already the supreme moment had arrived. So close had the vessel drifted to the reef that the coral might be seen many fathoms down through the clear water. This was the time to let go the anchor. As the whole weight of the vessel came upon it, we could see it tearing down trees of coral, breaking off portions of brittle rock, and starting innumerable fishes from their hiding-places. With the tremendous strain the chain groaned in every link, and for a moment seemed likely to break. But on this occasion the iron proved true, though shortly afterwards it played us an ugly trick. It was with feelings of no small relief, as may be imagined, that we saw the vessel safely anchored. Some thirty yards at most intervened between our bark and those great rollers that could have crushed her as easily as a steam-hammer could crush a nut. Many a good ship has come to grief in a similar way; and every man who navigates Fijian waters should look well to his ground-tackle. A few hours after sunset a breeze sprang up, and rescued us from a perilous position. Making the best of our way back to Wairiki, we remained there that night, and, starting early next morning, arrived at Vauna Levu about midday.

Twenty-four hours sufficed to put the little craft in order for the voyage. We took in some extra ballast, replenished the water-casks, laid in a store of cocoa-nuts for the Savage Island cook, and filling with a fair wind, shaped a course for Thicombia, the Land's End of Fiji to men bound northwards.

The navigation of the Straits of Somo Somo, through which it was necessary to pass, proved most intricate. The charts of this portion of the group are quite untrustworthy, not one-half of the dangers being accurately laid down. In such a narrow sea, however, no captain would think of trusting solely to his chart, but rather would keep a good look-out, and sail only by daylight, as Captain Cook and other sturdy old sailors were compelled to do. A watch was generally kept on board the cutter from the mast-head for reefs or shoal patches. These can, as a rule, be seen plainly enough from aloft, but not from the deck; hence the necessity for navigating your ship from the mast-head. In many parts of Fiji it is never safe to sail without this extra look-out, for no one can tell at what moment the vessel may come upon some isolated coral patch, technically known as a 'horse's head.' Such patches may be within a few inches of the surface or may be many feet below it; but, at any rate, if they are near enough to the surface to be dangerous they can always be seen from aloft, except, indeed, when the sun is shining directly upon them. As the mariner approaches the Island of Rabi these sunken dangers cluster round him more thickly than ever. He is entangled, as it were, in a network of reefs, and shoals, and 'horse's heads.' In fine, no man who does not know the coast well, and possesses withal a vessel easily handled, should attempt to leave Fiji by the Somo Somo passage.

At sunset we had worked clear of all danger, and could shape a straight course for Thicombia, whence, in nautical phrase, we were to take our 'departure' for Rotumah. The wind held fair, and by midnight we had passed the little island that stands like a sentinel before the Fiji group. Next morning no land was to be seen, for we were fairly launched on the broad Southern Ocean, which rolls unbroken, save by a few scattered islands, from Australia to Cape Horn, a vast expanse of restless heaving water, that realises to the voyager the 'ocean river' of Homeric song.

CHAPTER XI.

Voyage to Rotumah—Natives—Rotuman Mats—An extinct Volcano—Ancient Inhabitants—A Feast—Cocoa-nuts—I Practise Medicine with success—Missionaries—Civil War—Blown Away—Return to Fiji.

ROTUMAH is a small island, lying in mid-ocean, about four hundred miles north of Fiji. Having no chronometer on board, we had to trust for our longitude to what sailors call the 'dead reckoning;' but this mode of reckoning is of little use amid constant changes of winds and currents. On the third day the captain thought we must be near the island, and just as the sun was touching the horizon the mate was confident that he saw land. Others held the appearance to be only a cloud, and as no one could agree, the ship was 'laid to' for the night under easy sail, and all hands went to sleep. Next morning we looked in vain for the phantom of the night before, and, loth to abandon hope, even sailed resolutely in the direction where we had seen it for three hours. At last we were obliged to return to our former course, to which we held all that day and the next. Still Rotumah was nowhere to be seen. It was now to be feared that we had overshot the mark, for the sun not having been visible for two days, we did not exactly know where we were. The weather, too, looked threatening enough. Heavy rollers came toppling in from the east, while the wind at one moment would fall calm, and at the next blow in such furious gusts that we were obliged to lower all sail, and to watch the little craft very narrowly. But just as everyone on board had made up his mind for an uncomfortable night, the mist lifted, and Rotumah was seen broad on the lee, not five miles distant. We shook a reef out of the mainsail, and before evening were at anchor opposite a native town, and within a hundred yards of a sandy beach covered almost to the water's edge with most luxuriant vegetation.

By sunrise next morning I was ashore, enjoying the novelty of the scenery. Rotumah is a small island, some nine miles by seven, but is a perfect gem of beauty and fertility. It is covered by groves of cocoa-nut trees, in addition to which every tropical plant known in Fiji flourishes in abundance. My first care on landing was to become acquainted with any white men who might be residing on the island. The first I met was an old man of the name of Bill R——. He had called in at Rotumah originally on a whaling voyage, and had remained on the island more than forty years. He was a member of that large family of stray whites already noticed, who are to be found more or less scattered over all the Pacific archipelagoes. These men belong to a bygone age, and are themselves passing rapidly away; the means of communication are increasing every year throughout the Southern Ocean, and very soon there will be few places in the world that answer to the peculiar requirements of such persons. In fact, work in some shape or other is becoming a universal necessity, and soon the genus 'loafer' will scarcely find a suitable habitation on the globe. Like pirates, buccaneers, Spanish galleons, and sailors' pigtails, he will become a thing of history, to be spoken of, indeed, and wondered at, but never to be met with. Old Bill had settled on Rotumah when he was about twenty years of age. At that time there were over seventy whites on the island, all, with scarcely an exception, runaway convicts from Van Diemen's Land and Botany Bay, establishments then in full activity. One of these men had managed to extemporise a rough still, and the daily occupation of himself and fellows was distilling 'grog' from the shoots of the cocoa-nut trees. As might be imagined, these lawless men, freed from every restraint and inflamed by drink, abandoned themselves to every excess, scaring even the savage natives by the wildness of their orgies. Desperate conflicts with each other, and with the natives, gradually thinned their numbers, and old Bill assured me that of all the seventy men who were on the island when he first landed, there was not one who escaped a violent death. What a strange life this old fellow must have led, severed for so many years from the outer world, and mewed up in a small island with such desperate company! The blandishments of native beauties prevailed in his case over all weightier considerations, and though offered from time to time a passage in some passing whaler or ship-of-war, he could never bring himself to quit the island. At length he found himself the sole survivor of a bygone generation, and, moreover, surrounded by new men with whom, from his previous course of life, he could have but little sympathy. Against missionaries in general, and 'native teachers' in particular, he was possessed with the most hostile feelings, which he never took the slightest trouble to conceal; he was a 'thorn in the flesh' to more than one reverend gentleman, and an object of terror to many a Fijian and Tongan preacher. As might be supposed, Bill had a good deal of influence with the natives, and generally acted as the go-between in all dealings between ship-captains and the islanders. He could procure either seamen, or labourers, or provisions, or firewood, as the case might be, better than any other man in Rotumah. If allowed to have his own price he would see that no one else cheated you, and most shipmasters were glad enough to agree to his terms, and thus prevent further misfortunes. In his old age Bill had taken to purchasing cocoa-nut oil, and had amassed a good deal of money in this way, though what use his wealth could be in such a place no one, probably not even himself, could tell.

The natives of Rotumah are a genial and kindly set of people, the men handsome and courteous the women pretty, graceful, and retiring. As a rule, although they are not so handsome as the Samoans, nor so dignified as the Tongans, yet some of the prettiest women south of the Equator may perhaps be found in Rotumah. Like many other South Sea Islanders, they plaster their heads with quicklime; and, strange as it may seem, this fashion is, in some cases at any rate, far from unbecoming. One pretty girl I saw thus *coifféed*, looked for all the world like a court beauty of the days of Madame de Maintenon. Many of them stain their hands and skin with turmeric, a monstrous and unbecoming fashion, which yet in Rotumah finds favour with the other sex. The men of Rotumah make good sailors, and after a few years' service in sea-going vessels are worth the same wages as white men. Scarcely a man on the island but has been more or less of a traveller. It is no rare thing to find men who have visited Havre, or New York, or Calcutta, men who can discuss the relative merits of a sailors' home in London or Liverpool, and dilate on the advantages of steam over sailing vessels. Thus the average native of Rotumah is more than usually capable and intelligent. Of late years the wealth of the little community has largely increased, and the price of every kind of provisions has become so high that whalers have almost ceased to visit the island. We had no difficulty, however, in procuring plenty of fowls, pigs, yams, and cocoa-nuts at a moderate price, though not so cheaply as among the savages of the New Hebrides or Admiralty Islands. As regards the domestic life of the natives, it resembles very much that of the Fijians and other South Sea Islanders. The climate requires few clothes, and calls for little work from those who are lazily inclined. The houses are small, dark, and dirty, built of leaves, and thatched with reeds; the sides are of cocoa-nut leaves, tied loosely on to posts, so that the whole side of a house can be removed at a moment's notice without damage to the general structure. As a rule, during the day, one or more sides of the house are thus taken down, to admit light and air, and are replaced in the evening.

Among the industries of Rotumah, there is only one of any particular interest, namely, mat-making. A Rotumah mat is valued in other islands much as an Indian shawl is valued in Europe. Compared to Rotumah mats, the finest Batique mats from Fiji are coarse and ugly; while the mats of Samoa and Tonga do not deserve to be mentioned in the same breath. A good Rotumah mat will take many years to make, and will cost at least five pounds of our money. To an Englishman's eye, there is nothing in them of such surpassing excellence. I, however, brought two of them back with me to Fiji; and, on showing them to the Queen of Cakadrovi, she expressed such admiration, and begged so earnestly to have them, that I could not refuse her, particularly as friends at home would probably only have recognised in them a strong likeness to bass-matting, somewhat finer than that which gardeners use. The staple product of Rotumah, from a commercial point of view, is cocoa-nut oil. Like wool in Australia, or cotton in Fiji, it constitutes the wealth of the country. The mode of its preparation is simple enough. The natives gather the cocoa-nuts at that stage of their growth when all the so-called milk has been absorbed, and when the fleshy portion of the nut is thickest. They then break off the shell, and leave the kernel to putrefy in the sun. After a certain time the oil drains from the nut, and is collected in suitable vessels. Meanwhile, the process is extremely disagreeable to all not pecuniarily interested in the matter. The air round each primitive oil-press becomes laden with a pestilential smell, while the ground becomes covered with broken shells and decaying husks to an extent that makes walking almost impossible.

As the vessel was to stay but a short time at Rotumah, I took up my quarters on shore. Among other excursions, I made one to an extinct volcano which exists in the centre of the island, and to which Rotumah probably owes its existence. The path to this ancient crater lies through a dense forest, rich with all the wealth of the tropics. This portion of the island is not less fertile than the most fertile parts of Tavinni, while it surpasses most portions of Fiji as much as Fiji surpasses New Caledonia or Queensland. The predominant tree is the cocoa-nut; but trees and plants of many other species grow so luxuriantly that the traveller walks in twilight beneath their shade. Two chiefs accompanied me, and acted the part of guides. One had formerly been king of the island, until Christianity having created a political as well as a religious revolution, had displaced many of the old ruling families. The other chief was a man not less remarkable for mental power than physical strength. He had played a great part in a war which had lately resulted in the triumph of his party, and had throughout shown himself to be a brave and able general. He was a very Falconbridge in the 'huge composition' of his chest and brawny limbs. As he toiled up the steep, carrying a basket of provisions that would have been a load for two ordinary men, he might have served for a model of Samson bearing away the gates of Gaza. An old white man was also of the company, who, though weighted by a burden of threescore years, yet carried them bravely. He had become a settler in Rotumah by what might fairly have been called a series of accidents. He had been wrecked, in the first instance, on the island when a youth, and been taken off by a passing vessel only to be wrecked some years afterwards in almost the same spot. He had escaped once more, but was left a third time on shore by a rascally captain; and before escape was again possible, so long a time had elapsed that he did not care to leave the island.

After gazing down the ancient crater, whose fires had long been extinct, we descended a cave that penetrated for an unknown distance underground; some said even under the sea. This cave evidently owed its existence to some convulsion at a time when the island was an active volcano, and also bore traces of having once formed the bed of a stream. After descending along it for about a quarter of a mile, the air became as hot and oppressive as in the Great Pyramid, and we were forced to return. After all, there was not much to see, though it would have been difficult to have imagined a better hiding-place for a body of men, or a more typical robbers' cave. From this cave to the highest peak in the island was not a great distance. Apart from the view to be obtained from the summit, this hill was interesting for another reason. It was holy ground, having been for ages past the burying-place of the great hereditary chiefs of the island. Its top was covered with stones, each stone marking the resting-place of some departed sage or warrior. The air was here so cool and fresh that we would gladly have lingered longer, but the sun was already low, and many miles of forest still lay between us and the sea coast. Looking, therefore, for the last time at the old moss-grown tombstones, we prepared to descend the mountain. We had not proceeded far, however, before the two chiefs called a halt, and invited us to share a feast which had been prepared in their honour. Deep in the recesses of that forest there still lived two families, the sole survivors of an inland tribe that once formed the chief population of the island. The present inhabitants of Rotumah live entirely on a small strip of alluvial land lying between the central volcano and the sea. But there was a time when such was not the case. The interior of the country was at some period inhabited by tribes between whom and the coast natives there had existed one long feud. This had at length resulted in a permanent separation between the two sections of the population, namely, between the dwellers inland and the dwellers on the coast. This separation produced in time divergences in language and modes of thought, so that the dialect of one tribe became unintelligible to the other. The sole representatives of the inland inhabitants of former days were the two families whom we were now visiting. Their numbers were too few to justify any general conclusions regarding the race they belonged to. They seemed, however, decidedly inferior to the coast natives of the present day in physique and intelligence. It occurred to me that these people might be a remnant of an earlier migration to the island, and that on the arrival of the present inhabitants they had been driven to seek shelter in the mountains and forests, much as the Britons sought shelter in the fastnesses of Wales on the approach of the English. A study of their language would have tended to throw some light on this point, but in their present moribund condition it is not likely that any enquiry could be made conclusive. There can, however, be no doubt that at one time Rotumah supported a much larger population than at present. Tradition leads us to believe as much, while an examination of the island proves it. In all directions through the forest there are traces of large clearings. Flat stones arranged in a peculiar manner mark the sites of ancient houses and temples. Stone fences and walls, now meaningless, served at one time to divide the lands of one family from those of another. These remains point to some great changes having taken place in the population of the island. The population has decreased; but this decrease is not peculiar to Rotumah, for it is noticeable more or less throughout Eastern Polynesia. It is an ethnological fact of some importance, and seems to point to the conclusion that this particular subdivision of the human race is doomed to extinction. The distinction between coast tribes and inland tribes was probably at one time universal throughout the larger groups of the Pacific. Now, except in a few instances, it does not exist. A good example of it may still, however, be observed in Fiji, in the island of Viti Levu, where the mountaineers (Kai Colos) differ from the coast tribes of the present day in language, religion, and polity. Between these two tribal divisions an irregular warfare has been maintained from time immemorial, but there can be no doubt that both are descended from the same stock.

Having spoken about the people of Rotumah it would be ungrateful to suffer their hospitality to pass unnoticed. It was for the chiefs, indeed, that most of the good things had been prepared, but we white men came in for our share. The feast resembled in many points the one which Tiu Cakou had given at Wairiki. A large pig, heavy enough to try the strength of a strong native, had been baked in the oven, and was brought in whole Taro, yams, and bananas were eaten with it. All the food was served on broad leaves instead of plates, and in the absence of knives or forks we fell back on fingers. A lump of rock salt was placed on the floor. This the natives would not touch, but anyone who liked was at liberty to chip a piece off for his own use. Besides all these, there was given us a peculiar sauce or condiment not met without of Rotumah, though there its use is very extensive. It is prepared from young cocoa-nuts, by filling them with salt water, carefully sealing them up and then burying them in the ground for several weeks. Here they undergo a kind of fermentation, and when first opened emit an intolerable smell. Their taste, however, is by no means bad, resembling somewhat that of anchovies, and forming an excellent relish to the generally insipid fish or other food of the South Sea Islands. With a draught of the juice of young cocoa-nuts, the repast came to an end. Many persons in England derive their notions of a cocoa-nut from those which are sold in London or elsewhere. But in countries where cocoa-nuts grow, such old ones would be considered worthless, except for making oil or feeding animals. A young nut contains very little of the white 'flesh,' the shell is thin and comparatively soft, while the interior is filled with a subacid juice more resembling water than milk. A nut of average size contains about half a pint of liquid, which, mixed with some gin or other spirit, makes a very refreshing drink in hot weather. After the cocoa-nuts came the unfailing kava bowl, with the usual operations of chewing, straining, and handing round. By the time this was ended the sun had set, and we made our way back through the forest by moonlight as best we could.

During my time in Rotumah I lost no opportunity of visiting any sick persons whom I could find. One day Alberti, the principal chief of the island, sent for me, and invited me to come and live in his palace. It was not, indeed, a very palatial residence, although it was one of the best houses in the island. Alberti, it so happened, suffered from a surgical disease which had long baffled the skill of native doctors, but which required for its cure nothing beyond a very simple operation. He was, however, very nervous, and had promised the most liberal rewards to anyone who could cure him. To such a man, if he could meet with him, he would make over a corner of the island, many hundreds of acres in extent, a house or two, the labour of a certain number of men annually to gather cocoa-nuts and make oil, and finally a town to provide him with food—offers as liberal as those of the Persian monarch to Themistocles. But better than everything else, he promised to give the successful man the hand of his sister in marriage, and so make him equal in rank to the highest chiefs in the island. Such offers were not to be lightly rejected. After a good deal of hesitation, Alberti submitted to the necessary treatment, and in a few days was cured. He proved as good as his word, for his first act was to fulfil his previous promises. He granted me the land and houses, and I could not but be pleased at the extent and beauty of the gift so far. As to the lady, I had not yet seen her, for she was in a distant part of the island.

By the successful treatment of the chief my name soon got bruited about Rotumah, and I was well-nigh overwhelmed by the numbers of those who flocked to consult me. In order to put a stop to this I exacted some payment from each individual, and consented to receive yams, taro, fowls, mats, bread-fruit, cocoa-nuts, or indeed anything they chose to offer. Alberti himself took me under his special protection, made me live with him, and was never tired of hearing about England, Australia, and other distant countries. In a word, he presented that rarest of phenomena—a grateful patient. The moon was just at this time at its full, and the pleasantest part of the whole day in Rotumah was from sunset until the moon went down. There happened fortunately to be a concertina on board the ship, and this was brought ashore every evening by one of the sailors. First of all, the white men would dance a hornpipe or 'break-down,' then the natives would dance their own dances to their own wild music. Sometimes both parties would take hands and dance together, and then assuredly the measure would be one of the strangest ever stepped by sane people. When all had wearied of dancing, the girls would prepare kava, with which to refresh their partners. This they made so strong that some one or more imprudent sailors were generally overpowered and unable to get up from the ground. This was considered very amusing by all except the victims, whose brains were quite clear although their muscles were paralysed. These evening parties on the bright coral sand, beneath the pale light of a glorious moon, were indeed delightful. Everyone was in the highest spirits, and due restraints were present to check the general mirth. It was under these conditions that I first had the supreme pleasure of meeting my promised bride. A bevy of laughing girls presented her to me, all coyness and modesty, and the frequent blushes mantled her cheeks as she greeted me after the manner of her country. She was some sixteen years of age, brunette of course, and decidedly pretty. Her hair was braided with hybiscus flowers, while round her waist she had twined a girdle of some graceful plant like ivy. Her cheeks were unhappily dyed in one or two places with turmeric, but even this hideous fashion could not destroy her native beauty. Her dress was a mat of island workmanship, and hung as gracefully round her as the drapery on a Greek statue. Altogether, Alberti's sister was a very charming and piquante little creature, and from all accounts quite as well behaved as she was good-looking. It was difficult to resist the conclusion that it would be much nicer to remain among these kind folks than to go to sea in the uncomfortable little craft that was pitching and rolling in full view of the spot where we sat. And what, after all, was to be gained by tempting the hardships and dangers of the deep once more? By a freak of fortune, I had come into possession of all that might be looked on as a necessary basis of material happiness—a homestead and a position of independence, coupled with youth, health, and a fine climate; and, moreover, as if this was not enough, I had the offer of that which Bernardin de St. Pierre says is indispensable to happiness—a good wife.

I had brought a few letters of introduction from Fiji, and among others one to the Roman Catholic priests who were conducting a mission at Rotumah. Their success on this island had to all appearance been considerable, and they seemed to have accomplished a good deal in the way of civilising and instructing the natives. Both of them were men who had had experience in mission-work in other parts of the Pacific, and hence had brought some special qualifications to bear on their task. As usual with French missionaries, they had built their own house, made their own furniture, and were diligent workers with their hands as well as with their heads. From them the native converts received instruction in the useful arts of civilisation, and as an ignorant layman I could not but think that such was a far better way of educating the native mind than by merely cramming it with dogmatic theology. I spent many hours with these priests, and was struck by their earnestness and single-heartedness. Among such men the chivalry of the great missionaries of old is not yet dead. A lofty purpose carried out without flinching, a life-sacrifice offered without misgivings or regrets, a courage undaunted by difficulties or dangers, an enthusiasm that never waxes cold, are qualities that command respect wherever met with. For my own part, though opposed to their tenets, and doubtful of the ultimate value of their work, I cannot but admire the consistent and manly bearing of these soldiers of the cross, who confront heathenism and savagery, well knowing that their campaign can cease only with their lives. For them there are no domestic ties to soothe care or alleviate toil, no 'retiring allowance' to gladden their declining years, no 'fat offerings' to make their lives as luxurious as those of the natives who surround them. In their camp the stern discipline of active warfare is ever present, and they themselves are but the rank and file of that highly organised army whose skill and disciplined valour has so often proved a match for the best statesmanship of Europe. Before leaving the French mission, I was introduced to the chief of the 'Catholic party;' for society in Rotumah is split up into as many 'sets' as in Guernsey or the Isle of Man. He was a handsome gentleman-like young fellow, and spoke French remarkably well. He had gained his courteous bearing and polished manner in the school of the Vatican, and his French during a five years' residence at St. Omer and Paris. I conversed with him for some time, and was astonished at his general intelligence and knowledge of the world, though, as might be supposed, he saw everything through the glasses of his spiritual advisers. The Rev. J. Nettleton [1] speaks of him as 'a young native who has been to Rome and seen the Pope. To the conduct of a Rotumah heathen he adds the politeness of a Frenchman.' Which is the gravest crime in the eyes of the reverend gentleman, whether to have seen the Pope or to have the politeness of a Frenchman, it might be difficult to say. It is satisfactory, however, to know that most of the Wesleyan converts in Fiji and Rotumah are free alike from both these crimes or errors, more especially from the latter of the two.

It would not be fair to dismiss the subject without some reference to the Wesleyan mission, established in Rotumah, which has apparently been attended with a large share of success. The gentlemen who conduct it deserve credit for energy and perseverance, and for that skilful organisation which is found wherever Wesleyan enterprise has penetrated. Churches have been built, schools established, teachers imported from Tonga and Fiji, subscription lists opened amongst the natives, and in fact the whole missionary machinery fairly put in motion. Whether all this will ultimately increase the well-being of the people of Rotumah may reasonably be doubted. So far it certainly has not. As already stated, a Roman Catholic mission had been established on the island for some time. It was scarcely to be supposed, however much it might have been desired, that these two

---

[1] 'Fiji and Fijians,' p. 588. Hodder and Stoughton. 1870.

sections of Christians should work together amicably. The old contests of the League were after a time renewed on a smaller scale and a narrower field; and the two bodies of professing Christians, in their hatred to one another soon forgot their common hatred to heathenism and savagery. The newly-made converts on both sides were inflamed with an excess of religious zeal, and desired nothing better than an opportunity of showing how sincere their repentance and subsequent conversion had been. The enthusiasm of the teachers spread itself among the disciples, and unfortunately was held in check by no previous mental or moral training. Society in Rotumah soon became thoroughly unsettled. Two great factions came into being in the island, the Catholic and the Protestant. There was yet a third faction which was still powerful, and counted among its supporters many of the leading families of the island, namely, the heathen faction. A pretext was now only required for a religious war, and this pretext was soon found.

The first open rupture which occurred related to the payment of taxes. The king of the island was still a heathen, and, as is the rule in primitive states of society, was both king and priest. He united in his person the highest civil and religious offices, and received equally the revenues of the kingdom and the offerings of the faithful. But now a knotty question arose as to whether a Christian convert should pay tribute to a heathen ruler. There was indeed a precedent for paying to Cæsar the things which were

Cæsar's; but in this case apparently it was not held to be applicable. So far as I could learn on the spot, though I only give the information as I received it, and do not express any opinion as to its correctness or otherwise, the Wesleyans were the first to resist payment. The priests on their side recommended payment of the secular taxes, but in the same breath urged their converts to abstain from those heathen dances, feasts, sacrifices, and other abominations which concluded the annual ceremony. The Protestant minister advised the non-payment of any taxes whatever, for Christians, he argued, should have nothing, not even taxes, in common with heathens. When the king learned that his secular authority was about to be disputed he at once prepared to enforce it. This was the signal for a civil war, which was in reality a religious war, as everyone felt. It was prosecuted on both sides with a bitterness and cruelty beyond what was customary even in savage warfare. A great battle was at length imminent. Each party prepared to do its utmost, and religious fanaticism inflamed men already sufficiently brave to the highest pitch of frenzy. In the camp of the Protestant Dissenters, as in that of Cromwell before Naseby, nothing was heard save the solemn chanting of hymns and penitential psalms mingled with the fervid oratory of local preachers from Fiji and Tonga. In the Catholic camp the sacrament was administered to every warrior, while the banner that was to be borne aloft that day was honoured with the special blessing of the

Church. The battle was fought with determination on both sides; but the event was not long doubtful. The Wesleyans inflicted a crushing defeat on the combined forces of the heathens and Catholics. Then followed the usual period of wild excess. Chapels were demolished, lands laid waste, houses burned down, and the population of a whole district forcibly removed away. The priests' vestments were found and torn to pieces, and the fragments scattered over the island. The strong-box that contained the sacred oil, the vessels, the relics, and other valuables was broken open, and its contents set up as targets for the rifles by these fierce iconoclasts. At the time of my visit to the island the Catholic and heathen natives were reduced to great straits. They had been compelled to quit one portion of the island altogether, and had been deprived of their houses and stores of food. The position of the victors is, naturally, much better than before the war. Every native who had heretofore wavered in his religious belief at once declared for Protestantism. Arguments and proofs that had heretofore failed to convince became at once irresistible. Converts crowded round the Fijian preachers, blocked up the doors of the churches, and called loudly to be instructed. It seemed as though the days of the Primitive Church had returned. A great revival of religion had apparently taken place, compared to which the remarkable revival witnessed in the French Court towards the close of the reign of Louis XIV. was as nothing. The missionary reports are naturally full of these glad tidings, which at length reach the sacred precincts of Exeter Hall. To many, however, who were on the spot, the day of this great victory seemed a gloomy and disastrous one in the annals of Protestant missions.

With Alberti I fought the battle over again. His generalship had contributed much to the victory, and he showed me the various strategical points he had gained or defended on the eventful day. Along what had been the line of combat we passed several newly-made graves. Here had been laid many of the brave men who had died in defence of what they had held to be a righteous cause. One of these lowly graves was better tended than the others, and was decked with fresh flowers every day by the widow of the slain warrior. Gazing on these sad monuments of civil strife, one could not but regret that the introduction of Christianity should have brought about such untoward results. It seemed a hollow mockery that in this island, so small, so secluded, hitherto so peaceful, the tidings of good will to men should have been heralded by the crack of the rifle and the wail of widows and orphans. It would surely have been better that one party of Christians should have retired before the other rather than that the cause of Christ should have fallen into disrepute. Intelligent natives themselves told me that the island was in a far happier and better state before the rival missionaries settled in it. Looking round on the bare and blackened walls of many a homestead and on those newly-made graves, I could not but come to the same conclusion.

This religious war was one of the few topics on which Alberti and I could not agree, so we mutually allowed it to drop. The good fellowship still continued between the sailors and natives, though the moon now rose so late that the time for dancing was scarcely long enough. I had made up my mind to accept Alberti's offers, and remain for a time at any rate on the island and try the life. Such, however, was not to be. One morning, while the captain and most of the crew were on shore enjoying a bowl of kava, a native rushed into the house in great excitement to say that the vessel 'had gone away.' The news made everyone start to his feet, and in a few moments we were all on the beach. The vessel had indeed broken adrift from her anchor, and was going sideways out to sea. The two men on board were trying to make sail, but meanwhile seemed in imminent danger of drifting down upon a reef to leeward. A tropical squall had sprung up and had brought with it a 'chopping sea,' which had snapped the cable, already half rusted through. Had the wind not been off shore nothing could have saved the vessel. As it was a boat was soon launched, and, after many tears and adieus from Alberti, I jumped in, intending to return as soon as the vessel was safe. But scarcely were we outside of the shelter of the little bay when we found that a gale was blowing, against which our united efforts would not have moved the boat. All were glad enough to get on board the cutter, and, with three reefs in the mainsail and a storm-jib, we found it blowing quite hard enough. The most unpleasant part of the whole adventure was that both anchors had been lost, and consequently it became necessary to bear up for Fiji instead of completing the voyage. This was to me a most unexpected conclusion, and I begged to be put on shore again at Rotumah. But the captain was inexorable; and, indeed, with the wind and sea both rapidly rising, the further the vessel was kept off the island for safety the better. Soon, one by one, the familiar features of the landscape faded from the view. By sunset we were a good ten miles away from the land, and next morning the island was out of sight; nor have I ever again had an opportunity of seeing it or any of its kind-hearted and hospitable inhabitants.

CHAPTER XII.

Method of Procuring Labourers in Rotumah—Labour-producing Islands Trading with Savages—Pigeon English—Soloman Islanders—Banks' Islanders—Tokalaus—Dangers of Labour-getting—Head-money—Tricks of the Trade—Mr. Consul March and the 'Carl'—The Labour Trade not Slavery—Exaggerated Statements current in England—Causes of these—Treatment of Labourers on Plantations in Fiji—Traffic in Natives within the Limits of Fiji—Suggestions for the Conduct of the Trade generally.

As the vessel in which I had visited Rotumah had made the voyage with the object of procuring labourers, it became an important question for the owners how many she had brought back. The answer was four; and for this the voyage had lasted some six weeks. These four men had been procured just in the same manner in which nine-tenths of all labourers imported into Fiji have been procured, namely, fairly and honestly. As some misapprehension prevails in England as regards the labour-trade of Fiji generally, I shall make no apology for narrating exactly what I was myself witness to.

Immediately on arrival at the island the master of the vessel lost no time in communicating with the chiefs. He wanted, he said, so many young fellows to work in Fiji for a term of four years; their work was to be in boats and on a cotton plantation; they were to be fed and housed; and at the end of their term might either remain in Fiji or have a free passage back to Rotumah.

To facilitate matters the chief of the district and Old Bill were sent for on board. Various articles of trade were shown to the islanders, such as hatchets, knives, cloth, rifles, jew's-harps, and such like. In return for a certain quantity of these the chief promised to use his influence with the young men of the place to induce them to emigrate, or at any rate not to hinder them from doing so if they chose. The captain himself went on shore and invited the natives to visit the vessel and judge for themselves. This they did, but out of seven who promised to go with him to Fiji three subsequently refused, stating that the vessel was too small. Eventually four signed an agreement for four years, much in the same way that sailors sign 'articles' before proceeding on a voyage. There was neither deception nor coercion in the matter. Any attempt at such would have been most impolitic, besides being quite useless. An interpreter had been employed, and the conditions of the contract were thoroughly explained to the natives. As well as I remember they were to receive at the rate of about six pounds sterling a year for their work, besides board and lodging. Such will not appear bad pay to those who know the wages that an English agricultural lad can earn, and these natives were mere boys. On asking the father of one of them why he sent his son away he answered me much as an English parent might have done—it was for the boy's own good. He was desirous that he should see the world, and have better opportunities for improvement and education than a small isolated place like Rotumah could afford. And therefore he sent him to Fiji, justly arguing that there the boy could not help coming in contact with white civilisation, and could not but derive benefit from the comparative enlightenment by which he would be surrounded. As to the boys themselves they were delighted to get away. A new world was about to be opened to them and a career in life. Although they shed a few natural tears at first, no sooner was their sea-sickness over than they worked on board with a will. On landing at Wairiki they were at once taken possession of by their own countrymen who were already there before them, and comfortably housed, clothed, and fed. If such be slavery, I could point to many a poor white man who would not object to being a slave. This is, I believe, a fair sample of what the Fijian labour-trade is at its best.

But then this trade is not always at its best. There are many blots upon it, some of them foul enough. But before discussing the trade and its abuses it will be well to state from what islands the labourers are imported, and some of the methods which have been resorted to to obtain them.

The cruising-ground of the labour-vessel is very extensive. It stretches northward of Fiji some six hundred miles, and east and west about two thousand. It embraces the low-lying groups of sandy islands known as the Ellice and Gilbert and Radack chains; the New Hebrides, the Soloman Islands, New Ireland, New Britain, the Admiralty Group, the Loyalty Islands, and many more, whose names would convey but little information to the ordinary reader. Many of these islands are mere barren sandhills, producing nothing but cocoa-nuts; others are larger in extent than England, and more fertile than the most favoured parts of Australia. The New Hebrides and the Soloman Islands are pre-eminently the places which supply the Fijian labour-market. Their inhabitants are to the cotton-planter of Fiji what the coolies of the Malabar coast are to the sugar-planters of Mauritius or Demerara. Of all the islands of the New Hebrides group Tanna produces the best workmen. They are, if well treated, docile, intelligent, and active men, and further are excellent agents to employ in procuring labourers from their own or other islands.

As may be imagined, in such a vast extent of ocean there are many differences between the inhabitants of the various groups and islands. With these distinctive differences and with the most important characteristics of each tribe of natives the labour-captain must make himself acquainted. We have already seen how labourers were procured at Rotumah; but Rotumah is comparatively civilised. The man who would venture ashore at Malicolo or Santa Cruz as he would at Rotumah would have but a poor chance of ever returning. The mode in which the more savage groups of islands are generally traded with is as follows:—The labour-vessel makes first of all for Tanna. Here she takes on board as many men as are willing to come, say some twelve or so. From Tanna she makes for Malicolo, Espiritu Santo, Sandwich, Bougainville, or perhaps Banks Island. Here the Tanna men are told off into the long-boat, armed with muskets. The captain or mate sits in the stern-sheets, also well armed, with a large box placed in front of him. This box contains the articles of trade which are to induce the natives to visit Fiji. The Tanna men row steadily towards the shore, keeping the while an eye on the muskets which lie beside them. As the boat approaches, the shore is seen to be lined with naked men, armed with spears, bows and arrows, stones or clubs, as the case may be. If there be women among them, the trader may go on shore, as no immediate treachery is intended. If there be not, he had better keep his boat afloat in at least five or six feet of water. If none but a few solitary men are on the beach to meet him, he has still greater need of circumspection, for probably every bush and rock hides an armed savage ready to jump forth at a moment's notice. As soon as the trader has assured himself as far as he can that all is right, he opens his strong-box and proceeds to trade with the natives. Sometimes the sight of a musket or hatchet or gaudy handkerchief will at once induce a man to come on board. Generally one or two are to be found who can understand English, and are ready to act as interpreters. Sometimes the vocabulary of these interpreters is very limited, and signs have to be used freely to eke it out. A yam stands conventionally for a year; and thus an engagement for four years would be signified by the native presenting four yams; a moon stands for a month; a fathom of 'cloth' is the unit of length, and the fingers the readiest mode of numeration. Sometimes curious dialogues, unintelligible as the pigeon English of Shangai to the uninitiated, takes place between the trader and the natives, thus:—

Loquitur Trader: 'You likee come work Fiji?'

Native (laughing): 'Me no savy' (Don't know).

T.: 'Fiji very good. Plenty kai-kai bull-y-macow (beef to eat); big fellow yam, big fellow cocoa-nut; very good Fiji.'

N.: 'How many yam (years)? Too muchy work Fiji; no good.'

T. (holding up four fingers): 'S'pose you come by-and-by? Tanna man plenty trade, muskets, powder, plenty sulu (waist-cloth).'

N.: 'Me go; very good. Small fellow ship-a-ship no likee; me go next time.' And with this that particular native sheers off to make room for another.

If possible, the white man endeavours to get the ear of the chief of the village. Not unfrequently the chief will come on board the vessel. There he is shown the trade, and then a bargain is made for as many men as he will give, the chief receiving a douceur for his trouble. The chief simply returns to the village, orders the men on board—an order which they dare not refuse—and on their return pockets a great part of their earnings. Such is the paternal government of Western Polynesia.

In the Soloman Islands the *modus operandi* is somewhat different. Here the natives come off from the shore in large canoes, carrying some twenty or thirty men. The trade is shown to them, and they either remain on board or go ashore as they please. Sometimes, but rarely, the trader may venture to land here, especially if the natives make a fire, which is a signal that they want him. The Soloman Islanders are ferocious cannibals, and treacherous to the last degree, and no white man can with safety trust himself among them. They are very fond of coming off to a ship in large numbers, and, if they see any chance of success, attempting to capture her. If they are successful, the crew are at once butchered, while the ship is driven ashore, and then plundered. At present labourers are more easily procured at the Soloman Islands than elsewhere. But they are not popular in Fiji, where they are both feared and disliked. Some planters, however, will tell you that, if properly managed, they make good workmen.

At Banks Island the natives are exceedingly timid. They will not approach a vessel if they see a particle of sail set. They will put off from the shore one by one, not in canoes, but swimming on surf-boards. After a considerable time one man more plucky than the rest may, perhaps, venture on board, and, if he is well treated, may induce others to follow. Then a bargain is made, and for so much tobacco and so many jew's-harps the shipmaster will seldom fail to secure the services of a certain number of these natives.

From the groups and islands hitherto mentioned few women, as a rule, consent to come. But in the low sandy islands near the equator called the 'Tokalaus,' and sometimes the Kingsmill Group, women are more easily procured than men. The natives of these islands are not cannibals, but, nevertheless, they are very fierce and implacable. If not wronged or irritated they are probably quiet enough, but of late years they have committed some cruel murders. In procuring labour amongst such people the shipmaster must ever be on his guard against treachery. The Tokalaus are not timid or bashful, like the Banks Islanders, and will crowd on board and perhaps seize his ship when he least expects it. On the other hand, he may go on shore with safety, and without fear of being eaten. The Tokalaus are a weird, wild-looking race of men; their eyes are large and full, their hair long and straight, their complexions yellow, and their bodies, as a rule, seared all over with knife or spear wounds. The women are utterly destitute not only of virtue but even of modesty. They will come on board in great numbers, begging a passage to Fiji or anywhere else. Sometimes these women are married, sometimes single. A husband, however, is generally ready to sell his wife for a clay pipe and a little tobacco or a bottle of gin, or to send his daughters away with the white men for any trifling present. The islands they live in are not, indeed, very inviting places, being little more than sandhills, and producing scarcely anything except cocoa-nuts and fish. Hence, no doubt, the inhabitants are glad enough to leave them, arguing, perhaps, that they cannot be worse off anywhere than they are already. The Tokalaus are passionately fond of alcohol in every form, and one great article of trade with these islands is rum or gin. Within the last two years, I believe, the supply of natives from the Line Islands to Fiji, at any rate, has somewhat fallen off. They are not, after all, the 'best workers on a plantation, although the women and children make good cotton-pickers.

From the slight sketch given above of the localities from which labour is procured, it will be seen that a labour-cruise is not free from risks. These vary in kind at the different islands. In the New Hebrides the chief risk is incurred in going ashore with the trade-box. Here the natives will sometimes seize hold of the boat and carry her and her crew in a moment into the 'bush,' out of sight of the vessel and out of reach of all assistance. The fate of the white men is then soon decided. Sometimes when the boat is shoving off they will send a flight of poisoned arrows after her. These arrows are very deadly weapons indeed, the slightest scratch, as a rule, proving fatal. Their shafts are made of common cane, tipped with a splinter of human bone, which has previously been soaked in some vegetable poison. Sometimes, again, the natives will salute the trader, as he approaches them, with a volley of musket-balls, or, if they get him on shore, with a blow from a club. On the whole, although the New Hebrides are good islands to procure labour from, they are not by any means particularly safe to visit.

In the Soloman Islands a further source of danger is found in the propensity displayed by the natives to rush on board the ship in large numbers. They come off, not in outrigger canoes, but in large boats, containing from twenty to fifty men. If these boats are allowed alongside the ship, treachery may at once be apprehended. Without a moment's warning the savages will board a vessel, and, rushing from one end to the other, will club and spear every white man they meet. Great numbers of vessels have thus been captured in this archipelago. If the shipmaster attempts to go ashore his peril is, of course, extreme, and on some islands death would be the almost certain result. Nor are the Soloman Islanders to be feared only in their native wilds. On board ship they may mutiny at any moment. The mutiny of some Bougainville Islanders, as our readers are probably aware, was the immediate cause of one of the most hideous tragedies of modern times—the 'Carl Massacre.' But among the Tokalaus, already mentioned, the only danger, perhaps, to be apprehended is a sudden attack made when the decks are crowded with natives. These people are inveterate thieves, and will carry off anything from the ship that they can lay their hands upon. If detected in the act, they will frequently 'show fight,' and then a general *mêlée* may ensue, from which the white men do not always come off successfully. In addition to these personal dangers there are other risks for the ship which must not be overlooked. The navigation of most of the island-groups in the Western Pacific is most intricate. They have never been thoroughly surveyed, and not even the Admiralty charts of this portion of the globe can be depended on. Thus, what with the open hostility or secret treachery of natives, what with unknown reefs, shoals, and currents, a labour-voyage is a somewhat perilous undertaking. In the face of such unusual dangers it is not unreasonable that owners, masters, and crews should look for unusual profits. Hence the cause of many of the abuses that have crept into this trade. Those who are most anxious to see it placed on a proper footing will be the first to allow that such abuses have actually, on various occasions, taken place. When the uncertainty and risk that attend the getting of labour in the usual way is considered, it will not appear strange that many men should have endeavoured to find a more convenient and more certain method. The ingenuity of both masters and men was further stimulated by the mode in which they were paid. A large proportion of their wages has always been derived from what is called 'head-money,' that is, a small sum paid to each sailor for each labourer from his vessel landed in Fiji. This sum varies generally from 1*l.* sterling paid to the captain to 2*s.* paid to the sailors, who, in consideration of this extra source of gain, consent to take a lower rate of wages. It is not to be supposed that such a system could long continue without abuses. Masters and crews would not always be proof against the temptation of securing a large number of men at one 'haul.' What, for instance, easier than to put the hatches on when a number of natives were eating beef and biscuit in the hold? Or, if some natives were too wary to come off, might there not be found ways to induce them to do so? If there was a concertina on board, it might be played as the vessel coasted along certain islands, and its Siren notes would be sure to attract a crowd of delighted and astonished natives. Sometimes a timid islander would come on board, and be sent ashore with his face smeared with red and black paint, and a looking-glass wherewith to admire himself. Others would be envious of his good fortune, and would hasten to visit the white men before it was too late. Perhaps a dozen islanders would now come off—some swimming, some on surf-boards, some in canoes. Meanwhile the white men would be busy in their own way. Each man would, it is said, be provided with a saucer full of paint and a fragment of looking-glass, and might be seen carefully drawing humorous conceits on the swarthy face upturned before him. A philanthropist of Mr. Pickwick's school might have now remarked what a pleasant sight it was to see the storm-tossed mariners forgetting awhile their labours and their perils, and anxious only to please their less civilised brothers. Meanwhile, if the tale be true, the captain stands at the wheel, with a twinkle in his eye, and anon asks aloud, 'Are you ready, men?' 'Aye, aye, sir,' is the universal response. Then, in a voice that rings through the ship, comes the laconic order, '*Grab!*' In a moment every saucer is dashed down and each painter seizes his subject by the hair, rolls him over, and hurries him towards the open hold, where he is soon secured. In this way perhaps some half-dozen have been captured. This account was given to me by a man who said he had borne a part in the transaction; but I am at liberty to say that I do not believe one word of it.

Sometimes canoes are run down. This has undoubtedly been done many times, and the mode in which it is effected is somewhat as follows:—The vessel endeavours to get between her victim and the land. Then she gets 'to windward' of it, that is to say, gets between the canoe and the wind. The natives in the canoe meanwhile paddle away as fast as they can. But the vessel gradually approaches nearer and nearer, and steers as if she intended to pass close to leeward. But suddenly the main-sheet is hauled in, the head-sail let go, the helm put hard down, and in a moment, and almost within her own length, the ship comes to the wind. Meanwhile, in executing this manœuvre she has crashed through the slender outrigger, upset the canoe, passed over it, and scattered the occupants in all directions. In a moment the Tanna men have jumped off the deck like so many Newfoundland dogs and have singled out each one his man. A struggle now ensues, sometimes fierce enough, but eventually the ship's boat arrives and carries the captives on board. Other plans have also been adopted. One of the best known is perhaps that of counterfeiting a missionary ship. A white macintosh coat has done duty for a surplice, the ship's log-book for a Prayer Book; and as no one could sing a hymn, the sailors joined in chanting that impressive ditty, 'Give me some time to blow the man down.' The natives were then invited below to prayers, and a barrel of biscuit left open as if by accident. Many went down to the hold, but on attempting to return found the hatches had closed over them. An outrage of this kind led indirectly to the 'Carl massacre,' the details of which must be fresh in the minds of most readers. It may not, however, be generally known that what mainly led to the wounded being thrown overboard on that occasion was the fear that they might meet with a ship-of-war. Curiously enough, the ghastly work had scarcely been ended when the 'Rosario,' as I believe, hove in sight, examined the 'Carl,' and not seeing anything suspicious about her, let her pass on her way. A good deal of unjust blame was attached to the

British Consul in Fiji for allowing Murray, the instigator of the whole affair, to turn Queen's evidence.[1] I have it on the best authority that Mr. March simply gave him a *safe conduct to Sydney*, there to give evidence on the trial of certain of the crew. The Colonial authorities, however, soon perceived that Murray's evidence was absolutely necessary; indeed, no other witness was forthcoming. The trial had, therefore, either to be dropped or the Consul's safe conduct amplified into a permission to turn Queen's evidence. The latter alternative was wisely chosen.

The above details have been given in order that the reader may know the worst that can be said against this labour-trade. It is not slavery in any sense of the word, and to call it so is at once to state what is unjust and untrue. If the large number of vessels employed in it and the number of labourers annually imported into Fiji be taken into account, it can easily be shown that the abuses committed bear a very small proportion to the total work. When the extent of the ocean over which the labour-vessel sails, the class of men that from a variety of circumstances have of late years flocked to Fiji, and the fact that the whole traffic was for a long time entirely unrestrained by any law, are all taken into consideration, it would be little short of miraculous if no abuses had taken place. On the other hand, when the small size of the vessels, the weakness of

[1] 'Fiji Gazette,' February 12, 1873; 'Pall Mall Gazette,' October 30, 1872.

the crews, the danger of any systematic attempts at kidnapping, and above all the willingness of natives to go and labour without compulsion, are considered, any unprejudiced person will allow that there are good grounds for believing that the actual abuses of the labour-trade have been grossly exaggerated. To quote the words of an eloquent writer: 'After being four years about the South Seas I came to the conclusion that outrages in the labour-trade were (considering the wildness of the vast tract and the absence of all restraint) extremely rare.'[1] It may be asked, then, why this trade has obtained so bad a name in England? The question is one not difficult to answer.

In the first place, a great deal of ignorance prevails on the whole subject of Fijian labour both in England and the Australian colonies. To most people Polynesia is a *terra incognita*. Every outrage, therefore, that takes place in it, every white man that is murdered, every ship that is lost, is put down to 'that labour-trade.' This is of course simply absurd. Long before the labour-trade was ever thought of, long before cotton was planted in Fiji, the inhabitants of Western Polynesia were cruel, treacherous, and bloodthirsty, while the inhabitants of Eastern Polynesia were kind, hospitable, and semi-civilised. This has been the case from the days of Captain Cook to

[1] Lord Pembroke, in 'Temple Bar,' quoted, without number, in 'Fiji Times,' February 5, 1873. An able and truthful article on the state of Fiji before the attempt at self-government, and also on the labour-traffic generally.

the days of Bishop Patteson, whose death, I believe, is to be attributed to a cause very different from the labour-traffic. It will, moreover, continue to be the case until the savages of the New Hebrides and Soloman groups either become civilised by contact with white men or die out entirely.

In the second place, the missionaries are opposed to the emigration of islanders from their homes. They dislike it heartily, and do all in their power to put a stop to it. One cause for their dislike is to be found in the fact that it lessens the numbers of their flock by taking away a large proportion of the younger men. These men, if already converts, are exposed to new and strange temptations, and are in danger of ultimately falling away. To many persons it might seem useless to teach a body of men a system of ethics that will benefit them only in their native place, and under certain conditions, but which will be useless elsewhere. How this may be it is not, perhaps, for a mere layman to say. Again, a large proportion of missionary, especially Wesleyan, revenues are derived from natives. I was on one occasion very properly rebuked by a reverend gentleman for speaking of missionary 'taxes,' and learned then that the proper word to use was 'offerings.' These offerings are voluntary, and, though small in themselves, amount in the aggregate to many thousands of pounds annually.[1] They depend, of course,

---

[1] 'Fiji and Fijians,' p. 566. The total amount contributed in 1869 by the Friendly Islanders amounted to 5,689*l*. 6*s*. 2*d*.; or, in

for their continuance on the labours of the native community, and anything that would tend to lessen this labour would of course tend to lessen their 'offerings.' Hence if the labour-trade lessens the 'offerings,' it is a sound reason why the missionaries should dislike it. But there is yet a third reason. The more enlightened and civilised a tribe becomes, the more the individual missionary loses his *prestige*. He ceases after a while to be the oracle of a nation or district. He loses gradually his heroic proportions, and eventually dwindles down to the stature of common men. He becomes one of a crowd of white men, with whom the natives will eat and drink and make merry, but for whom they have no particular veneration. We cannot do better, in order to show the feelings with which the missionaries regard this trade, than quote the words of the Rev. L. Fison, himself a missionary. He writes: '. . . . We have one more proof that the traffic is of a nature that makes regulation impossible, and that I spoke no more than the truth when I said, "What is wanted in the South Seas is not a law court, but a shotted gun and a rope at the yardarm."'[1]

There are yet other reasons why the labour-trade has attained an evil notoriety in England. Only one side of the question has been heard; the other

excess of the expenses of the mission, upwards of 3,000*l.* See also Annual Reports of Wesleyan Missions *passim*.

[1] 'Melbourne Daily Telegraph,' quoted in 'Fiji Gazette' of Jan. 3, 1874.

side has been condemned unheard. The planters and others interested in the continuance of the labour-trade outnumber their opponents in the islands by a hundred to one. But then they are more occupied in making a living by hard work than in writing articles or addressing meetings. The missionaries are numerically a small body of men, but have made themselves loudly heard, especially among the English middle classes. They have spread over the country their reviews, reports, letters, and deputations. They have worked hard with pen and tongue to enforce their peculiar views, and have not worked unsuccessfully. Add to this that in England generally every rumour relative to 'Polynesian slavery' is eagerly caught up and multiplied by fame, till sober-minded people, who can have no personal knowledge of the original facts, are forced to believe what they hear asserted by one side and uncontradicted by the other. The very name of 'slavery' attached to any cause is quite sufficient to condemn it unheard in the present temper of England. Nor must it be forgotten that many of the reported outrages in the labour-trade have come from Australian sources. The comments of the press there have been reproduced in England by writers who have been satisfied to take all statements for granted. Such writers forget that in many of the colonies, especially in the southern parts of Queensland, the labour question is a political one. I have myself heard it proposed as a test question to a member on the hustings. It is only another of the Protean forms which the contest between labour and capital is constantly assuming. The labouring classes, who have a large representation in the democratic parliaments of Queensland and New South Wales, are strongly opposed to the importation of South Sea Islanders into the cotton and sugar plantations of Northern Queensland, and consequently are anxious to bring the trade as much into discredit as possible. This they do not from any philanthropic motives, but from motives of self-interest. The Polynesian immigrants lower the price of labour and compete with the poorer whites. In New York, in the same way, the Irishman considers himself aggrieved by the presence of the black man, and the German of the Western States by the presence of the Chinese. In Sydney there is only one local paper of any importance, the 'Sydney Morning Herald.' This has 'gone in' against the Fijian labour-trade, partly because it is Fijian (and everything Fijian has a bad name in Sydney), and partly because this particular journal is the organ of the Dissenters in the colony, and chronicles with minutest accuracy every tea meeting, missionary address, or religious gathering that can in any way be connected with the party it serves. And, finally, there is one more body of men who have unintentionally and unwittingly done this traffic a good deal of harm. I refer to some of the sailors and loafers who hang about the bars of public-houses and hotels in Levuka. These men, in their cups or out of them, are proud of narrating their adventures 'in the islands.' Their tales are as a rule quite unworthy of belief. By their own showing, indeed, they have borne a leading part in every venture and hairbreadth escape. In their own way they are all Captain Bobadils, and not unfrequently their foolish vapouring has been reproduced in the local or colonial papers, whence it has been copied into English journals.

Thus it may be shown that a variety of causes have tended to bring the labour-trade into discredit. These are :—1. The ignorance that prevails in England as regards Western Polynesia generally, and the fact that every reported outrage has been taken for granted before being proved. 2. Missionaries and the colonial press have done their best to stop the trade from a variety of motives. 3. Its advocates, either from supineness or inability, seldom take the trouble to make themselves heard or to correct misstatements or misrepresentations. In conclusion, it may be said that those who live at home at ease should be disposed to criticise with leniency the unhappy skipper who sails in charge of a set of savages. All the white men employed in the labour-trade are not scoundrels or desperadoes. The majority of them are quiet, peaceable men, who by fortune rather than from choice have been compelled to adopt this mode of gaining a living. In our censure of some parts of their conduct we should strive to realise, if ever so vaguely, a few of the strange conditions and hard necessities that beset intercourse with savage tribes. Nor must it be forgotten that some of the undoubted outrages, about which thrilling accounts have been written, have not been perpetrated by Englishmen at all. In Tahiti and New Caledonia there are large French plantations, and the labour for these is all procured from the same field as that for Fiji. They, as well as Fiji, should bear their share of the blame of supporting this 'odious traffic.'

Whatever abuses may have been perpetrated by labour-vessels, none of these abuses can justly be charged to the account of the cotton-planters of Fiji. The planter, as a rule, hires his men in Levuka. He is ignorant how they have been obtained, whether fairly or otherwise ; and yet the knowledge would be of no small importance to him, for it is on him that all the wrongdoings of the shipmaster, perpetrated hundreds of miles away, will eventually be visited. On a lonely plantation, far away from any chance of assistance, surrounded by savages and cannibals, the planter passes most of the year. His life is many times every day in the power of his labourers. He rules them by moral not by physical force. His interest and theirs is in most cases identical. Every outrage, therefore, inflicted on natives is a direct injury to the individual planter. To speak of the planters of Fiji as slave-owners is a cruel injustice. As a body they are strongly opposed to slavery in any shape or form. On the opening day of the first Parliament held in Levuka the Constitution Act was read aloud. One paragraph in it enacted that 'no man could be a slave on Fijian soil.' Anyone who heard the ringing cheer with which the House, composed mostly of planters, greeted this statement will not readily believe that such men are either slave-dealers or slave-owners. As to the treatment received by imported natives on plantations, it is with scarcely an exception all that the most humane man could desire. The natives are, indeed, better off in Fiji than in their own country. They are well-fed, not overworked, fairly paid, are protected in the enjoyment of their gains, and are relieved from a daily and hourly fear of being killed and eaten. It is no uncommon thing for natives to refuse to leave the vessel that has brought them back to their own home. It is no uncommon thing for them on their own islands to engage with the shipmaster to be taken to the plantation which they had left. I myself witnessed in Savage Island, in 1872, the arrival and departure of a labour-vessel. Out of seven return-labourers two refused to go on shore at all or quit the vessel; the other five went on shore, but though most anxious to return were prevented from doing so by their friends. On this occasion I saw several old men stationed round the boat with sticks in their hands, to prevent the younger men leaving the island and going off to the vessel.

Plenty of evidence is forthcoming as to the uniform good treatment experienced by labourers on plantations in Fiji. In the Island of Rabi fifty New Hebridean labourers had worked their time, and been paid off. 'They expressed themselves so satisfied with their treatment and remuneration that, upon being paid off, they re-engaged for another term.'[1] Sometimes vessels will go down to the labour-producing islands to hire men entirely for one plantation, thereby showing that the treatment adopted in the past has been such as to make it probable that some of the old hands may wish to return.[2] To all who know Fiji and her planters such evidence will appear unnecessary. To those who do not, possibly the following extracts from the official report of Commodore Goodenough and Consul Layard may prove reassuring : ' We here feel it due to the great body of planters to say that with regard to food, clothing, and houses the Polynesian labourers are far better off than when on their native islands.' And again, at page 10 : 'The abuses in the labour-traffic have taken place through the rapacity of the shipowner or master, and should not be laid entirely or chiefly to the account of the planters, who, as we have before remarked, treat their labourers for the most part kindly.'[3]

The conduct of the British Government towards this labour-traffic has not been marked either by discrimination or by firmness. At first the trade was practically left to regulate itself; then, when certain

---

[1] 'Fiji Times,' May 24, 1873.
[2] 'Fiji Times,' April 26, 1873.
[3] 'Report of Commodore Goodenough and Mr. Consul Layard on the Offer of the Cession of the Fiji Islands to the British Crown, July 1874,' p. 6.

abuses had been discovered, vessels were seized on charges which, in the absence of special acts of Parliament, could not be shown to be illegal. At last, however, an Act was passed to regulate the whole traffic and place it on a proper basis. Had this Act been passed in the first instance, and the Consul at Levuka invested with magisterial powers, in order to enforce the law, much subsequent expense, injustice, and official bungling might have been avoided. At one time in Fiji no one really knew who either owned or sailed in a labour-vessel. He might be seized at any moment on a charge of slavery and carried off to Sydney, where, as a rule, he would be acquitted, but without being awarded compensation for loss of time or money. I have often heard shipmasters in Fiji complain bitterly of the oppressive nature of the control exercised over them by vessels-of-war. Some cases of great injustice and hardship did undoubtedly occur. One of them, known as the 'Daphne' case, has become a *cause célèbre*. The 'Daphne' had returned from the Soloman Islands with some hundred and twenty natives on board. As she was entering Levuka harbour she was seized by the 'Rosario' and charged with being a 'slaver.' She was then sent to the Admiralty Court at Sydney, while the natives on board were handed over to the Acting British Consul, who found means to utilise them. After much litigation the 'Daphne' was released, and the British Government paid the legal expenses of the trial. But the unfortunate owner not only got no compensation but was actually deprived of the labourers whom he had brought to Fiji at his own expense. Under one pretence and another they were kept on various plantations, and ultimately he lost sight of them altogether. By this transaction he was ruined in pocket and broken in spirit, and learned perhaps, for the first time, that his countrymen could punish him, indeed, but could not restore to him what was legally his own. This case of the 'Daphne' is better known than some others which have taken place recently in Fiji, and which, though not so flagrant, have yet inflicted much loss and annoyance on innocent men. Thus the owner of the 'Beauty' schooner was, after a fortnight's detention, informed by H.M.S. 'Dido' that he might take his vessel back. No investigation had been held and no reparation offered.[1] And so on through many more. A small fleet of schooners is now employed in regulating this traffic; but as the law becomes better understood and more clearly defined it may be hoped that, as regards Fiji at any rate, there will be little need of their services.

Whatever objections can be urged against the general labour-trade, none can be urged against the insular trade, that is, the trade between one portion of Fiji and another. In this case Fijians are simply conveyed from one island of their own group to another place a few miles distant; just as Irishmen are conveyed from Ireland to England during harvest-

---

[1] The authority for this statement is the 'Fiji Times,' July 30, 1873. See 'Fiji Times,' April 26, 1873, for the seizure of the 'Woodbine.'

time. This fact is so well known to everyone who has even a slight acquaintance with Fijian matters that it does not admit of contradiction. It was, therefore, with some surprise that I read in the 'Fiji Times' (August 9, 1873) a notice from Commodore Stirling, stating 'that no fresh licenses would be issued to British subjects for the conveyance of natives from one island to another.' The evident intention of this notice is to stop the passenger traffic heretofore existing, and so cut off the supply of Fijian labour to the plantations. It is difficult to see what good can come of such interference. There can be no pretext of 'slavery' as regards the Fijians.[1] To attempt to kidnap men on the Ra coast for Tavinni would be about as successful an experiment as kidnapping Irishmen in Dublin to work the hop-gardens of Kent. The idea is so absurd to anyone acquainted with Fiji that it need only be mentioned to be dismissed.

In conclusion, it may be asked, What is to be done with the labour-trade? To put it down completely is almost an impossibility, as French, American, and German vessels are employed in it as well as English. To put it down partially would be to inflict a cruel injustice on our countrymen in Fiji and Queensland, and to postpone for generations the civilisation of Western Polynesia. Under such circumstances a middle

---

[1] See report of the deputation which waited on Earl Kimberley, May 12, 1874, where the following words occur: 'Apart altogether from kidnapping . . . British subjects are engaged in a *local slave-trade*.'

course ought to be adopted. Let the trade exist, but place it under proper supervision. In the first place, the importation of Pacific Islanders into Fiji should be made a distinctly Government matter. Until the coolie trade was subject to Government inspection it was, as everyone knows, in a far from satisfactory state; so will it be in Fiji. Let every vessel that clears out for any of the labour groups obtain a permission from the authorities. Let her be sailed by officers and men who have no direct or personal interest in procuring men. Above all, abolish head-money. If thought necessary, a Government official might accompany every vessel that started on a labour-voyage. Such a man should receive a liberal salary, be independent of owners or charterers, and not have too many local interests. No natives should be shipped from any islands without their consent having been previously procured to the terms of the voyage, through a qualified interpreter. As to procuring interpreters no difficulty would be experienced, for there are in nearly every island and group old whites who know the native languages thoroughly. Furthermore, a careful register should be kept at all the Consulates in Levuka of the number of immigrants that arrive each year, and where they arrive from, of the plantations to which they are distributed, of the deaths that take place amongst them, and of the date at which their term of service expires. At the conclusion of this period Government should undertake to return the natives to their own homes; or, if they preferred it, allow them to enter on a fresh period of work. The arrangements at present existing on board labour-vessels are quite sufficient for the comfort and health of the native during his passage to Fiji. Each vessel is permitted to carry only a certain number of men in proportion to her registered tonnage, and so overcrowding is avoided. Every captain may be trusted to lay in a sufficient supply of provisions for his own sake, in order to avoid the necessity of sailing with hungry cannibals. If these simple suggestions were followed out, the Fiji labour-trade would, in a short time, be on quite as legal and satisfactory a footing as the coolie trade. It must, however, be confessed that until the question of annexation is finally settled the labour question cannot be dealt with in a comprehensive manner. Were Fiji to be annexed to England to-morrow all practical difficulty in the matter would cease. The traffic might even be abolished altogether, and coolie emigration substituted for South Sea Island. The difference in value between the two classes of labourers would more than compensate for the extra expense.

CHAPTER XIII.

Political Changes—Social Condition of Fiji in 1871—Old and New Settlers—Business Relations between Fiji and the Australian Colonies—Anomalous Position of the British Consul—Causes which led to the Formation of a Government—*A coup d'état*—Previous Attempts to Form a Government—The Tovata League—Methods by which the Ministers Consolidated their Power—The Constitution Act—The House of Delegates—Position of Native Chiefs—*Personnel* of the Ministry—Maafu and Tiu Cakou Join the Government—Attitude of England towards the New State—Orders in Council—Ministerial Doctrines—The Government loses Popularity.

ON my return to Levuka, after an absence of several months, I found that important changes had taken place in the political world of Fiji. Cacobau, no longer merely chief of Bau, was now king of the whole group; Tiu Cakou and Maafu were no independent chiefs, but only his viceroys; his ministers bore the title of 'Honourable;' while many of his subjects, erstwhile subjects of Queen Victoria, thronged the beach and the bar-rooms of the hotels, and wasted their time in wondering what it could all mean. A daring and successful *coup d'état* had, just about the time of my return to Levuka, been effected by a few white men till now almost unknown in the general community. In a word, 'a Government' had been established in Fiji. Hitherto there had been no law in the land, no protection for life or property theoretically, no means of redressing a wrong or enforcing a right. Yet, strange as it may seem, until the close of 1870 the country had been both peaceful and prosperous. After three years' experience of constitutional government men even now in Fiji look back with regret to the good old times that preceded the inauguration of the so-called reign of 'law and order.'

In order to understand how the necessity for a government arose, and how the means used to establish it proved so far successful, it will be necessary to have a clear notion of the state of Fiji at the commencement of 1871. As already stated, the Australian colonies had for some years been in a very depressed condition. The price of wool had fallen preposterously low, the gold diggings had ceased to yield so prolifically as heretofore; the Maori war had ruined many settlers; in a word, things were as bad as they well could be in a new country. Hence in Australia and New Zealand there were many ready to accept anything that presented a chance of retrieving their fortunes. To such men a new field was offered in Fiji, and not a few availed themselves of it. Hitherto the chief representatives of the white man had been the so-called patriarch planters. These were with scarcely an exception men of respectability; many of them men of birth and education, and withal possessed of more or less capital. Naval and military officers, colonial 'squatters,' younger sons fresh from home, were the stuff of which the earlier settlers had been made. Many of them had come down to Fiji shortly after General Smythe's visit, induced in a great measure to do so by Dr. Seemann's favourable report on the cotton-producing power of the island. Here they had lived quietly enough, working hard, and, if not amassing wealth, at any rate doing fairly well. The new settlers were a totally different class of men. Their advent was far from being a benefit to Fiji. They were in many cases needy adventurers; and although some came with the intention of planting cotton or doing other good work, the majority came with intentions the very reverse. Not a few of the new settlers had left the colonies to avoid criminal proceedings for fraud or even worse offences. So long as there was no extradition treaty such men were of course free from arrest in Fiji. To go to Fiji was quicker, easier, and less expensive than to go to San Francisco, and San Francisco had hitherto been the city of refuge for such individuals. In 1871 the numbers of this semi-criminal class in the islands had increased to such an extent that the very name of Fiji was looked on in Sydney and Melbourne with loathing and contempt. 'Gone to Fiji' bore the same significance in Australia as 'Gone to Texas' did in America a few years ago. The colonial newspapers were accustomed to speak of Fiji as the 'modern Alsatia' and not without some reason.

The new-comers, as might be supposed, were, as

a rule, men of totally different tastes and habits from the older settlers. Levuka was, naturally and of necessity, the head-quarters of the former class. The verandahs of hotels and the taprooms of public-houses were their favourite haunts. Their business was to make business of any kind that did not involve the need of either money or hard work. Commission agents, arbitrators, advocates, auctioneers, notary-publics, brokers of every kind, thronged the narrow streets of Levuka. Some of the men who engaged in such pursuits may possibly have been qualified by previous experience or special training to perform what they undertook, but with the majority such was not the case. With most of them there was no pretence of business; they were neither more nor less than loafers in disguise, and their high-sounding titles were but assumed to deceive the public. There was not legitimate business in the whole of Fiji, much less in Levuka, to give employment to one-half of those who flocked down to the islands in the spring of 1871.

But besides these rogues, whose occupation was at any rate of a peaceful nature, came a number of turbulent fellows, to whom the lawlessness of Fiji was its chief recommendation. These were generally of the lowest class, and comprised runaway sailors, absconding tradesmen, and not a few convicted felons. It was not to be supposed that such men would scruple to take whatever advantages the unprotected state of their neighbours might afford them. Thus, although serious offences had hitherto been comparatively rare, everyone felt that this immunity was at best precarious, and might be rudely disturbed at any moment. There was at this period no way short of a trial of personal strength by which disputes could be settled. Arbitration, indeed, was sometimes resorted to, but it failed more often than it succeeded. 'Club law,' in fact, was the only law by which any redress or satisfaction could be obtained. It was a final court of appeal open to every man who chose to employ it. Had an American element predominated in Fiji at this time there is little doubt that Lynch-law or vigilance committees would have hewn out a rough-and-ready code that might have sufficed until superseded by a better. Had a Spanish element predominated there would have been assassinations, pronunciamientos, revolutionary juntas, and other political remedies. But, as the community was essentially English, and intent on making money, men worked quietly and steadily at this, the chief object of their lives, and paid little attention to anything save their cotton and their ledgers. An aggrieved person, as a rule, contented himself by calling a public meeting and thus making known his tale of wrong. His opponent did exactly the same, perhaps at the same time, in another part of the town. Then each man would write a long letter to the 'Fiji Times,' which, *en revanche*, would charge for them as advertisements, most of its available space being occupied by attacks on the British Consul. Here the matter generally ended. Although a good many hard names may have been exchanged on both sides the peace of the community had not been disturbed; but it was felt every day more strongly that such a result might happen at any moment. One or two instances had actually occurred in which two litigants had resorted to open violence. A dispute had taken place between two partners as to the ownership of a certain cotton plantation. The planter in possession refused, as was alleged, to pay over the proper share of the crop, and even refused to allow the other partner on the ground. To make his position more secure he fortified his house with a stockade, and armed his Tanna labourers. He himself kept watch and ward, and had filled his house with friends, all of whom were pledged to resist to the utmost any attempt to seize the place by violence. When the note of these warlike preparations reached the sleeping partner in Levuka he, in turn, hired a number of 'filibusters,' as they liked to be called, at an honorarium of thirteen pounds each, to go and recover his demesnes. A large boatful of these amateur officials landed on the shore and advanced towards the plantation with fixed bayonets. Their determined attitude or his own conscience overawed the planter, who forthwith surrendered at discretion. But had he been more determined it is difficult to understand how bloodshed could have been avoided. On another occasion a planter's boat was boarded on the high seas by a number of hired pirates, all armed, and the owner compelled by force to submit to their demands. The occurrence of a very few of such acts would be enough to render Fiji unbearable as a place of abode. Enough had already occurred to dispose men's minds to accept any scheme which would substitute a reign of law for one of capricious violence.

With the influx of population the commerce of Levuka had increased sensibly. Shiploads of provisions and what was known as 'trade for natives' arrived weekly from Australia and New Zealand. In return for these cocoa-nut oil and cotton were exported. From the commencement of its commercial history Fiji had always suffered from a scarcity of coined money. The reason of this was, that the precious metals did not exist in the country, could not be coined there, and had been only imported at rare intervals and in small quantities by private persons. But as every departing ship took away a certain amount of coin in return for the merchandise she had left behind, the stock in the country often ran very low. The scarcity thus produced had hitherto been met in a rough way by the use of debased Bolivian half-dollars, which had percolated into Fiji from Samoa. These coins were worth nominally two shillings in Levuka, but in Sydney only about one shilling and threepence. No shipmaster, therefore, would take them out of the islands, where they thus remained for years in circulation. There being no coined money available in Fiji, men naturally in their transactions dealt largely in paper. Bills of exchange, cheques on colonial banks, notes of hand, drafts, I O U's, were freely offered and accepted. In not a few cases much of this paper was worthless; this fact, however, could not be known until the paper came to be presented for payment in Melbourne or Sydney, a distance of two thousand miles, where redress was practically impossible. As there was a good deal of trade at this time carried on between the Australian colonies and Fiji, it will be worth while to examine the mode in which it was conducted. Let it be supposed, then, that a vessel has arrived in Levuka laden with provisions from Sydney. Part of her cargo will be sold on board by auction, the rest handed over to some agent on shore to dispose of to the best advantage. A little gold will be tendered to the captain, but most of the money he receives will be in the form either of Bolivian silver or paper. The silver is comparatively useless in Sydney, and therefore he must either take the paper or take his goods back to Sydney. The bills he finally accepts may be drawn by a planter on some Levuka merchant, at whose 'store' the planter has an account. The planter's security is his future cotton crop, which of course may or may not be a failure. It was a common practice for, let us suppose, A to draw a bill on B, who then drew in turn on C. Now, C had no money in hand; but though he could not pay just then he had no objection to write his name on a 'bit of paper.' In due time the bill was presented in Sydney and dishonoured. Under these circumstances the despised paper returned to Fiji, accompanied by a severe letter from the Sydney firm. A comes on B, who passes on the compliment to C, who of course was very sorry, but could not do anything further in the matter, and knows moreover that nothing could be done either to himself or to A or to B, seeing that there was no law in Fiji. The goods meanwhile have been disposed of; and after all it is only the Sydney firm that has lost anything by the transaction. Business matters between the colonies and Fiji used to be carried on on a most uncertain footing—so much so, indeed, that the smuggler's rule of one cargo in three must have been applicable to many colonial merchants. A good deal of raw material was, of course, from time to time exported from Fiji, and this it was probably that rendered any trade possible. 'Bad paper' at last became such a nuisance, and was so frequently met with, that to negotiate any paper money in Levuka became almost impossible. Such a state of affairs was simply intolerable in a mercantile community. Hence those who most loudly called for a government and who first initiated the movement were the merchants of Levuka. They perceived that there was plenty of latent wealth in Fiji; to develope this capital was absolutely necessary. But to have capital a bank must be established, and, as a further step towards commercial security, an insurance office. Under the existing system of actual or potential anarchy it was vain to hope for either. Some recognised form of government was imperatively necessary before colonial speculators would advance the required funds. Once, however, establish a government, and it was rightly believed that plenty of money would be forthcoming for all legitimate purposes.

But, bad as things were, probably no attempt would have been made to form a government for many years to come, if only the powers vested in the British Consul at Levuka had been increased by the English Government. It is impossible to speak of the rise and development of the Government of Fiji without mentioning the name of Mr. March. From the moment of his entering office in Fiji until he left the group his position was at once difficult and anomalous. His official instructions, as published (some think unnecessarily), showed the limited extent of his powers. He was directed to look after the interests of British subjects if compromised by foreigners, and especially to look after British shipping and sailors; but, under the peculiar or perhaps unparalleled circumstances that preceded the formation of the Government in Fiji, many things of necessity came before the Consul on which his official instructions were silent. In the state in which society at this time was in Levuka a Consul was a man of unusual importance. He was the only man who, by his position, was elevated above local interests. He was the only man of whose impartiality all men might be certain. British subjects, therefore, almost daily resorted to him to settle disputes between man and man, to obtain redress for grievances, and to seek advice or information on matters of importance. In all such cases Mr. March acted with firmness and integrity. He could not, of course, please everyone; many with whom he came in contact resisted even the mild authority claimed by the Consulate over shipping affairs. Some persons in Fiji had apparently been so long accustomed to the absence of all law that they resisted even such simple requirements as having the name of their vessel legibly painted, their flag of a certain colour and shape, or the payment of certain Consular fees. With such men Mr. March was, of course, unpopular. Moreover, he had no power to give effect to any of his judicial decisions except through the medium of a ship-of-war; but, after all, any interference between contending parties was completely beyond the powers of his office, and by attempting it, though for the benefit of the community at large, he only rendered himself liable to official censure. Many in Levuka understood this, and were shrewd enough to perceive the remedy. This was, that the English Government should grant the British Consul magisterial powers, and the means of making such powers practically felt. Had this been done before June 1871, in all probability the 'Government scheme' would never have been brought forward. But, as it was not done, the position in which Mr. March found himself was one of great difficulty. It was one, too, that an unscrupulous man might have turned largely to his own advantage; but to have done so he must of necessity have become a partisan, and have compromised more or less his official position. Not a few men would have yielded to the temptation, especially as thereby they might have enjoyed a 'quiet life,' a state of existence not to be despised within the tropics.

It will now be understood that several causes had been at work for some time in Fiji to produce a very general desire for government of some kind. These were: 1. The increase of population, and with it an actual or possible increase of lawlessness and crime. 2. The difficulty of carrying on trade or procuring money from the colonies in the then condition of the islands. 3. The inability of the British Consul to dispense law or justice while deprived of magisterial powers. 4. A widespread conviction that some form of government was necessary to develope the latent wealth of the group, and determine once for all the relations that were to exist between the native and foreign inhabitants.

On the morning of June 5, 1871, the town of Levuka was thrown into a state of unusual excitement. Loud noises were heard proceeding from the direction of the native village at Totoga. Some persons thought this disturbance might be a native *mekè*, or dance, but then natives did not dance in the daytime; others held that it might be a fight between Fijians and half-castes; others that it might be a feast; but no one supposed it was the inauguration of a responsible and constituted Government. But such in truth it was. On approaching the spot all doubts on the subject were speedily set at rest. The venerable and familiar form of Cacobau was seen swathed in ample folds of native cloth. On his right stood a few Fijian chiefs; on his left some half-dozen Europeans. A guard of Tongese and Fijian soldiers surrounded the group, and made all the noise by beating their native drums. Cacobau, or Cacobau Rex, may be supposed to have had but a faint notion of the part he was playing. He spoke a few words in Fijian, which were neither heard nor understood by the whites around him. Then one of the European gentlemen came forward and gave notice to all whom it might concern that a Government was now in existence; that Cacobau was King of Fiji, and that he (the speaker) was one of the King's ministers. Then followed more drumming and shouting; the King and his ministers retired incontinently, and Levuka resumed its usually quiet and, at that hour, even sleepy appearance. Such was the 5th of June in Levuka, a day which it was hoped would be as important in the annals of Fiji as the 4th of July has been in the annals of America.

The great majority of white settlers in Fiji considered the whole affair as an elaborate joke. It was not the first time that similar attempts had ended in failure. As long ago as 1865 Cacobau had granted a charter to the whites settled in Ovalan. In 1867 and even in 1870 similar charters had been granted, and power given to the inhabitants of Levuka to make their own laws. Arrangements somewhat similar had been made between other ruling chiefs and whites settled within their territories, as at Bua and Cakandrove. But by far the most successful of all these attempts was the so-called 'Lau Confederation.' This was a confederation of the chiefs in the extreme north and east of Fiji, a district sometimes called Loma-Loma, and embracing a subsidiary group of islands known as the 'Exploring Islands.' For this confederation Mr. Swanston, as the representative of the white planters, had drawn up a series of excellent rules, or more properly laws. Under the discriminating and comparatively enlightened rule of Maafu, a Tongan chief, these had worked admirably. The whites paid a yearly impost to Maafu, and received in return protection for life and property. The arrangement worked in a satisfactory manner for both parties, and in no long time after it had come into force Lau was known as one of the most populous and thriving districts of Fiji.

The attempt now made in Levuka was, however, far more ambitious than any previous attempts had been. It aimed at making Cacobau King of the whole group instead of a portion of it.[1] It aimed at making him an independent ruler, where previously he had been indeed a ruler, but surrounded by other rulers as wealthy, as independent, and as powerful as himself. It aimed at governing the whole native population through him, and not merely the native but the white population. The men who had that

[1] See 'Report of Commodore Goodenough and Mr. Consul Layard,' p. 1, s. 5.

morning proclaimed a constitution had undertaken this onerous task. They were to be the ministers, or real governors of the country, while Cacobau was merely to lend them the *prestige* of his name. No wonder the public thought the whole matter a joke.

When, however, their scheme is carefully examined into it is seen to have been arranged with no little skill. Some years before this Cacobau had been held responsible for certain injuries inflicted by Fijians on American subjects. He had been compelled by the United States to pay a large sum of money as compensation. He pleaded, but in vain, that those who had committed the outrages were not his subjects. The Americans recognised him as King of Fiji, saluted him with a royal salute, and mulcted him in the sum of nine thousand pounds. He had thus been recognised as King of Fiji by at least one great Power, and of this fact his white advisers hoped to be able to make political capital. If they could only induce Fiji to recognise him, as America had done, their task would be accomplished. They would then govern the country in his name, and if he ruled it *de jure* they would rule it *de facto*. The old man lent a ready ear to their overtures, all the more so as by the action of the powerful Tovata league his position as premier chief of Fiji was now almost untenable. The Tovata league [1] was a union of all the most powerful chiefs on the eastern islands of Fiji. Its object seems

---

[1] 'Fiji Times,' March 11, 1874.

to have been to lessen and ultimately destroy the power of Bau. Tui Cakou lent it all the aid of his powerful name, while the wily and ambitious Maafu presided over its counsels and directed its movements. In presence of this league Cacobau felt that his position was desperate, and gladly embraced the means of escape now unexpectedly offered to him.

A tangible head to the Government being thus secured, the next step was to induce a sufficient number of whites to join in the scheme. Here, indeed, was a difficulty, but not an insuperable one. Some money, however, was necessary before it could be overcome, and this the King and his ministers unexpectedly found themselves possessed of. A tribe of mountaineers called the Levonis had just submitted to Cacobau. As a punishment for their misdeeds they were made subject to Bau, were compelled to adopt Christianity (a political affair in Fiji), and finally their labour was sold to white planters for the space of five years. By this means eleven hundred pounds were realised,[1] a sum quite sufficient to launch the ministers fairly on their new career. By the aid of this money Government offices were hired; lucrative appointments given to some, and similar appointments promised to many more. It was, indeed, noticed that the men who were thus appointed were, with scarcely an exception, new arrivals from the colonies or personal friends of the ministers. A band of fifty men was thus brought together bound to

[1] This information I have derived from a private source. I have no doubt whatever of its truthfulness.

PREPARATIONS FOR A CHANGE.

its employers by self-interest and by common aims. This body of men, though nominally 'civil servants,' represented really a force in disguise—a fact which at the time only a few persons in Levuka had sufficient acumen to perceive. By skilfully holding out vague hopes of future employment and renumeration ministers succeeded in disarming a good deal of opposition. Every man who had anything to hope for became at once a more or less staunch supporter of the new order of things. Every man, in fact, whom it was worth while conciliating was carefully led to expect that he himself would be a direct gainer by the changes that were taking place. Levuka was first gained over; the outlying districts and islands followed with more or less rapidity. The white community was so small, and communication between different islands so difficult, that there was really no such thing in Fiji as public opinion, using the word in its broadest sense. There was also no press to fear. The only newspaper at this time published in the group was the 'Fiji Times.' This was more of an advertising sheet than a journal, and was badly edited, badly printed, and destitute of any literary merit or political influence whatever. There was but little concerted opposition to be feared from the whites scattered throughout Fiji. Moreover, public meetings on every topic from the conduct of the British Consul down to the price of yams or the unpunctuality of Fijian washerwomen, had been of late matters of daily occurrence in Levuka. A 'public meeting' became at last a by-word, and sensible men did not find much fault with the ministers for not taking this method of declaring to their fellow-citizens the advent of a constitutional government.

And yet, when allowance has been made for all these special influences, the unanimity with which the so-called *coup d'état* of June 5 was received by an English community is indeed remarkable. It can only be explained by supposing that its importance was very much underrated by many persons at first, and also that everyone was already anxious to see accomplished what a few men in an irregular manner had now undertaken to perform. In after-times, when the ministerial popularity had completely vanished, the most rabid oppositionist did not venture to declaim against government in the abstract. 'I was always a Government man, sir, and am so still,' was a common mode of prefacing a violent attack on an obnoxious minister. In fact, the benefits to be derived from any form of government honestly administered were so great and so obvious that a man must have been blind to his own interests who failed to see them. The Government from the first moment of its existence met with the greatest encouragement and consideration from the community generally. But within a few months a series of acts of gross folly, combined with a high-handed mode of procedure, alienated this majority of friends, and raised up a powerful and determined opposition.

A king being now secured with a sufficient number of white supporters, it was time to commence the real work of governing the country. To facilitate this the Fiji Islands were roughly divided into electoral districts. Each district was to send a *delegate* to examine on its behalf the constitution which Cacobau proposed to grant to all his subjects, both black and white. The House of Delegates, as these representatives were collectively called, might either amend or accept or reject this constitution. If accepted, it was to form the basis of all future legislation, and to be a standing declaration of the rights of every Fijian subject, naturalised or otherwise. As regards the Constitution Act itself much need not be said. It was a document which, from a literary point of view, reflected little credit on its framers. The first few paragraphs might have been extracted from some French Revolutionary documents of last century. The existence of a God was affirmed, together with the inalienable right of every man to happiness and liberty of action. After this came paragraphs relating to the Royal Family, the imposition of taxes, the machinery of government, and so forth. After some weeks of deliberation this document, slightly altered, was accepted, and from this moment the ministers, and many other persons besides, held that the Government had a constitutional existence. The Assembly of Delegates was now dissolved by the King in person, with many formalities and festivities, and writs issued for the election of the first Parliament.

Before dismissing the Constitution Act it will be

well to state that it was based on the Hawaiin or Sandwich Islands constitution. These islands in many respects, and in none more than their political condition, bore a considerable resemblance to the Fijis. They were, indeed, under the rule of one powerful chief, while Fiji was divided among several. Their white population had come gradually, while in Fiji it had been thrust on the unprepared natives within the space of a few years. On the other hand, however, in spite of all difficulties, the Sandwich Islanders had developed a government of their own, and had succeeded in gaining the good will of America, England, and France. Although representative government existed therein it was in a modified form. The King was ruler of the country, and could do no wrong. Under him came the Privy Council, composed of his ministers, who could be dismissed from office only by the King's permission. Any minister, therefore, who could gain a personal ascendency over the sovereign could practically hold office for an indefinite period. If defeated in Parliament he might go through the farce of resigning office, but the King would not accept his resignation, and there was an end of the matter. The obnoxious minister became more powerful than ever; and if he were a Richelieu or a Strafford nothing short of a civil war could unseat him. Read by the light of subsequent events there is little doubt that the Fijian constitution was covertly framed on the same model.

The self-appointed ministers were *protégés* of Cacobau, and some of them, at any rate, possessed great personal influence over him. To many of them the King was heavily in debt for gunpowder, beer, salt beef, and other humble but necessary items. He had constantly before his eyes the threat of some German or American ship-of-war enforcing prompt payment of these claims. In studying Fijian politics it must never be forgotten that Cacobau is not really a civilised man. He is utterly uneducated, and can with difficulty write his own name. Throughout the history of this movement he is seen to be a mere puppet in the powerful grasp of his white advisers. He is the *roi fainéant*, while Mr. Woods or Burt or Thurston is for the time being his Mayor of the Palace. Until past the middle period of life Cacobau was a savage and a cannibal. He subsequently adopted Christianity, but that did not necessarily make him the fit head of a constitutional government. It may safely be asserted that in most matters which affect the prosperity of a civilised community King Coffee Kalcalli would be quite as able a ruler as King Cacobau.

In the original draft of the constitution no reference had been made to separate Houses of Parliament. An equal number of white members and native chiefs were to sit together and frame laws for the general community. But, apart from the difficulty attending the use of a language not understood by one section of the Legislature, there was a yet more serious difficulty in the background. The native vote on any question was not an independent one. It was not merely influenced but entirely controlled by the known wishes of the King on the subject before the House. It would, in fact, always be found on the side of the minister, for, as we have seen, the King's policy would be that of his favourite minister, not that of the Parliament. Such an attempt to gain absolute power was too much for even the friendly and pliant Delegates. Yet it might have passed unnoticed for some time but for the want of tact displayed on a certain occasion by the Chief Secretary. It so happened that he had lost a measure by two white votes. In this division the native chiefs present had taken no part. They had looked stolidly on; and although somewhat surprised at the ringing of the bell for the division, had prudently refrained from meddling with what they did not understand. At a signal, however, from the Chief Secretary they came over as one man to the Government side, and changed the previous minority of two into a majority of twenty-eight. Such an episode in parliamentary government could not pass unnoticed. The Delegates broke up earlier than usual that day, and ministers felt that henceforth a separate native Assembly was inevitable. The chamber to which the Fijian Chiefs were relegated might be compared to the House of Lords, while the chamber where the whites sat might be compared to the House of Commons. The chiefs held their seats by virtue of hereditary rank. They could not propose a measure, but could veto it or send it back for further discussion to the Lower House. Every minister must be the representative in Parliament of some constituency; but a member by accepting office under Government did not vacate his seat. Finally, it was arranged that all legislative power was to be vested in the King and Legislative Assembly, and that ministers were to hold office only during the will of Parliament. Such were a few of the more important clauses of the Constitution Act, as amended by the Delegates. The suitability of the form of government chosen to the requirements of Fiji will be considered hereafter. Its leading idea was that of a constitutional monarchy. Representative government and free institutions were, indeed, conceded, but only in so far as was compatible with the simultaneous existence of a Venetian Council of Ten.

After the dismissal of the Delegates the ministers began in all seriousness to govern their fellow-whites. Mr. Sydney Burt, formerly an auctioneer in Sydney, and since his arrival in Fiji commercial agent to Cacobau, assumed the post of Chief Secretary, with the prefix of Honourable. To Mr. Woods, who had recently come to Fiji in order to survey a passage for the Mail steamers, was entrusted the portfolio of Foreign Affairs. Mr. J. C. Smith became Minister of Trade, Mr. Sagar of Native Affairs, and Mr. Hennings of Finance. To the two first of these gentlemen the concoction of the whole Government scheme was probably owing. They were undoubtedly the most able and most ambitious of the King's advisers. But they were also beyond all question the most unpopular. To their obstinate and indecent continuance in office against the wish of the community must be attributed much of the unpopularity which before long overtook the Government. Mr. W. Hennings was the pioneer merchant of Fiji. Few men were so popular and so universally respected as he was. While he remained in office his name was a source of as much strength to the Government as the names of Mr. Burt and Mr. Woods were a source of weakness.

Much had thus far been done by the ministers, but more still remained. The native population had yet to be conciliated and won over, and this could only be through their own chiefs. Cacobau, indeed, had been told by his advisers that he was King of Fiji, and had always been so. Yet he had not himself been aware of the fact. Like M. Jourdain, who had been talking prose all his life and never knew it, so Cacobau had been King of Fiji for a number of years and had not discovered the fact. Nor, indeed, had some other chiefs been any better informed on this important subject than Cacobau himself. Some received the news of the discovery with astonishment, others with incredulity, and some went even so far as to show signs of loss of temper. Tiu Bau did not know what to make of it, and drank more kava and gin than ever. Tiu Cakou, the haughty lord of Cacadrovi, held aloof from the whole business; while Ratu Kini, a self-made Napoleonic sort of man, swore roundly that he never intended to be subject to Cacobau or any other chief. But Fortune is said to favour the brave, and she certainly favoured these bold white men who intrigued so cleverly for place and power.

Nearly a generation before the time of which we write Maafu, a Tongan chief, had settled in Eastern Fiji. There he had established a powerful rule, and had exercised an ever-increasing influence on Fijian politics. He was a man of ability and ambition. He had shown himself to be both a general and a politician, and moreover to have a more thorough knowledge of the doctrines and requirements of civilisation than any other chief in the group. There is little doubt that he could have made himself King of Fiji long before this but for white influence, particularly American. Eventually he had been beaten back to his own district, whence, as from a centre, he still contrived to make his influence felt over the whole circle of the islands. He had already wrested some of Cacobau's fairest lands from him. He had formed a close alliance with Tiu Cakou, one of the greatest of Fijian chieftains. He was head of the Tovata league, perhaps the most powerful combination ever formed in Fiji against one man. Maafu's independent position and ambitious designs were so well known that it was with no small surprise that men learned that he had joined the nascent Government. Whether Maafu really thought the movement would be a success, and therefore feared it, or a failure, and therefore hoped to use it, is doubtful. At any rate, he accepted the title of Lieutenant-Governor of a district which he had formerly ruled as an absolute chief, and commuted all his revenues for the modest sum of eight hundred pounds a year. In addition to this, however, he received the rank of Viceroy, one thousand pounds in money, and a clear title to three islands, Moala, Motuku, and Totoya.[1] The adhesion of Maafu to the new Government was a great accession of strength. When he had been gained over there could be no doubt but that other chiefs would soon follow.

Hitherto things had gone on more smoothly than could have been expected; but now a hitch seemed likely to occur. Tiu Cakou, who did not as yet know of Maafu's defection from the Tovata, flatly refused to join the Government. His district, Cakadrovi, was one of the most important in Fiji, both from the wealth and the number of its white inhabitants. The relations hitherto subsisting between the chief and the whites had been excellent. He had afforded them a fair share of encouragement and protection, and of these benefits the white settlers were now not unmindful. As soon as the news of the Government movement reached Cakadrovi, meetings of the planters were at once convened. It was then determined among the whites to pursue whatever course their legitimate chief, Tiu Cakou, should pursue. Tiu Cakou declared against the Government, and conse-

[1] 'Fiji Times,' March 11, 1874.

quently no white or native Delegates from his kingdom attended the Assembly in Levuka. Cakadrovi was thus unrepresented in that House which had accepted Cacobau's constitution. Thus matters continued until the Delegates had quitted Levuka and returned to their respective constituencies. Meanwhile Tiu Cakou had learned that Maafu had joined the Government and seceded from the Tovata league. When Tiu Cakou first heard this news he was on board the 'Wainui' on a pleasure-trip, and his rage and disappointment was something terrible. His position indeed was by Maafu's conduct considerably altered. He had now not only Cacobau, but the whites of Levuka and Maafu and his Tongans against him. Such a position was clearly untenable, and he had no other choice but to join the Government. An American armed expedition, accompanied by two of Cacobau's ministers, also went at this time to Cakadrovi, to obtain redress for certain losses inflicted on American subjects. Whether any influence was thus exerted on the recalcitrant chief is not known certainly, although a statement to that effect was made plainly enough in Levuka, and was never contradicted. It is certain that the American Consul was warmly in favour of the new scheme, and possibly may have backed up the ministerial arguments by measures calculated to alarm a barbarous chief. Whether any coercion was used is not known; but it may be supposed that no direct or official influence on behalf of the American Government was brought to bear. A few weeks after this incident Tiu Cakou came to Levuka, and pitched his tent outside the town. His arrival caused but little stir, and, indeed, for some time was not generally known. To all who attempted to communicate with him his manner was distracted; his eyes were red and swollen, and he bore the appearance of a man who had attempted to escape from some great trouble by the aid of the gin-bottle. By the side of Maafu, with his clean-shaven face, bright eyes, and neat uniform, he cut but a poor figure. A few days after this it was publicly announced that Tiu Cakou had joined the Government of Bau. He had accepted the same annual stipend as Maafu. With him, of course, the whole of Cacadrovi also joined, and thus a most important accession was gained. Tiu Bau, who was at best a drunken sot, also about this time gave in his adhesion, so that before the meeting of the first Parliament all the really important subdivisions of Fiji had been brought under the nominal sway of Cacobau. Ratu Kini and the cannibals of Viti Levu still held out; but even they, or some of them, soon after yielded.

The success that had thus far attended the formation of the Government had been most striking. But now unforeseen difficulties were about to retard its further progress.

Before, however, mentioning these it will be well to place before the reader the exact position which the Government now occupied in the eyes of the general body of white settlers. It consisted of Cacobau and his nominee ministers and a few native chiefs. They had seized power, indeed, in a most irregular manner. But then the irregularity of their proceedings had been allowed by most persons to have been unavoidable in the state in which society then was in Fiji. The Delegates had consented to accept the constitution from the hands of the ministers, and by so doing had condoned their previous conduct. So strong was the desire felt by every class of the community for a government of any kind, that men were disposed rather to assist than to thwart those who had promised to provide them with this boon. The difficulties which, in spite of this friendly feeling, the ministers had had to meet had been by no means inconsiderable. The manner, however, in which they had thus far consolidated their power, and gradually won over one section of the white population or one province of the native after another, had been admirable. Their measures had been concerted with forethought and skill, and carried out with energy. In these preliminaries they had displayed an amount of administrative ability which had augured well for the future, and had won the respect and confidence of their fellow-citizens. They had seized office certainly, but were showing themselves worthy to hold it. Such were the feelings of the more intelligent portion of the white settlers towards the Government at the close of the year 1871. As regarded the native population the greater portion of it was profoundly indifferent and profoundly ignorant concerning the political events that were taking place. The natives followed their chiefs implicitly, and all the most important of these chiefs had already sworn allegiance to Cacobau. For the first time in the history of Fiji the whole group had been united under one ruler. The Kai-se, or Fijian serf, had been nominally emancipated. A barbarous feudalism had been converted in a moment into a representative and constitutional government. The English constitution, which had taken eight hundred years to develop, had been transplanted bodily to a country whose inhabitants had not yet learned to wear clothes. The experiment had been, indeed, a most ambitious one, and one in which failure was *primâ facie* more probable than success.

Perhaps what now occupied the most anxious thoughts of everyone in Fiji was the attitude which England would adopt towards the new state. The prevailing opinion among the politicians of Levuka was that she would be only too glad to be relieved from the necessity of meddling in Fijian matters, and would therefore readily recognise the new Government. There can be no doubt but that the previous action of England fully justified this opinion. She had already refused to accept the offer made to her of the islands, had refused to grant the Consul magisterial powers, and rather than take the islands under her protection had gone so far as to suggest that Australia should undertake to govern them. In a word, the English Cabinet had exhibited throughout a pitiable spectacle of weakness and indecision in the whole matter. Now, however, an unexpected chance of at once escaping all further perplexities, and yet of adopting a manly and intelligible policy, was presented. The best plan, under the circumstances, would have been to have recognised the new state *de jure* and *de facto*, and to have allowed English subjects to transfer their allegiance to King Cacobau. English influence ought to have been withdrawn from Fiji, and England should no more have thought of interfering for the future with the affairs of Fiji than with those of Hawaii or Tahiti. There would no doubt have been a short and sharp struggle among local factions for supreme power; but in the end peace and security would have been the result. England, however, would not recognise the Government of Cacobau, and consequently Englishmen domiciled in Fiji began to ask themselves even thus early whether they could at will become subjects of another state, and throw off their allegiance to Queen Victoria. Opinions from eminent counsel were procured from Sydney and elsewhere. Men could not answer the important question for themselves, and in their perplexity naturally betook themselves to the British Consul. Hitherto he had scrupulously avoided taking any public part in the Government movement. While other consuls countenanced the new Government, partook of the ministerial hospitalities, and deferentially waited, or pretended to wait, on King Cacobau, Mr. March preserved an immovable attitude. To

X

him officially the King was still only Cacobau, chief of Bau, the honourable the Chief Secretary was still only an unsuccessful Sydney auctioneer, and the assembly of the Delegates nothing but a public meeting, like scores of others that had taken place in Levuka. Mr. March, however, in common with everyone else, saw the advisability and even necessity of some Government. But, manifestly, he could not give an official sanction to the movement, particularly when so important a matter as the allegiance of British subjects was in question, without definite instructions from home. Before these instructions could arrive, circumstances had occurred which of necessity compelled him to adopt a hostile attitude towards the King's ministers.

Immediately after the dissolution of the House of Delegates, writs were issued for the election of members of Parliament, or as it was called, in imitation of the colonial phraseology, the 'Legislative Assembly.' In the interval while the members were being elected the whole executive power remained in the hands of the self-appointed ministers. Their position was not strictly a constitutional one; but yet might have passed without much questioning. Now, however, incredible as it may seem, that discretion which had hitherto marked the ministerial policy seemed suddenly to have deserted it. Day after day fresh enactments were promulgated 'by order of the King in Council.' By the Constitution Act, indeed, it had clearly been affirmed that all power was vested in the King and Legislative Assembly; yet here was the King in Council making laws without even the pretence of consulting the representatives of the people. Nor were these Orders in Council on mere trivial matters, or on such as were so manifestly for the benefit of the community at large that they might have passed unchallenged. On the contrary, they affected the liberty of the subject and the revenues of the kingdom. By a stroke of the pen the Criminal Code of Hawaii was appointed to be the code by which British subjects were to be tried; by another it was superseded within a week by the code of Victoria; by another a police-court was established in Levuka; by another an enormous issue of paper-money was authorised. Scarcely a Fiji Gazette was published that did not contain some new 'Order in Council.' Men were at first astonished, and then thoroughly alarmed, at the unexpected course things were taking. It was said, and justly so, that ministers should have waited for the meeting of Parliament. Under the peculiar circumstances in which the country found itself, any trifling exercise of power on their part would have been condoned; but such wholesale and even wanton legislation could not be tolerated. And now a constitutional cry was raised. It was said that the Delegates had only met to consider the Constitution, not finally to accept it. Their function had simply been to lay before their constituents the work they had done, and if their constituents approved of it, then indeed it would become law; but not till then.

The King's ministers, however, held a different view. They proceeded on the assumption that Cacobau was *de jure* and *de facto* King of Fiji. Every white man domiciled in the group was, theoretically at any rate, a subject of the King. In strict political logic those constituencies who returned members to the first Parliament accept *ex ipso facto* this position. Those constituencies or individuals who did not intend to recognise the Government of Cacobau should have abstained from all action whatsoever. Every man who did not thus abstain had compromised his position, and had tacitly pledged himself to abide by the opinion of the majority. The power of the King was absolute and indefeasible. It was merely as a gracious condescension on his part, and as a proof of his regard to the whites settled in his dominions, that he had granted to them a Constitution at all. He might have been an absolute ruler; he preferred to be a constitutional one. Meanwhile his gracious gift did not invalidate his power. Through his ministers he still could and would make decrees that had all the force of law. Those who did not like these plain truths, or who did not believe them, might, as the Attorney-General said, leave the country.

Everyone of course knows that the ministers really spoke of and for themselves, although they went through the formality of using Cacobau's name. It was even said that the King had, in many instances, been kept in ignorance of, and had not signed, the obnoxious Orders in Council at all. It was the ministers who were endeavouring to impose a yoke on their fellow citizens. The position they assumed might, from their own point of view, have been logical enough; but it was one which they could successfully maintain only by force of arms. It was one which a community, accustomed to the free institutions of Australia and America, or the still freer life of Fiji, would not readily accept. A little consideration might have shown the ministers that such men would never willingly consent to be the subjects of a despotic monarch. This monarch was moreover, be it remembered, a man whose title was not yet a month old, and whom men could remember as a naked savage; a man with whom they traded and jested times out of mind; a man who had before now consented to be solemnly crowned with an oil-can, as a mark of real dignity; a man whom every new comer to Fiji was accustomed to visit as one of the sights of Levuka, and to whom he would offer brandy or champagne in the same way as he might offer a biscuit to a bear in the Zoological Gardens. Need it be said that the ministerial doctrines, as soon as understood, were received with derision and defiance by all independent men from Loma Loma to the far-off Yassawas, and from Vanna Levu in the north to Kadavu in the south?

As might be supposed, the ministers now began to lose popularity in many quarters. A regular opposition was set on foot, composed mainly of British subjects. These persons declared that they preferred to remain Englishmen rather than become natives of Fiji. And now the evil of the hasty and arbitrary manner in which the Government had come into existence became abundantly evident. Every discontented man held that he had a right to refuse to submit to it, and might cease or otherwise to take any part in it, exactly when he pleased. To such opposition the Government applied the name of sedition, and declared that all who took part in it were rebels and traitors. The British Consul had up to this time remained perfectly neutral. But now, insomuch as he could not recognise the claims of Cacobau and his ministers to coerce British subjects, he became involuntarily, and, as it were *ex officio*, identified with the Opposition. In the absence of definite instructions from England, it is difficult to know what other course he could have pursued. In the midst of the excitement attending the opposition movement, the elections for Members of Parliament came off. Levuka had the right of returning three. Two of the King's ministers, one of them a most popular man personally, and the pioneer merchant of Fiji, were indeed successful; but only partially so. They were not at the head of the poll, where they expected to be. Dr. Ryley, one of the few Delegates who had opposed the passing of the Constitution Act, and who was known to be bitterly hostile to the new Government, was returned by a large majority. This was a significant sign of the altered temper of the people, a sign which the ministry failed to interpret rightly.

CHAPTER XIV.

The Government consolidates its Power—The Supreme Court—The Police Court—The case of Rees—Parliamentary Opposition disavowed—Issue of Paper-money—More Grievances—The Ku Klux—Fall of the Ministry—Accession of Mr. Thurston—Mr. Woods Premier—The Ba River District—Native Outrages—Conduct of the Minis'ers who visited the District—Political Action of the Planters—A Civil War imminent—Interference of H.M.S. 'Dido'—Last Session of the Triennial Parliament—Unsettled State of the Country generally—Threatened Secession of Maafu—Attempt to enfranchise Natives—Collapse of the Attempt at Self-Government—Arrival of Commodore Goodenough and Mr. Consul Layard.

IN spite of the growing opposition, which, however, was as yet confined almost entirely to Levuka, the ministers continued to consolidate and increase their power. Dr. Macartney, an ex-member of the Legislative Assembly of Victoria, was appointed, with a salary of 500*l.* a year; many bills, principally relating to the imposition of taxes and the administration of justice, were drafted; a budget was sketched out, a post-office established in Levuka, in opposition to the one already existing at the British Consulate; Levuka itself constituted a municipality; the construction of public offices, and a House of Parliament, commenced; and many other reforms either promised or undertaken.

As has been already stated, the Code of Hawaii and subsequently that of Victoria had been adopted by the King in Council as the statute law of Fiji. To administer this a Supreme Court was now established in Levuka, presided over by three judges. Minor courts were also established in most of the outlying districts. These were under the direction of the local chiefs, aided by some of the white planters of the district. Many of these planters were now placed on the commission of the peace—an honour which, in all cases, was accepted readily enough. In Levuka there was moreover a police-court, under the direction of a stipendiary magistrate, assisted by a Fijian colleague.

The Supreme Court was the highest court of appeal in the country. Under its various jurisdictions, such as admiralty, ecclesiastical, criminal, and so forth, it could take cognisance of offences of every nature and degree, from petty larceny to high treason. It was at once a civil and a criminal tribunal, a Court of Chancery, a court of Queen's Bench, and a police court in one. It represented the highest available legal talent in the kingdom, and not even Parliament could reverse its decisions. Under such circumstances it might be supposed that no pains would have been spared to place it beyond the reach of suspicion, and to secure for its decisions all the respect which high professional standing, or unblemished personal character in its judges. could confer. Such, however, was not the case. The chief justice had been, up to the time of his appointment, a law reporter to the 'Sydney Morning Herald.' He was an estimable man in private life, but scarcely the person to be appointed as chancellor of a kingdom, and Controller of its most important court. He had originally been consul-general for Hawaii in Sydney, and had been knighted by the King of the Sandwich Islands. Unfortunately this is an honour recognised by no court in Europe, or elsewhere, and cannot be said to have at all increased the personal importance of the chief justice. It tended rather to make him ridiculous in the eyes of all sensible men, and to bring himself and his court into contempt. The associate judge, when the court was constituted, was not a barrister at all, but a solicitor; while the third judge was Mr. Justice Marica, a Fiji man of mature years. From the very nature of the case he was of course ignorant of all law except club law. He could speak scarcely a word of English, and at every turn required the services of an interpreter. He was an excellent man, but utterly unsuited for a supreme court judge. On the bench his position to himself must have been exquisitely painful. He was daily called on to give his opinion on points of law which he could not possibly comprehend. He might indeed, in most cases, with just as much propriety, have been asked to give his opinion on the integral calculus or on the functions of the pineal gland. He was completely ignorant of the Hawaiian or any other code, and could no more interpret a knotty point of law than he could interpret the pleadings of the advocate who spoke before him in an unknown tongue. His presence on the bench might have been necessary in cases where Fijians were interested parties; but if so, he should have confined himself to such cases, and not have presumed to tread on unknown ground. It is not too much to say that this supreme court never did and never could command the confidence of the community. Its judges, too, were all more or less interested parties, especially in all trials of a political nature, a large number of which came before them every session. On the success of the Government movement depended the offices and salaries of the judges; and where such interests are at stake it is not to be expected of any man, even with the best intentions, that he can be perfectly unbiassed. Although no Impey sat on the Bench in Levuka, the supreme court of Fiji was probably not less useful to the Government than the supreme court of Calcutta had once been to Warren Hastings.

In Levuka a police-court had been established almost immediately after the inauguration of the government. It had been called into existence by an 'Order in Council,' and had given offence to many persons from the very commencement. Its constitution was by many declared to be illegal, inasmuch as it had been created before any parliament had sat that could sanction such a court. The opposition which the ministers were encountering in Levuka had been growing every day more intense, and now it was finally determined by a number of the citizens to resist forcibly the jurisdiction of this obnoxious court. An opportunity soon presented itself. An old sailor named Rees, in receipt of a pension from the British Government, had been employed to perform some work by the editor of the 'Fiji Gazette,' the Government organ, who was himself, of course, a 'Government man.' Mr. Murray, the editor, not satisfied with the conduct of Rees, took out a summons against him, and cited him to appear before the magistrate sitting in the police-court. Rees, it so happened, was one of those tough, sturdy men that are slow to be moved, but when once moved are formidable adversaries. He was well known and popular in Levuka, and altogether was an unfortunate subject for arbitrary experiments. He refused to obey the summons, and consequently a warrant was issued for his arrest. When arrested he appealed to the British Consul, who protested against the action that had been taken. Rees meanwhile was lodged in a narrow cell, in company with three natives, and certainly had every reason to complain of the way in which he was treated. The ventilation was bad, the food insufficient, and the jailors harsh, while his friends were not allowed to visit him without a magistrate's order. A committee of citizens was immediately formed to investigate the whole affair, and, if necessary, effect the deliverance of the prisoner by force.

Next day Rees was brought up for trial. He denied the jurisdiction of the court, and was remanded to prison for contempt. The magistrate publicly .

declared that it was his intention to commit the prisoner every day if necessary, until he should be brought to recognise the authority of the court. This, of course, made matters worse. Levuka was soon in a state of intense excitement. Armed men patrolled the streets, the shopkeepers closed their shops, and all business was for a time suspended. This trial had now become a Government affair. The Attorney-General prosecuted, while Mr. De Courcey Ireland, well known afterwards in connexion with certain matters on the Ba coast, defended the prisoner. With the consent of all parties, it was arranged that the matter really to be tried was the legality of the police-court. The case for the Crown was that Cacobau was absolute King of Fiji, and therefore had a right to establish any court or make any laws he chose. In support of this claim a mass of heterogeneous evidence was brought forward, consisting of documents from naval commanders, from the American Consulate, and a stray letter from the British Consul, where the word 'king' occurred. Mr. Ireland, on the other hand, contended that Cacobau was never king of the whole group in any sense of the word; and that, even supposing he had been, he had subsequently of his own accord abdicated his power in virtue of a constitutional form of government. The Constitution Act stated clearly that all legislative power was vested in the King and Legislative Assembly, and therefore the King's Order in Council could not alone be sufficient to establish a criminal code of foreign origin, or to impose pains and penalties on free men. The magistrate was judge of his own case, and decided that these arguments were of no avail, a decision in which, he was glad to find, his friend Justice Marika coincided. Rees was again relegated to jail, to be brought up next morning.

The morrow dawned anxiously enough for many persons in Levuka. During the night a committee of the citizens had sat, and, after careful consideration, had determined that there remained only an appeal to force. The majority of whites would not recognise Cacobau as absolute sovereign, would not recognise the pretensions of his ministers, and would not take the Attorney-General's advice and leave the country. Consequently they had determined to defend what they considered their rights with their lives if necessary. The civil servants, too, had dropped their sealing-wax and red tape, and had assumed the batons of special constables. As the hour appointed for the trial approached, public excitement ran very high. Every man in such a small community was obliged to be more or less of a partisan. Private friendships were forgotten in political enmities. In such a crisis no one could remain neutral; or if any did, they deserved the curse pronounced by the Greek lawgiver on those wretched beings who, in a civil commotion, took neither side. Great masses of men, all more or less armed, might be seen gradually moving up towards the police-court from various parts of the town. At length the long-expected hour arrived, and the prisoner was led into court. But no man appeared to accuse him, and he was discharged forthwith. This was at once understood to be a victory for the oppositionists, and rightly so. The ministers felt they had already proceeded too far, and were glad to seize the only chance that remained of retiring gracefully from the matter. The concession, however, had come too late. The release of another prisoner committed to jail about the same time as Rees was demanded and refused. A large body of citizens thereupon marched down to the jail, broke it open, took the prisoner to the other end of the town, and tried him before a jury. He was found guilty, and handed over to the British Consul, who, with a view to meet the ends of justice and as far as possible allay the ill-feeling that existed between the townspeople and the Government, sent him back to prison. Thus ended the first serious conflict between the new Government and the people. In it the Government were clearly defeated, and probably from this time the ministers secretly gave up all idea of ruling constitutionally, and determined to retain power by any means and at all hazards.

The first Parliament met in October 1871. At first it was supposed there would be a stormy opposition, and so indeed there was, but only for a few weeks. Within that time it had crumbled down before the dexterous method of attack employed by Messrs. Burt and Woods. New offices, such as Lands Commissions, were given to some unruly members, vague promises were freely made to others, and in a word everyone was made to believe that it would be to his interest to be on the side of the ministers. By such means all danger of a serious opposition was removed. A few men indeed still remained true to their principles, but they were in a hopeless minority, and their votes could not affect the general result. The few who could not be bought over—and they were very few—were thus left alone in the House, and found but little sympathy among their colleagues. The ministers, meanwhile, lost no time in passing various Acts, by which the whole governing power of the country was centred in their hands. The budget was fixed at about 25,000*l.*, but the actual expenditure for the nine months ending June 1872 amounted to nearly 30,000*l.*[1] Permission was obtained from Parliament to issue debentures to the value of 5,000*l.* bearing interest at 10 per cent. and secured on the revenues of the kingdom. The civil list was very large for such a small country as Fiji, but Parliament did not care to scrutinise it. Everything that the ministers asked for the Commons granted, until it seemed as if no member had any power of independent thought or action. Owing to the slowness of printing in Levuka, all members could not be furnished with copies of the bills before the House; consequently, many of them actually voted with Government without having read the

[1] See 'Report of Commodore Goodenough and Mr. Consul Layard.' p. 36.

measures they voted for. The first Parliament was in fact a burlesque on representative Government. It represented nothing but the ambitious designs of the self-constituted ministers. In Levuka, at any rate, men saw that if future Parliaments were to be as subservient as the first, there was little hope of a constitutional Government. On the other hand, it must be said that settlers in the outlying districts had as yet had no opportunity of understanding the drift of the ministerial policy. They were still dazzled by the prospects of an influx of capital into the group, followed by a general rise in the value of all property. Most of the representatives returned had been more or less favourable to the Government from the first. They were, moreover, quite unskilled in the practical work of legislation, and were glad to leave the conduct of matters they did not understand to the guidance of energetic men like Mr. Woods or Mr. Burt.

One of the first practical results of the setting up of a government was to flood Fiji generally with paper-money. A large number of debentures, varying in value from one to ten dollars, were printed and put in circulation. The interest on these debentures was to be paid in coin, and certain days were fixed at the Treasury for the payment in specie of the debentures themselves. But any man who had repaired to the Treasury on the appointed day with the expectation of receiving gold or silver for his paper would have been sadly disappointed. There was no specie in the country, not even the hitherto despised Bolivian half-dollars. In Sydney the Fijian 'Government notes' were treated as so much waste paper. Merchants or masters of vessels would not accept them, and the public followed their example. A few storekeepers, however, took them, but at a ruinous discount—some six or eight shillings in the pound. Meanwhile, it was necessary to have some medium of exchange by which business could be carried on. This was supplied by an extended system of I O U's. If a sailor went into the barroom of an hotel he at once gave his I O U for what he had drunk; planters gave storekeepers their I O U's instead of cotton or cocoa-nut oil; and storekeepers gave their *employés* I O U's instead of their weekly wages. Strange as it may seem, many preferred these worthless documents to the 'Government paper.' Those who still had gold or silver kept it carefully concealed. It was said that the natives had large sums in half-dollars buried near their villages, but were afraid to use them. Merchants and storekeepers treasured up every coin they could find, in order to give it to the shipmasters who brought their goods from Sydney, and who declared they would rather take the merchandise back than give it in exchange for bad paper. In most outlying districts planters refused to have anything to do with paper-money. The credit of the Government was, in fact, not sufficiently good to enable them to float their issues. Such a state of things could not, of course, last long, and by-and-by worked its own cure. People gradually were obliged to take Government notes, because they could get nothing else. About this time Mr. Hennings became Minister of Finance, and his signature attached to these Government debentures inspired the public with more confidence than any Acts of Parliament could have done. The Government policy in regard to finance all along seemed to be to mystify everyone as much as possible, and to keep every measure a profound secret. In a small community like Fiji this was not easily done, and in the position in which the ministers were was far from judicious even to attempt it. In December 1871 the first Parliament was prorogued, and its members returned to their cotton plantations and their constituencies. So far the ministers had had it all their own way. They had educated Parliament till it had willingly passed all their measures. The Government of the country was completely in their hands. A despotism, in fact, was all but established, and that by a few men, some of whom six months previously had been unknown and unnoticed in the general community of Fiji.

At the commencement of 1872 the Government, as represented by the ministers, had become extremely unpopular. Their conduct previous to the meeting of Parliament had already alienated many of their supporters. The obnoxious Orders in Council, by which a police court and paper-money had been forced on the community had not been forgotten.

To these were now added fresh grievances. At the time of the inauguration of Government many posts and offices had been promised to persons resident in Levuka whose opposition was feared, or whose good-will it was thought proper to conciliate. These promises had not been kept. Every vessel from Sydney or New Zealand had brought numerous strangers to Fiji, and these, the older residents perceived, were constantly appointed to all vacant places, or places even made for them. In most instances the individuals so appointed were personal friends of some one minister. This, indeed, in many cases, seemed their only recommendation, for their previous histories would have acted as a bar to their obtaining respectable employment in any settled country. The use of such men to the ministers was plain enough. Under the name of 'civil servants' they formed a compact body, depending for very food and raiment on those whom they served. Such men were ever ready to support their employers, and under the name of 'special constables' formed a well-organised and readily available force. Meanwhile, a host of claimants for place and power felt personally aggrieved by the promotion of these comparative strangers. If a few representative and popular citizens had been chosen to fill the more important Government places it would have done much to conciliate the people. But the opposite plan having been adopted, dissatisfaction, the result of disappointment or wounded vanity, became general.

The conduct of the late Parliament had also given great dissatisfaction. It was said that the budget was excessive, that an expensive and useless executive had been forced on the country, that the taxes were inordinate, and so forth. Those who had property feared they might be called on to pay for those who had not, as it was evident that the money which was being so freely spent must be supplied from some quarter. To these must be added the hauteur and arrogant bearing adopted by some of the ministers in public. Their conduct in this respect, in a small place like Levuka, was as absurd as it was injudicious. The Prime Minister was simply a shopkeeper, like scores of others in Levuka; and though he called himself the commercial agent of Cacobau, everyone knew that he was only a retail trader. The Minister of Finance had a shop close to the Minister of Trade. The Minister for Foreign Affairs had originally come to Fiji to survey a passage for Mail steamers, but had remained to conduct the diplomatic business of the country. When Peter, in the 'Tale of a Tub,' insisted on wearing three hats and being called 'my lord,' he did not display more extravagant airs or more absurd pretensions than did some of these self-appointed advisers of the King. Their pretensions were the more intolerable because they were unfounded. Everyone in Levuka knew that the antecedents of a few of the ministers were such as would not only have prevented their being employed in any Government capacity in the Australian colonies, but would further have ensured their expulsion from every decent club in Sydney or Melbourne.

Discontent at last assumed the form of open rebellion. Levuka was the head-quarters of the oppositionists. Among the most determined opponents of the Government was an old man named Keyse, who had been for some time a resident in Fiji. He had built a house, which, being extended on piles into the harbour, admitted of being easily fortified. This was now done, and 'Keyse's' became the head-quarters of the malcontents. Here they formed themselves into a secret society, called the 'Ku Klux,' and pledged themselves by terrible oaths to obey their leaders and to keep all their deliberations secret. The members of this society bore arms, and bound themselves at a certain signal to be at their posts, prepared for any emergency. The defence of the house and the general direction of the society's affairs were entrusted to a committee, presided over by a retired naval officer. This society was formidable both from the number and character of its adherents, and appeared all the more formidable because the real extent of its power could not be known. The Government met this new foe as best it could. The Houses of Parliament were fortified, and guns placed so as to bear on the fortifications of the opposition. The Government position was at one end of the town, while their opponents were at the other. Levuka thus lay at the mercy of both parties, and in case of a battle would have been placed between two fires. During such a time all business was necessarily more or less suspended. No one could tell the moment when the hostile factions would open fire on one another. A collision was hourly expected; and as the Ku Klux men were well-organised and thoroughly in earnest, such a contest would probably have overthrown the Government. As it was it compelled the resignation of Mr. Burt, the most obnoxious of the ministers. But here its further existence was summarily put an end to by the arrival of H.M.S. 'Cossack.' On this occasion the Fiji Government was recognised by England *de facto*, but not *de jure*. In other words, it was only partially recognised, a policy of half measures which was productive of much subsequent mischief. This was the first occasion on which the Fiji Government was supported by an English vessel-of-war, but it was by no means the last.

In March 1872 the body of self-constituted ministers finally lost power. Mr. Burt was forced to resign, but he was far too able a man to be allowed to remain in opposition. Accordingly, he was offered and accepted the Attorney-Generalship, and henceforth plays a minor part in the Government which he himself had been mainly instrumental in establishing. Mr. Thurston, who had at one time been Acting British Consul, and who had the confidence of all parties, was now asked to join the Government. He consented, and accepted the post of Minister of Foreign Affairs. Mr. Woods, meanwhile, went to Sydney, where he succeeded in raising a small loan. On his return he again became Prime Minister, much to the dissatisfaction of all moderate men. Mr. Woods was both an able and energetic man, and it was much to be regretted that he did not see the necessity of yielding to public opinion and resigning a post which he could only hope to retain by force. Had he done so it is possible that even at this late stage the Government might have been established on a secure and permanent footing. But Mr. Woods would not resign the Premiership, and therefore all hopes of a hearty union among politicians for the good of the country were now at an end.

While matters were in this unsettled state in Levuka they were in even a worse state in some of the outlying districts. In the north and north-west of Viti Levu, or Big Fiji, one of the wildest parts of the group, some adventurous settlers had bought land and formed homesteads and plantations. The Ba river, coming down from the highlands in the interior of the island, flows over an alluvial plain, some six miles in extent, before it empties itself into the sea. This plain consists of a soil well suited to the growth of cotton, and possesses a further advantage in being free from heavy timber, the clearing away of which is always an expensive and troublesome operation. The mountains which skirt this plain are lofty and inaccessible, and, moreover, are inhabited by a race of ferocious cannibals. These cannibals, or Kai Colos (mountain-men), as they were called, had never been subject to Cacobau. While the rest of Fiji had *lotued* or become Christian these tribes still remained heathen. They allowed their hair to grow long, and twisted it into fantastic shapes; they painted their bodies, and wore no covering except a narrow strip of native cloth. The country they lived in was long a *terra incognita*; several whites had tried to penetrate it, but had lost their lives in the attempt. The few who had succeeded gave a doleful description of it. They stated that it was rocky and sterile, covered in many places with dense brushwood, in others destitute of all vegetation, and abounding in precipices, which could be scaled only by paths known to the mountaineers. From the earliest times the Kai Colos had been the enemies of the lowlanders; they had been accustomed, like the Highlanders of Scotland, to make predatory excursions on the peaceful and fertile districts which lay between them and the sea. When short of food, they had never hesitated to come down through the passes and plunder the coast natives of their yams, or pigs or fowls. Hence the Ba district had long been one of the most unsettled in Fiji. But the very fact that it was so made land cheap, and this was a great recommendation in the eyes of some adventurous settlers. The soil was good, possessed the advantage of water-carriage, and could be purchased at a very cheap rate. A few pounds of gunpowder, a few yards of calico, an old musket or two, were in the Ba district of more value than five times the same quantity of trade or money in Ovalan or Tavinni. Hence in spite of all drawbacks the land on each side of the Ba river was taken up by planters for a considerable distance. Probably they did not know the risks to which they exposed their lives in occupying such an outpost of civilisation. Once settled, however, on their lands, retreat was impossible, and it remained, therefore, only to make the best of the situation.

Until the middle of 1871 no serious outrages had been attempted; but in July of that year two white planters, Messrs. Spiers and Macintosh, were murdered by the mountaineers under circumstances of peculiar atrocity. After death their bodies had been cut up into small fragments; each piece had been wrapped in a banana-leaf and sent as a present to some chief. The cannibal drums had been beaten all night long, and next day a hideous feast was proclaimed, at which native warriors attended in great numbers. After the murder of these two planters the mountaineers became every day more bold and aggressive. At length matters became so bad that the settlers had to arm their imported labourers, and to watch their houses day and night. Two expeditions of whites and Fijians had already proceeded against the mountaineers, and had destroyed several of their villages. But as soon as Cacobau had been declared King of all the Fijis the mountain tribes who still refused to acknowledge his sway were of course rebels, and their subjugation became a government matter. The white settlers on the Ba had never been warm supporters of the Government schemes. They were too far away from Levuka to benefit much by ministerial patronage, and had, moreover, been so long accustomed to defend themselves that they preferred to continue to do so still. This, however, did not suit the plans of the ministers. A large force of Fijian and Tongan troops were sent down to the Ba district, as much, it was said, to overawe the whites as to check the mountaineers. These troops were, indeed, useless as a means of conquering the disaffected tribes, but nevertheless formed more or less of a protection to the planters, and as such were appreciated by them. Most planters, however, still kept their imported labourers well-armed, and themselves never quitted their houses without a rifle or revolver in their hands. Matters had been in this state for some time, when towards the end of 1872 two of the King's ministers made a tour of inspection round the island of Viti Levu. Among other places they visited the Ba River. Here they severely rated the settlers for their lukewarmness and disloyalty, and declared that they had no right to defend themselves against the mountaineers, or to arm their imported labourers. These duties the King's troops could perform; and in such hands all planters were expected to leave the defence of their lives and properties. Meanwhile, in order to impress their counsel on the minds of the Tanna men, the two ministers took one of them and, placing a halter round his neck, pointed to the nearest tree, and informed him that if he shot any mountaineer he should certainly be hanged. When the planters heard of this transaction they were very indignant, and declared that the ministers were positively inviting the mountaineers to attack and murder them. This was scarcely true, though the conduct of ministers in thus interfering between the men and their employers, especially under the peculiar circumstances of the case, was injudicious and culpable. The ministers had hardly returned to Levuka when the whole of Fiji was electrified by the news of a fearful outrage in the Ba district. Mr. Burns, who inhabited a lonely and exposed plantation, had been murdered, together with his wife and children and several Apic labourers. Their bodies had been treated with every indignity, and at length cut into small pieces and eaten. The horrified settlers could hear the cannibal drums all night long, and each one of them felt that it might be his turn next.

The planters seem unanimously to have attributed this murder to the action of the ministers on the occasion of their visit, and also to the fact that the Government troops had been suddenly withdrawn from the district. Their indignation rose to the highest pitch, and they resolved to cut adrift from a Government which could thus leave them unprotected, and at the same time forbid them to protect themselves. In conjunction with the settlers of Nadi and Nadroga they formed a kind of provincial 'Ku Klux.' They pledged themselves to act together on all occasions as one man, and if necessary to take up arms against all who should attempt to coerce them. They then formally disowned the Government that had been established at Levuka, and refused to obey its decrees or pay its taxes. As soon as the Government heard of these warlike proceedings they dispatched a body of troops to the Ba; but the settlers met them, beat them off, and compelled them to return discomfited to Levuka. Meanwhile they called on their brother settlers to redeem their promise and to assist them. This their brethren did, and soon a large and determined body of men were in open rebellion to the Government of Cacobau. Troops were now sent down in much larger numbers from Levuka, officered by white men, and well drilled and disciplined. Affairs looked ominous. Both parties were drawn up at a town called Sogunu,[1] and only awaited the commands of their leaders to fire. But at this critical moment messengers arrived from Levuka stating that Captain Chapman, of H.M.S. 'Dido,' had declared against the settlers. The secessionists, though ready enough to cope with the Fijian Government, could not oppose such an antagonist as a ship-of-war. Accordingly they submitted their case to the arbitration of Captain Chapman, and agreed to abide by his decision. He decided they had been wrong in the course they had taken, obliged them to sign a document of obedience to the Government; placed two of the leaders, Messrs. Ireland and White, under arrest, and conveyed them as prisoners to

[1] 'Fiji Times,' October 22, 1873.

Levuka. The latter gentleman was subsequently conveyed by force on board a vessel and carried off to Sydney, where he was set at liberty. Under the name of 'deportation' this method of getting rid of troublesome opponents was frequently resorted to by the Fijian Government. It was generally done secretly, without any previous trial, and on the mere order of a minister. That such things could take place showed sufficiently the despotic character of the Government then in existence. The conduct of Captain Chapman in this instance gave deep offence to the settlers. They asked by what right he had transformed a British ship-of-war into a police-boat for the Government. They declared that they had taken up arms in defence of their liberties, as their countrymen had once taken up arms against Charles I. and James II. They had determined on resistance, and were prepared to abide any penalty the Government could have inflicted upon them.[1] Commodore Goodenough and Mr. Consul Layard are of opinion that had it not been for the intervention of the 'Dido' the organised resistance to Government on the part of the planters of Ba, Nadi, and Nadroga might possibly have been successful;[2] and such must be the opinion of anyone who knows the sturdy and inde-

---

[1] 'Fiji Times,' October 22, 1873. Captain Chapman states in a letter ('Fiji Times,' May 24, 1873) that he was induced to act as a mediator at the request of both parties.

[2] See 'Report of Commodore Goodenough and Mr. Consul Layard,' page 3.

pendent class of men who formed the bulk of the settlers in these wild districts.

In Levuka affairs had been for some time in quite as unsatisfactory a state as in the outlying districts. Parliament met in 1873, the last session of the first of those triennial Parliaments that had been fixed by the constitution. After this session ministers were well aware that an appeal to the country would be inevitable, and were aware also what the result of such an appeal must be. All the most respectable and most influential men throughout the islands were by this time thoroughly disgusted with the Government. A powerful society had been organised in Levuka, under the presidency of a late Supreme Court Judge. It counted on its committee-list the names of the most popular and substantial settlers in every district of Fiji. This society was called the 'White Residents' Political Association,' and had for its objects: '(1) to protect by all legitimate means the liberties and privileges of the white residents in Fiji; (2) to watch the action of the Government, and to protest in the strongest legal manner against all such action as may appear to the association to be opposed to the interests of this country.' Such an organisation was not to be despised, containing as it did so many representative names.

Even this, however, could not deter the ministers from acting in any manner they thought fit. They still preserved their arrogant bearing, and still ignored the constitutional rights of those whom they governed.

Their rule at this time was simply terrorism. They had succeeded in getting together a considerable body of native troops. These troops were practically independent of Parliament, and formed a standing army, always available in case of need. They had originally been organised to act against the mountaineers, but were subsequently found to be useful auxiliaries against troublesome citizens. They were officered by whites, and amounted, all told, to 750 men.[1] Meanwhile the country generally was in a wretched state. Cotton-planting had not paid as men had expected it would pay. There had been a great fall in price since 1868 and 1869, and the planting community in Fiji was in 1873-4 to all intents bankrupt. The taxes could only be collected by force, and the expenditure was in excess of the revenue by about 500*l.* a month. The fabric of government was gradually crumbling under the feet of those who had reared it. Native disturbances had already taken place in many parts of the group. Tui Cakou and Maafu were both anxious to secede, and probably would have done so but for the influence of the house of Hennings in one direction, and that of Captain Chapman, of H.M.S. 'Dido,' in another.[2] Had these two chiefs been allowed to secede the Government must at once have collapsed, for Cacobau could no longer have borne the title of King of Fiji. He might still, indeed, have

---

[1] 'Report of Commodore Goodenough and Mr. Consul Layard,' page 9.
[2] *Ibid.*

been King of Bau, as heretofore; but then Bau was too small a kingdom to satisfy the ambition of any minister. It became, therefore, of paramount importance that these two chiefs should not be allowed to secede. Maafu exercised great control over Tiu Cakou; and therefore, if the ministers could only influence Maafu, they had little to fear from Tiu Cakou. How they managed to retain the allegiance of Maafu is not very clear. It is said, however, though with what truth I do not know, that Maafu, just before he was about to secede, incautiously placed himself in the power of the Government, not dreaming of the length to which it was prepared to go. The ministers, however, informed him on his arrival at Levuka that he might either land as Viceroy of the kingdom or as a rebel prisoner. In the latter case he would be tried by court-martial, and probably shot the same day, for Cacobau would not have dared to let him live as a prisoner.[1] Previous to this Mr. Bailey, Maafu's secretary, had written to Captain Chapman in Maafu's name expressing his desire to secede. These letters were now disowned by Maafu,[2] together with much that he had said at various meetings relative to secession. Thus, for a time, at any rate, the allegiance of Maafu was secured, but none knew better than the ministers that it could not be depended on.

The Parliament which had assembled in 1873

---

[1] 'Fiji Times,' March 11, 1874.
[2] 'Fiji Gazette,' July 26, 1873.

had shown itself so decidedly hostile to the Government, that the ministers had had no other course open to them but to dissolve it. There could, however, be no doubt that the newly-elected Parliament would be still more hostile, and under such circumstances it might be thought impossible for the Ministry any longer to remain in office. So undoubtedly it would have been in any country where constitutional government really existed. But men who had held power for three years were not to be deprived of it in a moment or for a mere conscientious scruple. They yet held a card which it now seemed the proper time to play. They proposed that at the forthcoming elections the votes of Fiji natives should be taken along with those of the white electors. Such a proposition, in direct violation of the Electoral Act of 1871, called forth the most violent opposition from all parts of the group. Every white man felt himself personally aggrieved, and determined to resist to the utmost. The ministers, however, cared little so long as they had the native troops to fall back upon. They submitted a case to the Judges of the Supreme Court as to whether the Electoral Act was not in direct opposition to the sixtieth clause of the Constitution Act, wherein the franchise is conceded to 'every male subject of the kingdom who shall have paid his taxes and attained the age of twenty-one years.' The Judges held that the Act of Parliament was in opposition to the constitution, and therefore declared it null and void. Preparations were made meanwhile for natives to vote, and every precaution taken that they should vote as ministers wished.

In giving this opinion the Judges may have been right in law, though their ruling was disputed by every lawyer in the group. But it is impossible to conceive any decision more opposed to the whole spirit of the constitution as accepted by the Delegates. The representatives of the Fijian population were not elected, and it was never intended they should be. They sat in an Upper House of their own by hereditary right, just as peers sit in the House of Lords. The native element had always been governed by its chiefs, and in fact no other government was possible. At the time of the passing of the Constitution Act this truth was recognised and acted upon both by Cacobau, his ministers, and the Delegates. The Fijian chiefs were relegated to a House of their own where they could legislate as they pleased for their own subjects. The whites meanwhile legislated for themselves by means of their representatives, and carried on the government of the country through ministers who were theoretically, at any rate, responsible to Parliament. But, apart from all this, everyone at all acquainted with Fijian customs or character knew that the natives were utterly ignorant not only of the spirit but even of the forms of constitutional government. King Cacobau himself did not understand them; it was not, therefore, to be supposed that his subjects, in most cases unlettered barbarians, could understand the important issues involved in the election of a Member of Parliament. How could such men possibly weigh the merits of rival candidates or distinguish between one line of policy and another? They would simply be driven like so many sheep to the hustings, there to vote for the candidate whom their chief had chosen for them; and the chief would choose whomsoever the minister or the King had told him to choose. In such a way any minister could easily be rendered practically independent of Parliament, for he could swamp all the white votes at any general election, and could fill the House with members of his own nomination. Parliamentary government was, in fact, at an end, and the country was under an undisguised despotism.

As soon as the intention of the Ministers to allow natives to vote at the ensuing elections was published meetings were held against it in every electoral district throughout Fiji. Members pledged themselves not to hold their seats if any natives came to the poll. The returning officer of Levuka rather than register their votes resigned his office. Even the wives and daughters of planters for once came forth from their seclusion and petitioned Commodore Stirling to forbid a course of action which they feared would lead to a civil war. The Commodore, however, could not interfere with so purely local a matter as the meaning of a clause in the Constitution Act, and could only promise in case of war to protect the persons and properties of British subjects.

Towards the end of 1873 a new constitution was arranged by the Ministers, and the old one, which had been passed by the Delegates, and on the faith of which the Government was first formed, was superseded. The condition of the country was meanwhile becoming every day more unsatisfactory. The Government could only maintain its position by force of arms. It could not maintain order or collect any but a small portion of the taxes. It had, in fact, degenerated into a 'ring,' to use an American phrase, and could count only on the assistance of unscrupulous place-hunters or armed soldiers. Things continued in this state until the beginning of 1874, when Commodore Goodenough and Mr. Consul Layard, the Commissioners appointed to enquire into Fijian affairs, landed in Levuka, and practically put an end to the so-called 'Constitutional Government' which had for nearly three years harassed and distressed Fiji.

NOTE.

The formal annexation of the Fiji Islands to the British Empire, and the cautious language of the newly-appointed Governor with regard to the labour-traffic among these islands, justify the hope that the new era thus begun may realise expectations of permanent prosperity which have thus far been disappointed.

APRIL 1878.

GENERAL LISTS OF NEW WORKS

PUBLISHED BY

Messrs. LONGMANS, GREEN & CO.

PATERNOSTER ROW, LONDON.

HISTORY, POLITICS, HISTORICAL MEMOIRS &c.

Armitage's Childhood of the English Nation. Fcp. 8vo. 2s. 6d.
Arnold's Lectures on Modern History. 8vo. 7s. 6d.
Buckle's History of Civilisation. 3 vols. crown 8vo. 24s.
Chesney's Indian Polity. 8vo. 21s.
— Waterloo Lectures. 8vo. 10s. 6d.
Cox's General History of Greece. Crown 8vo. 7s. 6d.
— History of Greece. Vols. I & II. 8vo. 36s.
— Mythology of the Aryan Nations. 2 vols. 8vo. 28s.
— Tales of Ancient Greece. Crown 8vo. 6s.
Epochs of Ancient History :—
    Beesly's Gracchi, Marius, and Sulla, 2s. 6d.
    Capes's Age of the Antonines, 2s. 6d.
    — Early Roman Empire, 2s. 6d.
    Cox's Athenian Empire, 2s. 6d.
    — Greeks and Persians, 2s. 6d.
    Curteis's Rise of the Macedonian Empire, 2s. 6d.
    Ihne's Rome to its Capture by the Gauls, 2s. 6d.
    Merivale's Roman Triumvirates, 2s. 6d.
    Sankey's Spartan and Theban Supremacies, 2s. 6d.
Epochs of Modern History :—
    Church's Beginning of the Middle Ages, 2s. 6d.
    Cox's Crusades, 2s. 6d.
    Creighton's Age of Elizabeth, 2s. 6d.
    Gairdner's Houses of Lancaster and York, 2s. 6d.
    Gardiner's Puritan Revolution, 2s. 6d.
    — Thirty Years' War, 2s. 6d.
    Hale's Fall of the Stuarts, 2s. 6d.
    Johnson's Normans in Europe, 2s. 6d.

London, LONGMANS & CO.

Epochs of Modern History :—*continued.*
  Ludlow's War of American Independence, 2s. 6d.
  Morris's Age of Queen Anne, 2s. 6d.
  Seebohm's Protestant Revolution, 2s. 6d.
  Stubbs's Early Plantagenets, 2s. 6d.
  Warburton's Edward III., 2s. 6d.
Froude's English in Ireland in the 18th Century. 3 vols. 8vo. 48s.
— History of England. 12 vols. 8vo. £8. 18s. 12 vols. crown 8vo. 72s.
Gardiner's England under Buckingham and Charles I., 1624-1628. 2 vols. 8vo. 24s.
— Personal Government of Charles I., 1628-1637. 2 vols. 8vo. 24s.
Greville's Journal of the Reigns of George IV. & William IV. 3 vols. 8vo. 36s.
Howorth's History of the Mongols. Vol. I. Royal 8vo. 28s.
Ihne's History of Rome. 3 vols. 8vo. 45s.
Lecky's History of England. Vols. I. & II., 1700-1760. 8vo. 36s.
— — — European Morals. 2 vols. crown 8vo. 16s.
— Spirit of Rationalism in Europe. 2 vols. crown 8vo. 16s.
Lewes's History of Philosophy. 2 vols. 8vo. 32s.
Longman's Lectures on the History of England. 8vo. 15s.
— Life and Times of Edward III. 2 vols. 8vo. 28s.
Macaulay's Complete Works. 8 vols. 8vo. £5. 5s.
  — History of England :—
  Student's Edition. 2 vols. cr. 8vo. 12s. | Cabinet Edition. 8 vols. post 8vo. 48s.
  People's Edition. 4 vols. cr. 8vo. 16s. | Library Edition. 5 vols. 8vo. £4.
Macaulay's Critical and Historical Essays. Cheap Edition. Crown 8vo. 3s. 6d.
  Cabinet Edition. 4 vols. post 8vo. 24s. | Library Edition. 3 vols. 8vo. 36s.
  People's Edition. 2 vols. cr. 8vo. 8s. | Student's Edition. 1 vol. cr. 8vo. 6s.
May's Constitutional History of England. 3 vols. crown 8vo. 18s.
— Democracy in Europe. 2 vols. 8vo. 32s.
Merivale's Fall of the Roman Republic. 12mo. 7s. 6d.
— General History of Rome, B.C. 753—A.D. 476. Crown 8vo. 7s. 6d.
— History of the Romans under the Empire. 8 vols. post 8vo. 48s.
Osborn's Islam under the Arabs. 8vo. 12s.
Prothero's Life of Simon de Montfort. Crown 8vo. 9s.
Rawlinson's Seventh Great Oriental Monarchy—The Sassanians. 8vo. 28s.
— Sixth Oriental Monarchy—Parthia. 8vo. 16s.
Seebohm's Oxford Reformers—Colet, Erasmus, & More. 8vo. 14s.
Sewell's Popular History of France. Crown 8vo. 7s. 6d.
Short's History of the Church of England. Crown 8vo. 7s. 6d.
Taylor's Manual of the History of India. Crown 8vo. 7s. 6d.
Todd's Parliamentary Government in England. 2 vols. 8vo. 37s.
Trench's Realities of Irish Life. Crown 8vo. 2s. 6d.
Walpole's History of England. Vols. I. & II. 8vo. (*In October.*)
Wyatt's History of Prussia. A.D. 700 to A.D. 1525. 2 vols. 8vo. 36s.

BIOGRAPHICAL WORKS.

Burke's Vicissitudes of Families. 2 vols. crown 8vo. 21s.
Cates's Dictionary of General Biography. Medium 8vo. 25s.
Gleig's Life of the Duke of Wellington. Crown 8vo. 5s.

London, LONGMANS & CO.

Jerrold's Life of Napoleon III. Vols. I. to III. 8vo. price 18s. each.
Jones's Life of Admiral Frobisher. Crown 8vo. 6s.
Lecky's Leaders of Public Opinion in Ireland. Crown 8vo. 7s. 6d.
Life (The) of Sir William Fairbairn. Crown 8vo. 2s. 6d.
Life (The) of Bishop Frampton. Crown 8vo. 10s. 6d.
Life (The) and Letters of Lord Macaulay. By his Nephew, G. Otto Trevelyan, M.P. Cabinet Edition, 2 vols. post 8vo. 12s. Library Edition, 2 vols. 8vo. 36s.
Marshman's Memoirs of Havelock. Crown 8vo. 3s. 6d.
Memorials of Charlotte Williams-Wynn. Crown 8vo. 10s. 6d.
Mendelssohn's Letters. Translated by Lady Wallace. 2 vols. cr. 8vo. 5s. each.
Mill's (John Stuart) Autobiography. 8vo. 7s. 6d.
Nohl's Life of Mozart. Translated by Lady Wallace. 2 vols. crown 8vo. 21s.
Pattison's Life of Casaubon. 8vo. 18s.
Spedding's Letters and Life of Francis Bacon. 7 vols. 8vo. £4. 4s.
Stephen's Essays in Ecclesiastical Biography. Crown 8vo. 7s. 6d.
Stigand's Life, Works, &c. of Heinrich Heine. 2 vols. 8vo. 28s.
Zimmern's Life and Philosophy of Schopenhauer. Post 8vo. 7s. 6d.
— — — Works of Lessing. Crown 8vo. 10s. 6d.

CRITICISM, PHILOSOPHY, POLITY &c.

Amos's View of the Science of Jurisprudence. 8vo. 18s.
— Primer of the English Constitution. Crown 8vo. 6s.
Arnold's Manual of English Literature. Crown 8vo. 7s. 6d.
Bacon's Essays, with Annotations by Whately. 8vo. 10s. 6d.
— Works, edited by Spedding. 7 vols. 8vo. 73s. 6d.
Bain's Logic, Deductive and Inductive. Crown 8vo. 10s. 6d.
      PART I. Deduction, 4s. | PART II. Induction, 6s. 6d.
Blackley's German and English Dictionary. Post 8vo. 7s. 6d.
Bolland & Lang's Aristotle's Politics. Crown 8vo. 7s. 6d.
Bullinger's Lexicon and Concordance to the New Testament. Medium 8vo. 30s.
Comte's System of Positive Polity, or Treatise upon Sociology, translated :—
    VOL. I. General View of Positivism and its Introductory Principles. 8vo. 21s.
    VOL. II. Social Statics, or the Abstract Laws of Human Order. 14s.
    VOL. III. Social Dynamics, or General Laws of Human Progress. 21s.
    VOL. IV. Theory of the Future of Man; with Early Essays. 24s.
Congreve's Politics of Aristotle; Greek Text, English Notes. 8vo. 18s.
Contanseau's Practical French & English Dictionary. Post 8vo. 7s. 6d.
— Pocket French and English Dictionary. Square 18mo. 3s. 6d.
Dowell's Sketch of Taxes in England. VOL. I. to 1642. 8vo. 10s. 6d.
Farrar's Language and Languages. Crown 8vo. 6s.
Finlason on the New Judicial System. Crown 8vo. 10s. 6d.
Geffcken on Church and State, translated by E. F. Taylor. 2 vols. 8vo. 42s.
Grant's Ethics of Aristotle, Greek Text, English Notes. 2 vols. 8vo. 32s.
Kalisch's Historical and Critical Commentary on the Old Testament; with a New Translation. Vol. I. *Genesis*, 8vo. 18s. or adapted for the General Reader, 12s. Vol. II. *Exodus*, 15s. or adapted for the General Reader, 12s. Vol. III. *Leviticus*, Part I. 15s. or adapted for the General Reader, 8s. Vol. IV. *Leviticus*, Part II. 15s. or adapted for the General Reader, 8s.

London, LONGMANS & CO.

Latham's Handbook of the English Language. Crown 8vo. 6s.
— English Dictionary. 1 vol. medium 8vo. 24s. 4 vols. 4to. £7.
Lewis on Authority in Matters of Opinion. 8vo. 14s.
Liddell & Scott's Greek-English Lexicon. Crown 4to. 36s.
— — — Abridged Greek-English Lexicon. Square 12mo. 7s. 6d.
Longman's Pocket German and English Dictionary. 18mo. 5s.
Macaulay's Speeches corrected by Himself. Crown 8vo. 3s. 6d.
Macleod's Economical Philosophy. Vol. I. 8vo. 15s. Vol. II. Part I. 12s.
Mill on Representative Government. Crown 8vo. 2s.
— — Liberty. Post 8vo. 7s. 6d. Crown 8vo. 1s. 4d.
Mill's Dissertations and Discussions. 4 vols. 8vo. 46s. 6d.
— Essays on Unsettled Questions of Political Economy. 8vo. 6s. 6d.
— Examination of Hamilton's Philosophy. 8vo. 16s.
— Logic, Ratiocinative and Inductive. 2 vols. 8vo. 25s.
— Principles of Political Economy. 2 vols. 8vo. 30s. 1 vol. cr. 8vo. 5s.
— Utilitarianism. 8vo. 5s.
Müller's (Max) Lectures on the Science of Language. 2 vols. crown 8vo. 16s.
Rich's Dictionary of Roman and Greek Antiquities. Crown 8vo. 7s. 6d.
Roget's Thesaurus of English Words and Phrases. Crown 8vo. 10s. 6d.
Sandars's Institutes of Justinian, with English Notes. 8vo. 18s.
Swinbourne's Picture Logic. Post 8vo. 5s.
Thomson's Outline of Necessary Laws of Thought. Crown 8vo. 6s.
Tocqueville's Democracy in America, translated by Reeve. 2 vols. crown 8vo. 16s.
Twiss's Law of Nations, 8vo. in Time of Peace, 12s. in Time of War, 21s.
Whately's Elements of Logic. 8vo. 10s. 6d. Crown 8vo. 4s. 6d.
— — — Rhetoric. 8vo. 10s. 6d. Crown 8vo. 4s. 6d.
— English Synonymes. Fcp. 8vo. 3s.
White & Riddle's Large Latin-English Dictionary. 4to. 28s.
White's College Latin-English Dictionary. Medium 8vo. 15s.
— Junior Student's Complete Latin-English and English-Latin Dictionary. Square 12mo. 12s.
Separately { The English-Latin Dictionary, 5s. 6d.
            { The Latin-English Dictionary, 7s. 6d.
White's Middle-Class Latin-English Dictionary. Fcp. 8vo. 3s.
Williams's Nicomachean Ethics of Aristotle translated. Crown 8vo. 7s. 6d
Yonge's Abridged English-Greek Lexicon. Square 12mo. 8s. 6d.
— Large English-Greek Lexicon. 4to. 21s.
Zeller's Socrates and the Socratic Schools. Crown 8vo. 10s. 6d.
— Stoics, Epicureans, and Sceptics. Crown 8vo. 14s.
— Plato and the Older Academy. Crown 8vo. 18s.

MISCELLANEOUS WORKS & POPULAR METAPHYSICS.

Arnold's (Dr. Thomas) Miscellaneous Works. 8vo. 7s. 6d.
Bain's Emotions and the Will. 8vo. 15s.
— Mental and Moral Science. Crown 8vo. 10s. 6d. Or separately: Part I. Mental Science, 6s. 6d. Part II. Moral Science, 4s. 6d.
— Senses and the Intellect. 8vo. 15s.
Buckle's Miscellaneous and Posthumous Works. 3 vols. 8vo. 52s. 6d.

London, LONGMANS & CO.

General Lists of New Works.

Carpenter on Mesmerism, Spiritualism, &c. Crown 8vo. 5s.
Conington's Miscellaneous Writings. 2 vols. 8vo. 28s.
Froude's Short Studies on Great Subjects. 3 vols. crown 8vo. 18s.
German Home Life; reprinted from *Fraser's Magazine*. Crown 8vo. 6s.
Hume's Essays, edited by Greene & Grose. 2 vols. 8vo. 28s.
— Treatise of Human Nature, edited by Green & Grose. 2 vols. 8vo. 28s.
Kirkman's Philosophy Without Assumptions. 8vo. 10s. 6d.
Macaulay's Miscellaneous Writings. 2 vols. 8vo. 21s. 1 vol. crown 8vo. 4s. 6d.
— Writings and Speeches. Crown 8vo. 6s.
Mill's Analysis of the Phenomena of the Human Mind. 2 vols. 8vo. 28s.
— Subjection of Women. Crown 8vo. 6s.
Müller's (Max) Chips from a German Workshop. 4 vols. 8vo. 58s.
Mullinger's Schools of Charles the Great. 8vo. 7s. 6d.
Owen's Evenings with the Skeptics. Crown 8vo.   [*Just ready.*
Rogers's Defence of the Eclipse of Faith Fcp. 8vo. 3s. 6d.
— Eclipse of Faith. Fcp. 8vo. 5s.
Selections from the Writings of Lord Macaulay. Crown 8vo. 6s.
Sydney Smith's Miscellaneous Works. Crown 8vo. 6s.
The Essays and Contributions of A. K. H. B. Crown 8vo.
    Autumn Holidays of a Country Parson. 3s. 6d.
    Changed Aspects of Unchanged Truths. 3s. 6d.
    Common-place Philosopher in Town and Country. 3s. 6d.
    Counsel and Comfort spoken from a City Pulpit. 3s. 6d.
    Critical Essays of a Country Parson. 3s. 6d.
    Graver Thoughts of a Country Parson. Three Series, 3s. 6d. each.
    Landscapes, Churches, and Moralities. 3s. 6d.
    Leisure Hours in Town. 3s. 6d.
    Lessons of Middle Age. 3s. 6d.
    Present-day Thoughts. 3s. 6d.
    Recreations of a Country Parson. Two Series, 3s. 6d. each.
    Seaside Musings on Sundays and Week-Days. 3s. 6d.
    Sunday Afternoons in the Parish Church of a University City. 3s. 6d.
Wit and Wisdom of the Rev. Sydney Smith. 16mo. 3s. 6d.

ASTRONOMY, METEOROLOGY, POPULAR GEOGRAPHY &c.

Dove's Law of Storms, translated by Scott. 8vo. 10s. 6d.
Hartley's Air and its Relations to Life. Small 8vo. 6s.
Herschel's Outlines of Astronomy. Square crown 8vo. 12s.
Keith Johnston's Dictionary of Geography, or Gazetter. 8vo. 42s.
Nelson's Work on the Moon. Medium 8vo. 31s. 6d.
Proctor's Essays on Astronomy. 8vo. 12s.
   — Larger Star Atlas. Folio, 15s. or Maps only, 12s. 6d.
   — Moon. Crown 8vo. 15s.
   — New Star Atlas. Crown 8vo. 5s.
   — Orbs Around Us. Crown 8vo. 7s. 6d.
   — Other Worlds than Ours. Crown 8vo. 10s. 6d.
   — Saturn and its System. 8vo. 14s.
   — Sun. Crown 8vo. 14s.
   — Transits of Venus, Past and Coming. Crown 8vo. 9s. 6d.
   — Treatise on the Cycloid and Cycloidal Curves. Crown 8vo. 10s. 6d.

London, LONGMANS & CO.

Proctor's Universe of Stars. 8vo. 10s. 6d.
Schellen's Spectrum Analysis. 8vo. 28s.
Smith's Air and Rain. 8vo. 24s.
The Public Schools Atlas of Ancient Geography. Imperial 8vo. 7s. 6d.
— — — Atlas of Modern Geography. Imperial 8vo. 5s.
Webb's Celestial Objects for Common Telescopes. Crown 8vo. 7s. 6d.

NATURAL HISTORY & POPULAR SCIENCE.

Arnott's Elements of Physics or Natural Philosophy. Crown 8vo. 12s. 6d.
Brande's Dictionary of Science, Literature, and Art. 3 vols. medium 8vo. 63s.
Decaisne and Le Maout's General System of Botany. Imperial 8vo. 31s. 6d.
Evans's Ancient Stone Implements of Great Britain. 8vo. 28s.
Ganot's Elementary Treatise on Physics, by Atkinson. Large crown 8vo. 15s.
— Natural Philosophy, by Atkinson. Crown 8vo. 7s. 6d.
Grove's Correlation of Physical Forces. 8vo. 15s.
Hartwig's Aerial World. 8vo. 10s. 6d.
— Polar World. 8vo. 10s. 6d.
— Sea and its Living Wonders. 8vo. 10s. 6d.
— Subterranean World. 8vo. 10s. 6d.
— Tropical World. 8vo. 10s. 6d.
Haughton's Principles of Animal Mechanics. 8vo. 21s.
Heer's Primæval World of Switzerland. 2 vols. 8vo. 28s.
Helmholtz's Lectures on Scientific Subjects. 8vo. 12s. 6d.
Helmholtz on the Sensations of Tone, by Ellis. 8vo. 36s.
Hemsley's Handbook of Trees, Shrubs, & Herbaceous Plants. Medium 8vo. 12s.
Hullah's Lectures on the History of Modern Music. 8vo. 8s. 6d.
— Transition Period of Musical History. 8vo. 10s. 6d.
Keller's Lake Dwellings of Switzerland, by Lee. 2 vols. royal 8vo. 42s.
Kirby and Spence's Introduction to Entomology. Crown 8vo. 5s.
Lloyd's Treatise on Magnetism. 8vo. 10s. 6d.
— — on the Wave-Theory of Light. 8vo. 10s. 6d.
Loudon's Encyclopædia of Plants. 8vo. 42s.
Lubbock on the Origin of Civilisation & Primitive Condition of Man. 8vo. 18s.
Nicols' Puzzle of Life. Crown 8vo. 3s. 6d.
Owen's Comparative Anatomy and Physiology of the Vertebrate Animals. 3 vols. 8vo. 73s. 6d.
Proctor's Light Science for Leisure Hours. 2 vols. crown 8vo. 7s. 6d. each.
Rivers's Rose Amateur's Guide. Fcp. 8vo. 4s. 6d.
Stanley's Familiar History of Birds. Fcp. 8vo. 3s. 6d.
Text-Books of Science, Mechanical and Physical.
    Abney's Photography, small 8vo. 3s. 6d.
    Anderson's Strength of Materials, 3s. 6d.
    Armstrong's Organic Chemistry, 3s. 6d.
    Barry's Railway Appliances, 3s. 6d.
    Bloxam's Metals, 3s. 6d.
    Goodeve's Elements of Mechanism, 3s. 6d.
    — Principles of Mechanics, 3s. 6d.
    Gore's Electro-Metallurgy, 6s.
    Griffin's Algebra and Trigonometry, 3s. 6d.

London, LONGMANS & CO.

Text-Books of Science—*continued*.
    Jenkin's Electricity and Magnetism, 3s. 6d.
    Maxwell's Theory of Heat, 3s. 6d.
    Merrifield's Technical Arithmetic and Mensuration, 3s. 6d.
    Miller's Inorganic Chemistry, 3s. 6d.
    Preece & Sivewright's Telegraphy, 3s. 6d.
    Shelley's Workshop Appliances, 3s. 6d.
    Thomé's Structural and Physiological Botany, 6s.
    Thorpe's Quantitative Chemical Analysis, 4s. 6d.
    Thorpe & Muir's Qualitative Analysis, 3s. 6d.
    Tilden's Chemical Philosophy, 3s. 6d.
    Unwin's Machine Design, 3s. 6d.
    Watson's Plane and Solid Geometry, 3s. 6d.
Tyndall on Sound. Crown 8vo. 10s. 6d.
—   Contributions to Molecular Physics. 8vo. 16s.
—   Fragments of Science. Crown 8vo. 10s. 6d.
—   Lectures on Electrical Phenomena. Crown 8vo. 1s. sewed, 1s. 6d. cloth.
—   Lectures on Light. Crown 8vo. 1s. sewed, 1s. 6d. cloth.
—   Lectures on Light delivered in America. Crown 8vo. 7s. 6d.
—   Lessons in Electricity. Crown 8vo. 2s. 6d.
Woodward's Geology of England and Wales. Crown 8vo. 14s.
Wood's Bible Animals. With 112 Vignettes. 8vo. 14s.
—   Homes Without Hands. 8vo. 14s.
—   Insects Abroad. 8vo. 14s.
—   Insects at Home. With 700 Illustrations. 8vo. 14s.
—   Out of Doors, or Articles on Natural History. Crown 8vo. 7s. 6d.
—   Strange Dwellings. With 60 Woodcuts. Crown 8vo. 7s. 6d.

CHEMISTRY & PHYSIOLOGY.

Auerbach's Anthracen, translated by W. Crookes, F.R.S. 8vo. 12s.
Buckton's Health in the House; Lectures on Elementary Physiology. Fcp. 8vo. 2s.
Crookes's Handbook of Dyeing and Calico Printing. 8vo. 42s.
—   Select Methods in Chemical Analysis. Crown 8vo. 12s. 6d.
Kingzett's Animal Chemistry. 8vo.   [*In the press.*
—   History, Products and Processes of the Alkali Trade. 8vo. 12s.
Miller's Elements of Chemistry, Theoretical and Practical. 3 vols. 8vo. Part I. Chemical Physics, 16s. Part II. Inorganic Chemistry, 21s. Part III. Organic Chemistry, New Edition in the press.
Watts's Dictionary of Chemistry. 7 vols. medium 8vo. £10. 16s. 6d.

THE FINE ARTS & ILLUSTRATED EDITIONS.

Doyle's Fairyland; Pictures from the Elf-World. Folio. 15s.
Jameson's Sacred and Legendary Art. 6 vols. square crown 8vo.
    Legends of the Madonna. 1 vol. 21s.
    — — — Monastic Orders. 1 vol. 21s.
    — — — Saints and Martyrs. 2 vols. 31s. 6d.
    — — — Saviour. Completed by Lady Eastlake. 2 vols. 42s.

London, LONGMANS & CO.

Longman's Three Cathedrals Dedicated to St. Paul. Square crown 8vo. 21s.
Macaulay's Lays of Ancient Rome. With 90 Illustrations. Fcp. 4to. 21s.
Macfarren's Lectures on Harmony. 8vo. 12s.
Miniature Edition of Macaulay's Lays of Ancient Rome. Imp. 16mo. 10s. 6d.
Moore's Irish Melodies. With 161 Plates by D. Maclise, R.A. Super-royal 8vo. 21s.
— Lalla Rookh, Tenniel's Edition. With 68 Illustrations. Fcp. 4to. 21s.
Redgrave's Dictionary of Artists of the English School. 8vo. 16s.

THE USEFUL ARTS, MANUFACTURES &c.

Bourne's Catechism of the Steam Engine. Fcp. 8vo. 6s.
— Handbook of the Steam Engine. Fcp. 8vo. 9s.
— Recent Improvements in the Steam Engine. Fcp. 8vo. 6s.
— Treatise on the Steam Engine. 4to. 42s.
Cresy's Encyclopædia of Civil Engineering. 8vo. 42s.
Culley's Handbook of Practical Telegraphy. 8vo. 16s.
Eastlake's Household Taste in Furniture, &c. Square crown 8vo. 14s.
Fairbairn's Useful Information for Engineers. 3 vols. crown 8vo. 31s. 6d.
— Applications of Cast and Wrought Iron. 8vo. 16s.
Gwilt's Encyclopædia of Architecture. 8vo. 52s. 6d.
Hobson's Amateur Mechanics Practical Handbook. Crown 8vo. 2s. 6d.
Hoskold's Engineer's Valuing Assistant. 8vo. 31s. 6d.
Kerl's Metallurgy, adapted by Crookes and Röhrig. 3 vols. 8vo. £4. 19s.
Loudon's Encyclopædia of Agriculture. 8vo. 21s.
— — - Gardening. 8vo. 21s.
Mitchell's Manual of Practical Assaying. 8vo. 31s. 6d.
Northcott's Lathes and Turning. 8vo. 18s.
Payen's Industrial Chemistry, translated from Stohmann and Eugler's German Edition, by Dr. J. D. Barry. Edited by B. H. Paul, Ph.D. 8vo. 42s.
Stoney's Theory of Strains in Girders. Roy. 8vo. 36s.
Ure's Dictionary of Arts, Manufactures, & Mines. 3 vols. medium 8vo. £5. 5s.
Supplementary Volume of Recent Improvements. 42s. (*Nearly ready.*)

RELIGIOUS & MORAL WORKS.

Arnold's (Rev. Dr. Thomas) Sermons. 6 vols. crown 8vo. 5s. each.
Bishop Jeremy Taylor's Entire Works. With Life by Bishop Heber. Edited by the Rev. C. P. Eden. 10 vols. 8vo. £5. 5s.
Boultbee's Commentary on the 39 Articles. Crown 8vo. 6s.
Browne's (Bishop) Exposition of the 39 Articles. 8vo. 16s.
Colenso on the Pentateuch and Book of Joshua. Crown 8vo. 6s.
Colenso's Lectures on the Pentateuch and the Moabite Stone. 8vo. 12s.
Conybeare & Howson's Life and Letters of St. Paul :—
 Library Edition, with all the Original Illustrations, Maps, Landscapes on Steel, Woodcuts, &c. 2 vols. 4to. 42s.
 Intermediate Edition, with a Selection of Maps, Plates, and Woodcuts. 2 vols. square crown 8vo. 21s.
 Student's Edition, revised and condensed, with 46 Illustrations and Maps. 1 vol. crown 8vo. 9s.

London, LONGMANS & CO.

General Lists of New Works.

D'Aubigné's Reformation in Europe in the Time of Calvin. 8 vols. 8vo. £6. 12s.
Drummond's Jewish Messiah. 8vo. 15s.
Ellicott's (Bishop) Commentary on St. Paul's Epistles. 8vo. Galatians, 8s. 6d. Ephesians, 8s. 6d. Pastoral Epistles, 10s. 6d. Philippians, Colossians, and Philemon, 10s. 6d. Thessalonians, 7s. 6d.
Ellicott's Lectures on the Life of our Lord. 8vo. 12s.
Ewald's History of Israel, translated by Carpenter. 5 vols. 8vo. 63s.
— Antiquities of Israel, translated by Solly. 8vo. 12s. 6d.
Goldziher's Mythology among the Hebrews. 8vo. 16s.
Griffith's Behind the Veil; an Outline of Bible Metaphysics. 8vo. 10s. 6d.
Jukes's Types of Genesis. Crown 8vo. 7s. 6d.
— Second Death and the Restitution of all Things. Crown 8vo. 3s. 6d.
Kalisch's Bible Studies. PART I. the Prophecies of Balaam. 8vo. 10s. 6d.
Keith's Evidence of the Truth of the Christian Religion derived from the Fulfilment of Prophecy. Square 8vo. 12s. 6d. Post 8vo. 6s.
Kuenen on the Prophets and Prophecy in Israel. 8vo. 21s.
Lyra Germanica. Hymns translated by Miss Winkworth. Fcp. 8vo. 5s.
Manning's Temporal Mission of the Holy Ghost. 8vo. 8s. 6d.
Martineau's Endeavours after the Christian Life. Crown 8vo. 7s. 6d.
— Hymns of Praise and Prayer. Crown 8vo. 4s. 6d. 32mo. 1s. 6d.
— Sermons; Hours of Thought on Sacred Things. Crown 8vo. 7s. 6d.
Mill's Three Essays on Religion. 8vo. 10s. 6d.
Monsell's Spiritual Songs for Sundays and Holidays. Fcp. 8vo. 5s. 18mo. 2s.
Müller's (Max) Lectures on the Science of Religion. Crown 8vo. 10s. 6d.
O'Conor's New Testament Commentaries. Crown 8vo. Epistle to the Romans. 3s. 6d. Epistle to the Hebrews, 4s. 6d. St. John's Gospel, 10s. 6d.
Passing Thoughts on Religion. By Miss Sewell. Fcp. 8vo. 3s. 6d.
Sewell's (Miss) Preparation for the Holy Communion. 32mo. 3s.
Shipley's Ritual of the Altar. Imperial 8vo. 42s.
Supernatural Religion. 3 vols. 8vo. 38s.
Thoughts for the Age. By Miss Sewell. Fcp. 8vo. 3s. 6d.
Vaughan's Trident, Crescent, and Cross; the Religious History of India. 8vo. 9s. 6d.
Whately's Lessons on the Christian Evidences. 18mo. 6d.
White's Four Gospels in Greek, with Greek-English Lexicon. 32mo. 5s.

TRAVELS, VOYAGES &c.

Ball's Alpine Guide. 3 vols. post 8vo. with Maps and Illustrations:—I. Western Alps, 6s. 6d. II. Central Alps, 7s. 6d. III. Eastern Alps, 10s. 6d. Or in Ten Parts, 2s. 6d. each.
Ball on Alpine Travelling, and on the Geology of the Alps, 1s. Each of the Three Volumes of the *Alpine Guide* may be had with this Introduction prefixed. price 1s. extra.
Baker's Rifle and the Hound in Ceylon. Crown 8vo. 7s. 6d.
— Eight Years in Ceylon. Crown 8vo. 7s. 6d.
Brassey's Voyage in the Yacht 'Sunbeam.' 8vo. 21s.
Edwards's (A. B.) Thousand Miles up the Nile. Imperial 8vo. 42s.
Edwards's (M. B.) Year in Western France. Crown 8vo. 10s. 6d.

London, LONGMANS & CO.

Evans's Through Bosnia and Herzegovina during the Insurrection. 8vo. 18s.
— Illyrian Letters. 8vo. (*Nearly ready.*)
Grohman's Tyrol and the Tyrolese. Crown 8vo. 6s.
Hinchliff's Over the Sea and Far Away. Medium 8vo. 21s.
Indian Alps (The). By a Lady Pioneer. Imperial 8vo. 42s.
Lefroy's Discovery and Early Settlement of the Bermuda Islands. Vol. I. Royal 8vo. 30s.
Packe's Guide to the Pyrenees, for Mountaineers. Crown 8vo. 7s. 6d.
The Alpine Club Map of Switzerland. In four sheets. 42s.
Wood's Discoveries at Ephesus. Imperial 8vo. 63s.

WORKS OF FICTION.

Becker's Charicles; Private Life among the Ancient Greeks. Post 8vo. 7s. 6d.
— Gallus; Roman Scenes of the Time of Augustus. Post 8vo. 7s. 6d.
Cabinet Edition of Stories and Tales by Miss Sewell :—

Amy Herbert, 2s. 6d.
Cleve Hall, 2s. 6d.
The Earl's Daughter, 2s. 6d.
Experience of Life, 2s. 6d.
Gertrude, 2s. 6d.
Ivors, 2s. 6d.
Katharine Ashton, 2s. 6d.
Laneton Parsonage, 3s. 6d.
Margaret Percival, 3s. 6d.
Ursula, 3s. 6d.

Novels and Tales by the Right Hon. the Earl of Beaconsfield. Cabinet Edition, complete in Ten Volumes, crown 8vo. price £3.

Lothair, 6s.
Coningsby, 6s.
Sybil, 6s.
Tancred, 6s.
Venetia, 6s.
Henrietta Temple, 6s.
Contarini Fleming, 6s.
Alroy, Ixion, &c. 6s.
The Young Duke, &c. 6s.
Vivian Grey, 6s.

The Atelier du Lys; or, an Art Student in the Reign of Terror. By the Author of 'Mademoiselle Mori.' Crown 8vo. 6s.

The Modern Novelist's Library. Each Work in crown 8vo. A Single Volume, complete in itself, price 2s. boards, or 2s. 6d. cloth :—

By Lord Beaconsfield.
    Lothair.
    Coningsby.
    Sybil.
    Tancred.
    Venetia.
    Henrietta Temple.
    Contarini Fleming.
    Alroy, Ixion, &c.
    The Young Duke, &c.
    Vivian Grey.
By Anthony Trollope.
    Barchester Towers.
    The Warden.
By the Author of 'the Rose Garden.'
    Unawares.
By Major Whyte-Melville.
    Digby Grand.
    General Bounce.
    Kate Coventry.
    The Gladiators.
    Good for Nothing.
    Holmby House.
    The Interpreter.
    The Queen's Maries.
By the Author of 'the Atelier du Lys.'
    Mademoiselle Mori.
By Various Writers.
    Atherstone Priory.
    The Burgomaster's Family.
    Elsa and her Vulture.
    The Six Sisters of the Valley.

Whispers from Fairy Land. By the Right Hon. E. H. Knatchbull-Hugessen M.P. With Nine Illustrations. Crown 8vo. 3s. 6d.

Higgledy-Piggledy; or, Stories for Everybody and Everybody's Children. By the Right Hon. E. M. Knatchbull-Hugessen, M.P. With Nine Illustrations from Designs by R. Doyle. Crown 8vo. 3s. 6d.

London, LONGMANS & CO.

POETRY & THE DRAMA.

Bailey's Festus, a Poem. Crown 8vo. 12s. 6d.
Bowdler's Family Shakspeare. Medium 8vo. 14s. 6 vols. fcp. 8vo. 21s.
Conington's Æneid of Virgil, translated into English Verse. Crown 8vo. 9s.
Cayley's Iliad of Homer, Homometrically translated. 8vo. 12s. 6d.
Ingelow's Poems. First Series. Illustrated Edition. Fcp. 4to. 21s.
Macaulay's Lays of Ancient Rome, with Ivry and the Armada. 16mo. 3s. 6d.
Poems. By Jean Ingelow. 2 vols. fcp. 8vo. 10s.
    First Series. 'Divided,' 'The Star's Monument,' &c. 5s.
    Second Series. 'A Story of Doom,' 'Gladys and her Island,' &c. 5s.
Southey's Poetical Works. Medium 8vo. 14s.
Yonge's Horatii Opera, Library Edition. 8vo. 21s.

RURAL SPORTS, HORSE & CATTLE MANAGEMENT &c.

Blaine's Encyclopædia of Rural Sports. 8vo. 21s.
Dobson on the Ox, his Diseases and their Treatment. Crown 8vo. 7s. 6d.
Fitzwygram's Horses and Stables. 8vo. 10s. 6d.
Francis's Book on Angling, or Treatise on Fishing. Post 8vo. 15s.
Malet's Annals of the Road, and Nimrod's Essays on the Road. Medium 8vo. 21s.
Miles's Horse's Foot, and How to Keep it Sound. Imperial 8vo. 12s. 6d.
    — Plain Treatise on Horse-Shoeing. Post 8vo. 2s. 6d.
    — Stables and Stable-Fittings. Imperial 8vo. 15s.
    — Remarks on Horses' Teeth. Post 8vo. 1s. 6d.
Moreton on Horse-Breaking. Crown 8vo. 5s.
Nevile's Horses and Riding. Crown 8vo. 6s.
Reynardson's Down the Road. Medium 8vo. 21s.
Ronalds's Fly-Fisher's Entomology. 8vo. 14s.
Stonehenge's Dog in Health and Disease. Square crown 8vo. 7s. 6d.
    — Greyhound. Square crown 8vo. 15s.
Youatt's Work on the Dog. 8vo. 12s. 6d.
    — — — — Horse. 8vo. 6s.
Wilcocks's Sea-Fisherman. Post 8vo. 12s. 6d.

WORKS OF UTILITY & GENERAL INFORMATION.

Acton's Modern Cookery for Private Families. Fcp. 8vo. 6s.
Black's Practical Treatise on Brewing. 8vo. 10s. 6d.
Bull on the Maternal Management of Children. Fcp. 8vo. 2s. 6d.
Bull's Hints to Mothers on the Management of their Health during the Pregnancy and in the Lying-in Room. Fcp. 8vo. 2s. 6d.
Campbell-Walker's Correct Card, or How to Play at Whist. 32mo. 2s. 6d.
Crump's English Manual of Banking. 8vo. 15s.
Longman's Chess Openings. Fcp. 8vo. 2s. 6d.
Macleod's Theory and Practice of Banking. 2 vols. 8vo. 26s.
    — Elements of Banking. Crown 8vo. 7s. 6d.

London, LONGMANS & CO.

M'Culloch's Dictionary of Commerce and Commercial Navigation. 8vo. 63s.
Maunder's Biographical Treasury. Fcp. 8vo. 6s.
— Historical Treasury. Fcp. 8vo. 6s.
— Scientific and Literary Treasury. Fcp. 8vo. 6s.
— Treasury of Bible Knowledge. Edited by the Rev. J. Ayre, M.A. Fcp. 8vo. 6s.
— Treasury of Botany. Edited by J. Lindley, F.R.S. and T. Moore, F.L.S. Two Parts, fcp. 8vo. 12s.
— Treasury of Geography. Fcp. 8vo. 6s.
— Treasury of Knowledge and Library of Reference. Fcp. 8vo. 6s.
— Treasury of Natural History. Fcp. 8vo. 6s.
Pewtner's Comprehensive Specifier; Building-Artificers' Work. Conditions and Agreements. Crown 8vo. 6s.
Pierce's Three Hundred Chess Problems and Studies. Fcp. 8vo. 7s. 6d.
Pole's Theory of the Modern Scientific Game of Whist. Fcp. 8vo. 2s. 6d.
The Cabinet Lawyer; a Popular Digest of the Laws of England. Fcp. 8vo. 9s.
Willich's Popular Tables for ascertaining the Value of Property. Post 8vo. 10s.
Wilson's Resources of Modern Countries 2 vols. 8vo. 24s.

MUSICAL WORKS BY JOHN HULLAH, LL.D.

Chromatic Scale, with the Inflected Syllables, on Large Sheet. 1s. 6d.
Card of Chromatic Scale. 1d.
Exercises for the Cultivation of the Voice. For Soprano or Tenor, 2s. 6d.
Grammar of Musical Harmony. Royal 8vo. 2 Parts, each 1s. 6d.
Exercises to Grammar of Musical Harmony. 1s.
Grammar of Counterpoint. Part I. super-royal 8vo. 2s. 6d.
Hullah's Manual of Singing. Parts I. & II. 2s. 6d.; or together, 5s.
Exercises and Figures contained in Parts I. and II. of the Manual. Books I. & II. each 8d.
Large Sheets, containing the Figures in Part I. of the Manual. Nos. 1 to 8 in a Parcel. 6s.
Large Sheets, containing the Exercises in Part I. of the Manual. Nos. 9 to 40, in Four Parcels of Eight Nos. each, per Parcel. 6s.
Large Sheets, the Figures in Part II. Nos. 41 to 52 in a Parcel. 9s.
Hymns for the Young, set to Music. Royal 8vo. 8d.
Infant School Songs. 6d.
Notation, the Musical Alphabet. Crown 8vo. 6d.
Old English Songs for Schools, Harmonised. 6d.
Rudiments of Musical Grammar. Royal 8vo. 3s.
School Songs for 2 and 3 Voices. 2 Books, 8vo. each 6d.
Time and Tune in the Elementary School. Crown 8vo. 2s. 6d.
Exercises and Figures in the same. Crown 8vo. 1s. or 2 Parts, 6d each.

London, LONGMANS & CO.

www.ingramcontent.com/pod-product-compliance
Lightning Source LLC
Chambersburg PA
CBHW020237240426
43672CB00006B/553